This is a tasty collection of well researched and conceptualised chapters on the urgent matter of decolonising higher education in post-colonial Africa. The book contributes substantially to unravelling a prevailing conceptual paralysis on the subject of decolonising higher education and will be an excellent companion for researchers, students, policy makers and practitioners with a focus on disrupting the stranglehold of the western canon on Africa's higher education.

—**Felix Maringe,** *Professor of Higher Education, University of the Witwatersrand*

A profoundly sterling scholarly discourse on decolonising African higher education from its current colonial umbrage. Knaus, Mino, and Seroto have assembled a volume that highlights the need for higher education in Africa to be relevant to the African socio-cultural, political and economic contexts. Their collection should be of interest to educators, scholars, and policy makers on African education.

—**Edward Shizha,** *Professor of Youth & Children's Studies, Wilfrid Laurier University*

Decolonising African Higher Education vibrates with interruption, reclamation and repair. Across nine focused chapters, the authors wrestle with the legacies of epistemic, racial and material injustice and inequality that persist in the current geopolitical and geocultural conditions of higher education in their midst. With ethical wisdom born of resistance and desire, they share the ways in which their transformative imaginaries of Indigeneity will operate and flourish, discussing specific examples, cases and studies from across the complex ecology of knowledges and knowledge systems, curricula, academic citizenry and engagement of the African university.

—**Dr. Dina Zoe Belluigi,** *School of Social Science, Education and Social Work, Queen's University Belfast; and Chair of the Study of the Critical Studies of Higher Education Transformation, Nelson Mandela University*

This book covers diverse topics across the Higher Education curriculum, with contributions from academics across the African continent. Knaus, Mino, and Seroto emphasize Indigenization, contextualization, Africanisation and the use of African epistemologies as key aspects towards a transformative agenda for the decolonization of African Universities. I fully endorse this work.

—**Soul Shava,** *Ph.D., Professor, University of South Africa*

Most often, colonisation is seen in the context of physical colonisation of territory. However, physical colonisation went with, among others, the mission civilisatrice which sought to denigrate and decimate all Indigenous knowledge and lifestyle, leading to the colonisation of the mind. This insidious element of colonialism extended to the highest echelons of formal education. Yet, the formal end of colonialism did not extend to decolonisation of the mind. Thus, the basis of higher education in Africa, as this book seeks to establish, remains colonised. The book, therefore, represents an important contribution to decolonising higher education in Africa to pave the way for the recognition and application of Indigenous knowledge and Indigenous means of knowledge production.
—**Kwadwo Appiagyei-Atua,** *Professor, University of Ghana Legon*

Knaus, Mino, and Seroto provide a roadmap for transcending the antiquated colonially imposed confines of Africa's formal education. Readers will be equipped to leverage on emerging opportunities offered by changing global dynamics—such as increased internet access and the effects of COVID-19 across Africa—to establish authenticity in education towards accelerated individual, community and societal advancement across the region.
—**Dr. Chika Ezeanya Esiobu,** *Visiting Lecturer, University of Rwanda College of Business and Economics and Adjunct Professor in the Department of Africana Studies at California State University, Dominguez Hills*

Knaus, Mino, and Seroto offer more than an alternative perspective on how to re-imagine higher education. Readers are provided African-centered paradigmatic perspectives, research, and praxes that are entrenched in Indigenous wisdom, serving to decolonise African education as well as disrupt epistemic apartheid. If we are who we've been waiting for…then we are ready!
—**Dr. Venus E. Evans-Winters,** *research and policy scholar, clinician in private practice, and Former Professor of Education, Women & Gender Studies, and African American Studies*

DECOLONISING AFRICAN HIGHER EDUCATION

Across the African continent, college student activists have long fought to decolonise African institutions. Reflecting ongoing Western colonisation, however, Indigenous African languages, thought, and structures remain excluded from African universities. Such universities remain steeped in Eurocentric modes of knowing, teaching, researching, and communicating. Students are rarely afforded the opportunity to learn about the wealth of knowledge and sustainable wisdom that was and is generated by their own home communities. Such localised Indigenous African perspectives are critical in a world committed to anti-Black racism, capitalist materialism, and global destruction.

This book thus clarifies decolonial efforts to transform higher education from its anti-Black foundation, offering hope from universities across the continent. Writers are university administrators and faculty who directly challenge contemporary colonial education, exploring tangible ways to decolonise structures, curricula, pedagogy, research, and community relationships. Ultimately, this book moves beyond structural transformation to call for a global commitment to develop Indigenous African-led systems of higher education that foster multilingual communities, local knowledges, and localised approaches to global problems. In shifting from a Western-centric lens to multifaceted African-centrism, the authors reclaim decoloniality from co-optation, repositioning African intellectualism at the core of global higher education to sustain an Ubuntu-based humanity.

Christopher B. Knaus is a global critical race practitioner focused on collaborative disruption of anti-Black education and the centring of Black and Indigenous affirming systems. Dr. Knaus serves as a Professor of Education at the University of Washington Tacoma and Professor Extraordinarius at the University of South Africa.

Takako Mino is a scholar-practitioner, who studies and strives to actualise a humanising education. Dr. Mino serves as an adjunct lecturer at Ashesi University in Ghana and co-founder of upcoming Musizi University in Uganda.

Johannes Seroto is a research practitioner in Indigenous knowledge systems, the history of South African education, and colonial, post-colonial, and decolonisation studies. Dr. Seroto serves as a Professor of the History of Education at the University of South Africa.

DECOLONISING AFRICAN HIGHER EDUCATION

Practitioner Perspectives from Across the Continent

Edited by Christopher B. Knaus, Takako Mino, and Johannes Seroto

NEW YORK AND LONDON

Cover image: Getty Images

First published 2022
by Routledge
605 Third Avenue, New York, NY 10158

and by Routledge
4 Park Square, Milton Park, Abingdon, Oxon, OX14 4RN

Routledge is an imprint of the Taylor & Francis Group, an informa business

© 2022 selection and editorial matter, Christopher B. Knaus, Takako Mino, and Johannes Seroto; individual chapters, the contributors

The right of Christopher B. Knaus, Takako Mino, and Johannes Seroto to be identified as the authors of the editorial material, and of the authors for their individual chapters, has been asserted in accordance with sections 77 and 78 of the Copyright, Designs and Patents Act 1988.

All rights reserved. No part of this book may be reprinted or reproduced or utilised in any form or by any electronic, mechanical, or other means, now known or hereafter invented, including photocopying and recording, or in any information storage or retrieval system, without permission in writing from the publishers.

Trademark notice: Product or corporate names may be trademarks or registered trademarks, and are used only for identification and explanation without intent to infringe.

Library of Congress Cataloging-in-Publication Data
Names: Knaus, Christopher Bodenheimer, editor. | Mino, Takako, 1989- editor. | Seroto, Johannes, editor.
Title: Decolonising African higher education : practitioner perspectives from across the continent / edited by Christopher B. Knaus, Takako Mino, and Johannes Seroto.
Description: New York, NY : Routledge, 2022. | Includes bibliographical references and index.
Identifiers: LCCN 2021056806 (print) | LCCN 2021056807 (ebook) | ISBN 9780367745196 (hardback) | ISBN 9780367745189 (paperback) | ISBN 9781003158271 (ebook)
Subjects: LCSH: Education, Higher--Social aspects--Africa. | Educational change--Africa. | Postcolonialism--Africa. | Afrocentrism.
Classification: LCC LC191.98.A35 D424 2022 (print) | LCC LC191.98.A35 (ebook) | DDC 378.6--dc23/eng/20220218
LC record available at https://lccn.loc.gov/2021056806
LC ebook record available at https://lccn.loc.gov/2021056807

ISBN: 978-0-367-74519-6 (hbk)
ISBN: 978-0-367-74518-9 (pbk)
ISBN: 978-1-003-15827-1 (ebk)

DOI: 10.4324/9781003158271

Typeset in Bembo
by SPi Technologies India Pvt Ltd (Straive)

To Africa's future generations of Indigenous educators, knowledge-holders, and resistance fighters, who sustain Blackness, African solidarity, and live Ubuntu with pride.

CONTENTS

List of Illustrations		*xi*
Acknowledgements		*xii*
About the Contributors		*xiv*
1	Decolonising Higher Education: Definitions, Conceptualisations, Epistemologies Christopher B. Knaus, Takako Mino, and Johannes Seroto	1
2	Centring African Knowledges to Decolonise Higher Education Mishack T. Gumbo, Velisiwe Gasa, and Christopher B. Knaus	21
3	Curriculum Transformation to Decolonise African Higher Education Ngepathimo Kadhila and John Nyambe	37
4	Removing and Recentring: Student Activist Perceptions of Curricular Decolonisation Khazamula J. Maluleka	55
5	Localising Knowledge Systems Ferdinand Mwaka Chipindi, Ane Turner Johnson, and Marcellus Forh Mbah	74

6 Reclaiming Indigenous Epistemes: *Entenga* Drums
  Revival at Kyambogo University   91
  James Isabirye

7 On Language, Coloniality, and Resistance: A
  Conversation between Abdirachid Ismail and Christopher
  B. Knaus   108
  Abdirachid Ismail and Christopher B. Knaus

8 (De)Colonising Physical Education in Ghana   120
  Bella Bello Bitugu and Austin Wontepaga Luguterah

9 The Re-Assimilation of Indigeneity in Education: A
  Long-Term Journey   139
  Takako Mino and Elaine Alowo-Matovu

Index   *157*

ILLUSTRATIONS

Tables

4.1	Participants	64

Figures

6.1	Musisi Mukalazi Livingstone, the Entenga master musician	99
6.2	Musisi scaffolding Entenga student	100
6.3	New generation of Entenga players at coronation 2016 anniversary of the Kabaka	102
6.4	Entenga performance at Kasanda on July 31, 2017	103
8.1	Ampe	123
8.2	Tumatu	124
8.3	Pilolo	125
8.4	Oware	126
8.5	Chaskele	127
8.6	Ole	128

ACKNOWLEDGEMENTS

The editors would like to acknowledge the many Indigenous African elders, scholars, resistance fighters, and mothers, who have struggled against European coloniality to survive long enough to foster love and strength. We specifically recognise the superstar also known as Jordan Gonzales at Academic Mechanic for his generosity, guidance, and beautiful editorial love to help this book become readable. Jordan's care for words, for centring justice and humour in bureaucratic processes, and his eternal commitment to strengthening others offers hope for what education—and writing—could be. We additionally acknowledge the supportive team at Routledge/Taylor and Francis, especially Matthew Friberg, without whom this book project would not have come to fruition.

Dr. Johannes Seroto would like to acknowledge the principal editor of this book, Dr. Christopher B. Knaus, who continuously shares the gift of mentoring and developing others. A very big thank you also goes to my other collaborator, Dr. Takako Mino. I want to say thank you to individuals I had an opportunity to lead, led by, and to watch their leadership from a distance. Thanks to the Department of Educational Foundations at University of South Africa for being my inspiration and foundation.

Dr. Takako Mino would like to acknowledge my dear friends across Africa for teaching me the spirit of being fully human. Thank you Bobhuti, Dr. Christopher B. Knaus, and Dr. Johannes Seroto, for your mentorship, friendship, and support in this process of co-editing my first book. Afwoyo swa Dr. Jane Frances Alowo and webale inho Dr. James Isabirye for your efforts to revive Indigeneity and your constructive feedback. Thank you Larissa Rwenaga Kacence for your thoughtful input and passion for Uganda. Medaase paa Dr. Joseph Oduro-Frimpong for having the coolest office and indulging me in discussions about how to make research more inclusive. Weebale nnyo Elaine Alowo-Matovu for welcoming me back to Uganda and for being a living example of Obuntu Bulamu. To Ma Sankofah, oyi wala doŋ for taking care of me as your daughter and modelling the pursuit and preservation of Indigenous knowledge. To my students, past and present, thank you for inspiring me to continually improve myself as an educator and as a human being. To my colleagues at Ashesi University, for your unshakeable commitment to educating the future of Africa. I want to say arigato to Obachan, my grandmother, who still harbours hope for world peace, and arigato to Kazuko and Yoshiaki Mino, for showing me that happiness comes from dedicating one's life to helping others.

Dr. Christopher B. Knaus would like to acknowledge my beautiful collaborators, Dr. Johannes Seroto and Dr. Takako Mino. Sisi Takako is proof that we can meet incredible future colleagues on a bus; the more present we are, the more likely we can expand our community. And while COVID interrupted our plans to break bread, Bhuti Johannes served as a beautiful welcome into the UNISA family. Administrative hugs to Dr. Velisiwe Gasa, who facilitated my visits to Tshwane and UNISA with open arms and a shared commitment to lift while climbing. Sisi Veli makes things happen despite working within limited resource spaces designed to squash creativity. To my brother Dr. Karel Prins, whose initial conversations sparked this book idea, in part because we recognised, over morning cups of rooibos, that there were simply not enough spaces for administrators to write.

Any work I do in South Africa extends the day-to-day brilliance of school leader and other-mother Nososi Ntshuntshe, a sparkling heart in a war-torn region. Sisi Nososi, your gentle and loving soul are exactly what we need as foundations for an Ubuntu-based education. Dr. Dina Belluigi, who brings fiery creativity and artistic expression to the work of decoloniality, has been an intellectual blessing across these oceans, helping keep me grounded in tangible hope when fighting daily nonsense. And always love to Sisi Samu Mhkize, whose presence reminds me that no matter how horrible oppression may be, we can choose to live vibrantly, with soul-filled purpose. Last, and always most important, Dr. Cyndy Snyder continues to be my light and breath, an eternally patient coach as I hold other people's traumatic experiences with my own.

ABOUT THE CONTRIBUTORS

Editors

Christopher B. Knaus, Ph.D., is a Professor Extraordinarius at the University of South Africa and a Professor of Education at the University of Washington Tacoma. The founding director of University of Washington Tacoma's first doctoral programme, Dr. Knaus has 26 years of experience teaching, researching, and writing about intersectional racism in education. A critical race theory practitioner, Dr. Knaus cultivates educational leaders committed to transforming and decolonising educational institutions. A former Fulbright Scholar to South Africa, Dr. Knaus has served as visiting faculty at the University of the Western Cape and held positions at California State University East Bay and the University of California, Berkeley. His research aims to support creative, healing-centric, abolitionist education that prepares youth and adults to navigate and transform global anti-Blackness. When not agitating against racism, Dr. Knaus is an avid runner, aspiring home chef, and global traveller in support of resistance to global anti-Blackness.

Takako Mino, Ph.D., is an educator with ten years of teaching experience in the U.S., Ghana, and Uganda, and she is co-founder of the upcoming Musizi University. Dr. Mino was born in Japan and grew up in the U.S. She obtained her Bachelor's in International Relations from Claremont McKenna College. One of her major turning points was studying abroad in Uganda and being deeply moved by the warmth and humanism of the Ugandan people. After working with non-governmental organisations to introduce a public debate programme that reached 50,000 students in East Africa, Dr. Mino served as a high school English teacher in California public schools for six years. Dr. Mino obtained her doctorate in Education from Claremont Graduate University. She served as a lecturer in the Humanities and Social Sciences Department of Ashesi University in Ghana for three years and continues to teach at Ashesi as an adjunct. Throughout her career, Takako has explored the role of education in cultivating humanity in young people. She has published peer-reviewed journal articles on topics spanning humanising higher education in Africa, comparative studies of African traditional education and Soka education philosophy, and institutional mentorship in West Africa.

Johannes Seroto, D.Ed., is a full professor in the History of Education at the University of South Africa. He holds a master's and doctorate in the History of Education. Dr. Seroto has authored numerous journal articles, contributed chapters in academic books and has presented a number of scientific papers at local and international conferences. His areas of research include missionary education in South Africa, Indigenous knowledge systems, the history of South African education, and comparative education. He is one of the editors of the celebrated book project, *Decolonising Education in the Global South*. Dr. Seroto's research has made a contribution in debates and research in the field of colonial and postcolonial studies, which continue to critique power relations in various contexts.

Contributors

Elaine Alowo-Matovu is an education entrepreneur and co-founder of The North Green School and upcoming Musizi University. The North Green School is an affordable school in its fifth year, committed to giving a quality, value-based education to middle- and lower-middle-income families in Uganda. From 30 students when it first opened in 2017, the school now has nearly 700 students and a steadily growing waiting list. Elaine is also a lawyer and has extensive experience in engaging with start-ups, corporate law, and land acquisitions. Elaine obtained her Bachelor's in Law from Makerere University and diploma in legal practice from the Law Development Centre. As a mother of four and a proud Ugandan, Elaine is deeply passionate about creating viable alternative education models within the Ugandan context. Elaine is committed to conserving the environment and grooming young individuals who are intentional about making an impactful change in their communities. She has had a longstanding interest in exploring Uganda's history and Indigenous knowledges, the majority of which she accomplished through her own efforts to learn outside of formal schooling. In her research, she employs a sociological lens to analyse development in Africa.

Bella Bello Bitugu, Ph.D., is the Director of the Sports Directorate at the University of Ghana, Legon. Dr. Bitugu is an expert in Development through Sports which uses the strength and power of sports to address development and other societal issues, with a specific focus on addressing all forms of discrimination and racism. Dr. Bitutu is credited with several publications, interventions, and contributions relating to development through sports, North-South, South-South, and Global Dialogue. Educated in Ghana and Austria, Dr. Bitugu is what can be described as *Brain Gain*, as he relocated to Ghana in 2012 after 20 years studying, working, and living in Austria. Aside from his responsibility as the Director of Sports, Dr. Bitugu teaches at the University of Ghana and across universities in Europe. He serves on numerous boards and provides consultancy services to organisations and governments. Prior to his current role, Dr. Bitugu taught at the University of Innsbruck in Austria for 15 years and coordinated Sports for Development projects across Europe and Africa. Dr. Bitugu served as the Country Manager of Right to Play, Ghana, one of the biggest Sport for Development and Peace organisations in the world.

Ferdinand Mwaka Chipindi, Ph.D., is a senior lecturer at the University of Zambia's School of Education. His research interests are at the intersection of higher education, political economy, and decolonisation. Ferdinand currently leads the department of Educational Administration and Policy Studies, where he teaches a range of courses in education and development.

Velisiwe Gasa, Ph.D., is a Professor and Head of Graduate Studies and Research in the College of Education at the University of South Africa. She leads various research and community engagement projects. Dr. Gasa's research interests include postgraduate supervision, research administration and management, decoloniality in higher education, distance learning, learners' aggressive/challenging behaviour, family dynamics, inclusive education, and gender studies.

Mishack T. Gumbo, Ph.D., is a Professor in the Department of Science and Technology Education at the University of South Africa. He leads research and community engagement projects. Dr. Gumbo's range of research interests include: Indigenous Technology Knowledge Education, Decolonisation, Africanisation, and Indigenisation of Curriculum and Postgraduate Programme/Supervision, Teachers' Professional Development and Pedagogical Content Knowledge in relation to technology, and Distance Education and E-Learning.

James Isabirye, Ph.D., is an educator, musician, cultural revivalist and manager, and researcher. Dr. Isabirye teaches Music Education and Music in the Department of Performing Arts at Kyambogo University in Kampala, Uganda. Dr. Isabirye earned his doctorate in Music Education from Oakland University in Rochester, Michigan, U.S. His research interests include Indigenous knowledge and ways of knowing; decolonising education, being, and the research practice; music and dance heritage practices and contexts; and a constructivist vision of knowledge and learning. Dr. Isabirye has researched Indigenous education in Busoga and Buganda, the value of identity, agency, and joy-filled passion in music education and cultural revival contexts; relevancy of Indigenous music education in school settings; and music and dance as mediation of ritual and healing. Dr. Isabirye has presented research papers and music and dance workshops at conferences at universities and cultural development institutions in Uganda, Kenya, Tanzania, Ethiopia, Sweden, Denmark, Norway, the United Kingdom, the U.S., China, Hungary, and France. He has also led Indigenous music and dance revival projects in Busoga and Buganda kingdoms in Uganda with funds from UNESCO and Singing Wells and engaged in development and networking activities of the cultural and creative industries across the world.

Abdirachid Ismail, Ph.D., is a founding member and current Vice President of the Independent Research Institute of the Horn of Africa (IRICA). For the past 18 years, he has served as a senior lecturer in the University of Djibouti, teaching linguistics and communication. Dr. Ismail has worked in various French and international companies, as an industrial purchaser and professional promoter. Past administrative posts include serving as Head of Literature and Linguistics Department and Chief Executive of the Continuing Education Center of Djibouti University. Dr. Ismail has directed numerous transformational projects, including Djibouti's *Ten-Year Strategic Plan for Higher Education*, 2010 and the *Creation of the Intergovernmental Academy of Somali Language in 2013*. Dr. Ismail's research interests include language, culture, communication, and organisational management. Recent publications include English and French language engagements, using Somali history, folktales, and current experiences to argue for transforming the foundations of education across the Somali Coast, and the Horn of Africa.

Ane Turner Johnson, Ph.D., is a professor of educational leadership at Rowan University in New Jersey, USA. She has published and presented on higher Education in Africa, focusing on governance and policy-making. Dr. Johson's recent work addresses Indigenous knowledge, sustainable development, and qualitative research methods.

Ngepathimo Kadhila is a Director of Quality Assurance at the University of Namibia. He holds a Ph.D. in Higher Education with a focus on Quality Assurance from the University of the Free State, South Africa; Master's in Education and Bachelor in Education from the University of Namibia; as well as Postgraduate Diploma in Higher Education from Rhodes University in South Africa. His research interests include academic development, curriculum development in higher education, teaching and learning in higher education including assessment, and quality assurance.

Austin Wontepaga Luguterah, Ph.D., is a sports management and governance specialist in the department of Physical Education and Sports Studies of the University of Ghana. Dr. Luguterah has 25 years of teaching physical education and sports from basic school through to the university. He obtained his bachelor's degree in English Language and Physical Education from the University of Education, Winneba, Ghana. He has two master's degrees, including in public administration from the University of Ghana, and in sports management from the Johan Cruyff Institute. Dr. Luguterah obtained his Ph.D. in Public Administration and Management from the University of South Africa. He has international certificates in Sports Management, Event Management, Coaching Effectiveness, and several coaching certificates. His area of expertise includes Physical Education, Sports Management and Governance, Contemporary Sports Leadership, and volleyball coaching.

Khazamula J. Maluleka, Ph.D., was a Senior Education Specialist for Technology Education in Gauteng Province. He is presently a senior lecturer in Educational Foundations at the University of South Africa, where he teaches Comparative and International Education. He holds a Ph.D. from Vista University. Dr. Maluleka's research interests are embedded in Indigenous Knowledge Systems, including culturally responsive pedagogy, curriculum decolonisation, and Indigenous technology. He has published several articles and chapters based on these areas of interests.

Marcellus Forh Mbah, Ph.D., is a senior lecturer in the Institution of Education in the School of Social Sciences, Nottingham Trent University. He contributes to teaching a range of modules, providing research supervision and leading a fortnightly digest seminar. As an active researcher, Dr. Mbah also leads a special interest group (SIG) on Education and International Development across the University. His research interest captures the overarching themes of education for climate change adaptation and higher education's contribution towards sustainable development and specifically looking at the role of Indigenous knowledge systems.

John Nyambe is currently the Associate Dean of the School of Education at the University of Namibia. Dr. Nyambe's research interests are in the areas of higher education, covering learning and teaching, curriculum development, assessment and quality assurance. Further to this, Dr. Nyambe also does research in teacher education and educational reform. Dr. Nyambe has held various leadership positions in higher education.

1
DECOLONISING HIGHER EDUCATION

Definitions, Conceptualisations, Epistemologies

Christopher B. Knaus, Takako Mino, and Johannes Seroto

2020 got off to a rough start, with news of a deadly virus spreading fears about a possible global contagion. By March, much of the world began closing borders, shutting down basic aspects of society, and limiting non-essential human movement. Many African countries were quick to respond, shutting down all but essential services when the first trickle of cases came in. Others downplayed the virus, with some leaders denying the virus existed, paralleling historic and ongoing treatment of those with HIV and AIDS. Some of this fear and denialism reflected historic (and ongoing) Western medical research that withheld healthcare, forced sterilisations, and tested vaccines on unwitting populations (who later would be kept from accessing those very vaccines, as has been the case with COVID-19 in South Africa) (Washington, 2008). Regardless of response, however, testing capacity was limited, and enforcement of social distancing was nearly impossible in areas where people live in tight quarters, sharing washrooms and limited water access. Universities across the continent struggled to adapt to the unexpected lockdown; some shifted to remote learning within weeks, while others shut down completely, awaiting government directions on re-opening. In July of 2020, despite COVID's continued spread and increasing deaths, many economies across Africa began to re-open to reduce the impact of the first continent-wide recession Africa has experienced in 25 years (Giles & Mwai, 2020). As people returned to work and travel restrictions were eased, a daily balancing act between risking COVID contraction and personal survival became the new normal. COVID heightened pre-existing inequities and threatened to push millions more into poverty (Lakner, Mahler, Negre, & Prydz, 2020). These disparities only increased in 2021, as vaccines that were shared amongst Europe, the U.K., and the U.S., were largely withheld from Africa.

DOI: 10.4324/9781003158271-1

Global racial tensions rose as the pandemic dealt a disproportionate blow to Black Americans in the U.S. (Laurencin & McClinton, 2020; Shah, Sachdeva, & Dodiuk-Gad, 2020). On top of these strains, the killing of George Floyd by U.S. police officers sparked a national wave of anti-Black police brutality protests, renewing the global momentum of the #BlackLivesMatter movement. A multiracial coalition across the globe protested at police stations and civic offices, and for a short while, the world saw statues of racist historical figures toppled (McEvoy, 2020; Taylor, 2020). The 2020 #BlackLivesMatter protests continued a long-standing tradition of global struggle against the structural whiteness that enables violence against Black lives on every continent (Marx, 1998). For many Africans, the #BlackLivesMatter movement re-opened painful memories of colonisation, imperialism, and the imposition of a white supremacist doctrine that justified slavery and the killing of untold hundreds of millions of Black people on the continent, and that still persists in shaping modern African societies.

As these dual pandemics collided across the globe and extenuated disparities, displaced Black communities in South Africa erupted into protests, conducting coordinated mass movements to occupy land. These protests continued the #RhodesMustFall movements that emerged into prominence in 2015 with an aligned effort to challenge structural racism (Brown, 2020). These movements specifically called for higher education curricula to centre on African discourses. Contributing to decolonising higher education efforts, these anti-racism protests called for a full stop to the entire educational system's fostering of racism and coloniality (Chantiluke, Kwoba, & Nkopo, 2018). The historic and contemporary linkages between South African anti-Blackness and American anti-Blackness are both historically and currently rooted in a white settler coloniality, wherein the structures of whiteness have remained intact, ensuring coloniality as the way of organising all aspects of society (Knaus & Brown, 2016; Rosenberg, 2020). Thus, Black South Africans agitated, not just for access to land and higher education, but for decolonial orientations to both.

Across much of the rest of the African continent, however, discussions on the inherent anti-Blackness in colonially imposed structures can be more muted, in part because many African institutions of higher education are predominantly Black. In South Africa, however, apartheid-era segregation remains normalised in racially disparate higher education institutions, with larger numbers of Black staff, faculty, leaders, and students serving in resource-depleted institutions. In South Africa, the connection between historic anti-Blackness and contemporary conditions is impossible to ignore (Carter, 2012; Marx, 1998). As Makhubela (2018) argues, 'The South African academy is a colonial-apartheid invention and continually seeks to reproduce this status quo' (p. 2). This commitment to the status quo of coloniality is precisely what South African students have protested in the ongoing #RhodesMustFall movements.

The lack of such overt structural whiteness in opposition to Blackness across much of the rest of the African continent, however, complicates resistance to contemporary coloniality. Indeed, when those who organise and lead higher education infrastructures are ethnically, culturally, and linguistically diverse, in reflection of a country's Black populace, considerations of colonial infrastructures are murkier. Such is the case with colonisation; when countries overthrew their colonial rulers, the infrastructures, particularly in education, remained (Belluigi & Thondhlana, 2019; Lulat, 2005; Teferra & Altbach, 2003). While white colonial rulers may have been overthrown, the machinery of linguistic and capitalistic domination was not. The liberation struggle may have removed symbolic European colonialism, but Arabic domination of Black populations, for example, were not so easily dislodged. Within these nuanced oppressive constraints, higher education has largely continued its colonial foundation unabated, even as the need for Indigenous African methods has been expressed through research, publications, and recently created academic departments (Chilisa, 2020).

The opportunity for higher education to offer solutions to pandemics, poverty, racism, and disparities, and to foster local and global leadership that can break economic and social dependency from the West, is ever growing (Moyo, 2009). Yet the higher education institutions imposed upon Africa were not designed, nor have they been transformed, for such. Despite thousands of years of higher education, African nations have largely transitioned to a Western-based approach to post-secondary education, embracing a model colonised into existence (Lulat, 2005). This approach has led to a focus on Western notions of research, limited to dissemination in obscure academic channels often hidden behind paywalls and monolingual instructional approaches geared towards standardised colonial languages (Ramoupi, 2014). Even though multilingual and Indigenous African learners make up the majority of students in Africa, most attend woefully unresourced basic education systems, and the cultural, linguistic, and historical wealth of these communities remains structurally excluded from official knowledge (Lulat, 2005). Thus, despite the vast intellectual wealth that Pan-Africa represents, including the continual infusing of African identities and ideologies into the fabric of colonial systems (Falola, 2003), decolonising all aspects of higher education in Africa—after centuries of colonial rule and continued reliance upon the West—remains as Bob Marley (1976) sang, 'a fleeting illusion, to be pursued, but never attained.'

The work of decolonisation is not only limited to higher education institutions but is a process requiring transformation on multiple levels—from the global to the individual—across economic systems, housing, food, electricity, basic education, representational politics, transportation, and other societal functions. This book focuses on the future of African universities because of their current role in reinforcing structural oppressions, and because of their potential to disrupt colonial legacies. Indeed, as the ongoing COVID-19 and anti-Black racism pandemics demonstrate, higher education can emerge from its colonial roots to lead the way towards addressing our most pressing global issues. We argue that no other resource is equipped to foster such decoloniality on a continental level. This book will thus accomplish two primary objectives. First, we make the case for why elevation of ongoing processes of higher education decoloniality across Africa is essential to fully release from the chains of colonialism and anti-Blackness. We demonstrate how definitions of decolonising education engage contemporary African higher education contexts and clarify complexities of Indigenous African modes of decolonial thought (Falola, 2003). Second, we engage the complicated and often contradictory transformative efforts that are contained within overused, oft-appropriated, heavily theorised notions of decoloniality (Manthalu & Waghid, 2019; Ndlovu-Gatsheni, 2015a; Shepard, 2015; Tuck & Yang, 2012; Tuck, McKenzie, & McCoy, 2014). This chapter also frames how Africa-based authors grapple with various levels of and orientations to higher education decoloniality, offering insights by practitioner-scholars who lead within institutions of African higher education.

Why Decolonise Higher Education

Centuries of enslavement, racism, land theft, systemic exploitation, environmental degradation, genocide, war, violence, eradication of family structures, implementation of colonial schooling, disruption of such schooling, and the continual exodus of people trying to survive have dramatically shaped the backdrop of African societies. Higher education similarly reflects these historical and contemporary realities, systematically privileging whiteness, European and American subjectivities, and European linguistic domination, while largely ignoring (and/or justifying) the fabric of sustained racialised impoverishment (Lulat, 2005). Yet countless examples of resistance strategies, programmes, and entire academic departments exist in opposition to the colonial mission, consequently fostering Indigenous African knowledge systems. While many examples of higher education challenge such structured devastation by infusing Indigenous African knowledge and providing leadership through localised circumstances, the bulk of African higher education remains committed—in shape, scope, and form—to Western approaches, despite how these approaches continue to disrupt African societies. The core of higher education decoloniality, then, must build from these pockets of resistance, to challenge the pressures and powers that normalise colonial structures that silence and limit Black-affirming efforts to implement institutional and societal decoloniality.

One recent example illustrates how the commitment to Western-framed higher education promotes racism as knowledge, further silencing conversations that challenge whiteness. In May 2020, the South African Journal of Science published an article entitled, 'Why are black South African students less likely to consider studying biological sciences?' The article reported on Nattrass's (2020) survey, which 211 University of Cape Town (UCT) students completed during their lunch breaks. Questions asked if respondents had 'considered studying the biological sciences,' and a seemingly random selection of opinions, such as if they agree that 'Addressing social inequality is more important than wildlife conservation' or that 'Humans evolved from apes' (Nattrass, 2020). Additional questions assessed if respondents agree 'that disciplines like conservation biology are colonial and should be scrapped at UCT,' and that 'many of South Africa's national parks should be scrapped and the land given to the poor' (Nattrass, 2020). Natrass also assessed if respondents had ever owned pets, then ran regressions of these overly simplistic questions, presenting findings that suggested linkages between 'anti-conservative' views, 'religiosity,' and 'materialist values,' even though these undefined concepts were not surveyed.

Methodological concerns were raised immediately. Makoni (2020) reports that UCT's Black Academic Caucus (BAC), among many who protested the article's lack of context, said it was 'not surprised when white academics design research framed in a fashion that belittles the aspirations of black people because they are meant to feed a narrative that "they are not good enough or they don't deserve to be here."' Makoni further reported that the BAC leveraged a challenge for all higher education institutions: 'Let us not have more of this patronising and dehumanising research. Instead let's have research that affirms the humanity of all and doesn't seek to insidiously fault black people for institutionalised structures beyond their control.' Underneath the charge of dehumanising research lays the reality that, as BAC argued, 'institutional structures,' including lingering apartheid-era effects, directly limit access into predominantly white universities like UCT in the first place.

Nattrass (2020) ignored South Africa's context of dramatic racial disparities, avoided engagement with the extensive literature base on higher education access for students of colour in science fields, and did not consider individual respondent background, as if student career aspirations can be summarised by apartheid-era racial categorisation (Fadiji & Reddy, 2020; Marginson, 2016; McCoy, Luedke, & Winkle-Wagner, 2017; Walker, 2018; Wilson-Strydom, 2017). The methodological weaknesses of the study include a lack of engagement with racial, ethnic, and linguistic identities, which have a profound importance for South Africa's diverse populations under the umbrella of 'Black,' as well as a lack of assessing intersectionalities such as gender, sexuality, ability, social economic class, and related social identities that are widely oppressed (Boonzaier & Mhkize, 2018; Bornman, Álvarez-Mosquera, & Seti, 2018; Gouws, 2017; Walker, 2005). In short, Nattrass's entire study was based upon stereotypical preconceptions, reinforcing a deficit agenda that blames Black students for white oppression (McKay & Devlin, 2016; O'Shea, Lysaght, Roberts, & Harwood, 2016).

Two examples reinforce this publication designed to promote an anti-Black agenda. The first is the linkage between anti-conservationist views based on questions like, 'Addressing social inequality is more important than wildlife conservation.' This question is a false comparison; one can think wildlife conservation is incredibly important, and just slightly less so than social inequalities. Similarly, linking a two-part statement 'that disciplines like conservation biology are colonial and should be scrapped at UCT' conflates issues. One can certainly see conservation biology as colonial, particularly given that access into universities is based upon colonial structures. But scrapping the entire field is a different question requiring nuance: Some might prefer to decolonise and transform, rather than remove entirely. Regardless, opinion on coloniality of the field is not the same as the desire to scrap or transform. The survey instrument, in short, did not allow for the human capacity to hold multiple thoughts at once. Just as Nattrass's (2020) approach denies racial identities, languages, cultural heritages, and individuality, her approach to surveying humans is overly simplistic and stereotyping.

But a deeper underlying issue remains: What is the purpose of this research, particularly given that it was conducted at a state-supported public university? Why (and how) did a scientific journal publish a study that so clearly violates almost every basic tenet of social scientific research? That a study utilising racist research methods was conducted and disseminated via proper scientific channels suggests a sinister white supremacist alignment across state and scientific institutions. Such alignments collude to promote white supremacist thinking over decolonial efforts. Makoni (2020) reports that the journal will publish a special compilation issue based on Nattrass's (2020) article, giving the author a further elevated platform. It is not enough that the journal published a poorly conducted, racist study, but the journal's response is to feature that article as the centre of debate, further entrenching the white privilege of the author's racism. This process highlights the whiteness of academia, and how the agenda of what counts as knowledge is legitimated by those who hold the power to publish, frame scholarly discussions, and foster denial of context, exclusion, racism, power, and humanity (Boaventura de Sousa, 2014; Ndlovu-Gatsheni, 2013; Ramoupi, 2014; Walker, 2005; Wilson-Strydom, 2017). In short, rather than promote diverse forms of knowledge, including Black and Indigenous-centric engagements, the journal and the university collude to highlight white supremacy as a legitimate ground for debate.

This article, the journal that published it, and continued anti-Black racism are precisely why decoloniality across higher education on the continent is so urgently needed. Indeed, rather than invest in faculty to conduct racist-driven research, disseminate such through racism-supportive journals, and then foster conversation about an idea that is clearly anti-Black, a transformational agenda recentres the role and purpose of higher education. Underlying this focus on racist-driven research is a charge that most research conducted by African academia is simply not up to the task of decolonising, much less simply helping to improve daily life for the continent's impoverished communities. Falola, the well-known writer and scholar of Indigenous African knowledge, clarified an argument about Nigeria that applies across the continent: 'Tell me one problem facing Nigeria that the academia has been engaged to resolve successfully' (Falola, as quoted in Adeyemi & Agboluaje, 2020). Falola notes a lack of infrastructure to fund cutting-edge research that meaningfully engages societal problems: 'I don't even think we have well-funded research institutes capable enough to carry out the research we are talking about here' (Falola, as quoted in Adeyemi & Agboluaje, 2020). Lulat (2003) laid the ground for Falola's point, some 17 years earlier:

The fact is that the remarkable quantitative progress that African higher education has registered to date sadly masks a proportionate qualitative degeneration on a massive scale. It is symptomatic of the emergence (to varying degrees of course, depending on what part of Africa one is looking at) of an enduring pattern of woes: Crippling budgetary constraints as institutions are starved of funds; large scale deterioration of physical plant; overflowing classrooms; poorly equipped laboratories and other similar facilities set against a logistical background of intermittent supply of even such basics as water and electricity (not to mention consumables like chemicals); shrinking and outdated libraries as collection development has come to a virtual standstill against a backdrop of widespread looting of holdings; overworked and underpaid faculty who often must moonlight to make ends meet; inefficient administrations as talented and able administrators have left for greener pastures; teaching, learning and research that is bereft of even the most basic logistical support (such as chalk, textbooks, photocopy machines, etc.); almost complete loss of autonomy as governments vilify and obliterate academic freedom; and the list goes on.

(p. 596)

The overall context of academic disparity spans the continent, with many countries lacking in sufficient infrastructure, while countries with sufficient capacity provide unequal access, particularly in relation to race, language, and economic access.

The three traditional functions of a university, research, teaching, and service are intended to promote the public good, at least if mission statements of higher education institutions are to be believed. In essence, universities exist to support and enhance life in our many diverse forms, through these three primary approaches. Yet without substantive research infrastructure, African universities remain vastly underrepresented at the global level. Despite comprising 12.5 % of the world population, Africa contributes less than 1 % of world research (Duermeijer, Amir, & Schoombee, 2018). This means that African voices are often excluded from global discourse, further marginalising African scholarship. This is of detriment to both Africa and the rest of the world. Research produced by universities has the potential to shape policy-making and inform public thinking on societal challenges. Yet faculty are expected to publish in internationally ranked journals requiring a basis in Western logic and theory that deny the existence of other ways of thinking. By requiring research dissemination that adheres to colonial infrastructures, logics, and languages, universities bolster this unjust power dynamic. Fostering a decoloniality through scholarship is critical in enabling Africans to develop homegrown solutions to societal issues rather than seeking to import solutions prescribed by other countries and conducted within a framework designed to promote whiteness (Chilisa, 2020; Ndlovu-Gatsheni, 2015b).

Similarly, teaching serves as a foundational process through which to develop future generations of leaders, professionals, educators, and public servants, and has the potential to shape democratic values. University graduates are more likely to be able to access opportunities that will place them into positions of influence that impact many others, yet only nine per cent of college age youth are enrolled in university across Africa (World Bank, 2018). Limiting college access ensures university education remains a privilege available primarily to future generations of the already elite. Within this limited population, knowledge dissemination across African institutions continues to reflect Freire's notion of the banking system, wherein students are treated as objects, provided opportunities to withdraw knowledge held by instructors confined by academic disciplines and ultimately assessed by those with intellectual authority (Freire, 1970). Morreira, Taru, and Truyts (2020) clarify:

> In the social science disciplines, furthermore, most undergraduate teaching is lecture-theatre or classroom based and is removed from concrete engagements with the material world. Lecture theatres allow one expert academic citizen (the lecturer) to teach many non-expert academic subjects (the students), which fulfils both an economic and a hierarchical imperative.
>
> *(pp. 3–4)*

While there are efforts to provide more humane instructional engagements (Behari-Leak et al., 2019), by and large, university instruction remains lecture-driven. These orientations privilege Western-rooted students more familiar with such individualised, abstract learning, reinforcing a colonial mindset to devalue multiple ways of thinking, teaching, and learning (Morreira et al., 2020).

Often subsumed beneath the economic engines of teaching and research, university service to communities remains a distant third function of higher education. Dismissed by many as ivory towers, in part due to the intentional exclusion of applicants and reliance upon elitist frameworks, universities attempt to counter privileged aloofness through claiming relevance specifically through service commitments (Fourie, 2003). Yet service to communities reflects a lack of investment in higher education and a disengagement from addressing societal problems, in part due to limited institutional support for such engagements (Buckley, 2012). Similar to aid agencies operating within an outside-in framework to solve community problems for the community (Knaus & Brown, 2016), universities often rely upon notions of service learning that take from, rather than collaborate with, communities (Rautenbach & Mitchell, 2005). Such service-learning frameworks position students to adopt Western frameworks, paralleling some international aid agencies' adversarial relationships within African countries (Knaus & Brown, 2016; Santiago-Ortiz, 2019). The deficit-based perspective in such service orientations guide university service perceptions, reinforcing the ivory tower in ways that position local people as a source of labour and the community as a space for student or faculty field work rather than as equal partners in sustainable development. This third foundation of higher education simply echoes the coloniality of research and teaching, perhaps even more nefariously, by hiding beneath claims of helping while fostering reliance and elitist engagement.

Thus, however well-intended individual faculty, students, staff, and leaders may be, the university at its core remains committed to a robust, continually renewing, coloniality. Combined with disparately provided resources, racial and class-based exclusions built into the walls and WiFis of campuses, woefully inadequate infrastructures, and governmental limitations, higher education in its current form is simply inadequate for the task of leading decoloniality across the continent. Rather than address these historic and contemporary inadequacies piecemeal, however, we suggest that decoloniality must coincide with a strategic reinvestment in higher education. The two efforts must be conjoined, wherein investments that are based in 'adopting and examining an epistemic lens that recognise multiple knowledge forms as legitimate' (Morreira, 2017, p. 288), and that are tied to access, relevance, and a commitment to preparing local solutions to localised problems, with a concurrent global lens, are the only way forward to a transformed notion of higher education committed to modelling, fostering, and continually decolonising.

Conceptualising African Colonialities

Moving towards a coherent platform of decoloniality and reinvestment in transforming higher education requires engaging in conversations on what 'Indigenous,' 'African,' 'coloniality,' and 'decoloniality' all mean to whom. Yet this book is written in a colonial language, reflecting the European linguistic domination that remains the norm across the continent. Similarly, any definitions of terminologies confined to the parameters of the very English used to colonise remains extremely problematic. At the same time, a cursory overview of terminologies is essential to engage in specificities of any sort; in short, decoloniality may require multilinguality, but will also likely engage multiple forms of English to transform the very languages used to colonise. In this text, we use Black, African, and Indigenous interchangeably, as they are commonly used across the Sub-Saharan continent, while we intentionally designate Indigenous African to connote pre-colonial heritage, that is, the culture and knowledge of people who existed on the continent prior to white coloniality and which persists in various forms in modern African society.

As a reflection on memory and history, we assert that first and foremost, thinking about Indigenous African decoloniality requires recognition that the African continent has seen waves of imperialism and enslavement for thousands of years. African people have resisted settler colonialism, genocides, mass enslavement, and imperialism from the very beginning. The impact of colonisation on cultural ways of organising life and the violence inflicted on local populations varied dramatically. While many waves intended to colonise, such as the European domination of North Africa, and Arab settlements across North, West, and East Africa, there was integration across cultural contexts, with some semblances of limited linguistic, racial, and religious tolerance across the centuries (Azumah, 2014; Lodhi, 1994).

The point is not to minimise historic violences and wars but to contextualise types of coloniality based on intentional migration and patterns of settler coloniality. These waves complicate notions of Indigeneity, as many of the people with claims to being the first inhabitants violently displaced and settled upon those who were there before, who had similarly settled upon those who were before them, and these waves historically included European, Arabic, Christian, Islamic, and African empires (De Bruijn, 2001; Kopytoff, 1987; Lentz, 2006).

From Europe, since the 1500s, came new sinister waves of colonisation focused more intently on systemic resource extraction, settler-domination, and the imposition of societal segregations by race, language, religion, and ethnic affiliation. As Du Bois (1925) observes, 'With nearly every great European empire today walks its dark colonial shadow' (p. 423). As Europe thrust itself upon the rest of the globe, colonising vast land and diverse peoples as far as their ships—powered by enslaved Africans—could reach, Africa became a resource through which to fund global domination (Rodney, 2018). The sheer impact of this intentional devastation cannot be understated, as the mass disruption in ways of life across the continent cannot ever fully recover. There is no going back. In addition to lives and languages killed, societal destruction, family obliteration, and genocide, Europe created borders that largely remain intact, carving up regions from which to instill their specific versions of white supremacist coloniality, so that any notion of Africa is, at its core, impacted and defined by the West (Benyere, 2020; Said, 1978).

Colonialism cannot be simplistically understood as a phenomenon where outsiders come to stay in a country and establish territorial sovereign political orders (Ndlovu-Gatsheni, 2015b). Colonialism is about the practice of power, subjugation of society, and production of knowledge by a dominant political group. Maldonado-Torres (2007) explains that colonialism is 'a political and economic relation in which the sovereignty of a nation or a people rests on the power of another nation, which makes such a nation an empire' (p. 203). The colonisers not only succeeded in taking over Africa's resources but also captured African minds long after they packed their bags and left Africans to govern themselves. The worst form of colonialism in the African continent, according to Ndlovu-Gatsheni (2013) is thus the epistemological one. Under colonial frameworks, the epistemologies of Indigenous people were suppressed and destroyed. This process of killing Indigenous knowledge systems has been described as epistemicide (Santos, 2014). Césaire (2000) defines colonialism as 'a disruptive, "decivilising," dehumanising, exploitative, racist, violent, brutal, covetous, and "thingifying" system' (p. 32). In this way, Indigenous Africans were taught to see themselves through the eyes of the coloniser, which rendered Indigenous ways of life barbaric and uncivilised (wa Thiong'o, 1986; Wright, 1957).

Fanon (1963) cautions that colonialism disfigures and distorts the past of oppressed peoples. Colonialism is hidden in institutions and governance structures. The knowledge hidden in the colonial African university replaced Indigenous

African knowledge with Western notions. During the post-independence period, freedom fighters who worked to secure independence dreamed of a reclaimed African identity free from colonial legacies that influenced how Indigenous Africans viewed themselves and lived their lives. Newly independent governments saw universities as centres of Africanisation and tasked them to propel Africanisation throughout society, supporting ambitious projects such as Nyerere's (1987) Ujamaa and Nkrumah's (1963) Pan-African vision. Quijano (2000a, 2000b) and Mignolo (2000) explain how colonialism continues to enforce domination and exploitation to undervalue Indigenous people. Morreira (2017), writing about Mignolo (2011) and Quijano (2007), summarises that 'whilst colonialism may have been and gone, the colonial matrix of power is still very much seen, lived, and felt in the present day' (p. 292). For the purposes of this book, then, we define coloniality as the ongoing self-replicating practices that structure white supremacy's resource theft through intersectional racism, sexism, classism, heterosexism, religious persecution, Islamophobia, ableism, colourism, and related oppressions across all organising systems within African societies.

Conceptualising Decolonialities

Definitions of decolonisation have taken on different meanings from post-independence to modern times. Decolonisation should not only be understood as the 'undoing' of colonisation processes, that is, the act of undoing establishing colonies, but should be framed as disrupting the political, economic, and paternalistic philosophies that continue to undermine Indigenous ways of living, thinking, and expressing (Mignolo, 2017). Decoloniality must be both a challenge to the status quo of colonial racism and an imagination of what could organise African societies instead (Mbembe, 2016). Thus, decolonisation encompasses complicated, contradictory, contested terrains, including coloniality, Indigeneity, language, individual and collective identities, and higher education infrastructures designed to maintain societal fragmentation to justify and promote a world of white supremacy. For the purposes of this book, we define decoloniality as intentional, systemic recentring of Indigenous African thought, languages, people, ideas, and ways of organising societies. These cultural hybridisations transform higher education into a people's collective engagement with thinking about past oppressions and resistances to inform present conditions and strategies and build futures that foster anti-oppression as fundamental to Indigenous African knowledges.

Such previous and contemporary decolonial Indigenous African efforts, within a context of ongoing coloniality, have always been targeted for eradication. Indeed, the very act of defining what counts as decoloniality represents a privilege of space and time. As colonial schools were implemented to foster Christianity and whiteness as social order, decoloniality was forced underground, as elders created and told stories to sustain cultural and linguistic traditions and directly countered the white supremacy of the formal organisational structure of newly independent

African countries (Mpofu, 2013). Because the West's attempts to obliterate collective African memory of decoloniality, including the devaluation of the very languages in which such memories are held, decolonisation of contemporary African societies must sustain a foundation in historical resistances and multilinguality (Mbembe, 2016). As Ngugi wa Thiong'o (2005) argues, 'We must reconnect with the buried alluvium of African memory and use it as a base for further planting of African memory on the continent and the world' (p. 164). Recognition of the horrors that have been heaped upon Africa, combined with memories of resistances and culturally sustaining practices provide a hopefulness from which to conceptualise decoloniality in the contemporary African context (Mpofu, 2013).

Looking to Indigenous African philosophies as a source of inspiration plays an important role in shaping contemporary movements. By Indigenous African philosophies, we mean Indigenous ways of life and thinking that pre-existed colonisation but have also remained engrained in contemporary realities. Indigenous philosophies are based on an understanding that a spirit moves within and around all lives and differs from rational Newtonian Cartesian epistemologies that tend towards an over-reliance on logic and scientific experimentation, excluding spiritual and non-material realms of life (Goduka, 1999). Even though most Africans can be considered Indigenous, in terms of originating from the continent prior to European coloniality, much Indigenous culture has been lost. Indigenous Africans remain the numerical majority across most of the continent, whereas settler coloniser populations remain a small minority; even in South Africa, whites represent less than eight per cent of the total population (CIA, 2020).

While Indigenous languages may be fading, they are still normalised in everyday conversations. In many cases, colonising and local languages have integrated into hybrid languages, such as Pidgin and Creole, but also Afrikaans in South Africa (Faraclas, 2013). This is the same with religion. While the majority of Africans may identify as Christian or Muslim, Indigenous religions have informed African spiritual blends and given birth to reformist movements such as Black liberation theology (Maluleke, 2004). Therefore, Indigeneity is not a static concept stuck in the past but is a living and breathing praxis that continues to shift and morph through exposure to and adaptation with other cultures. Furthermore, we recognise that Africa is home to diverse Indigenous groups that have been violently categorised into various ethnic and racial groups through multiple approaches, mostly imposed by Western policies and exploitative practices. Similarities exist among these diversities that require continual unpacking as part of a decolonial movement to reflect the fluidity of socially constructed racial identities.

Core principles of Indigenous African epistemologies often differ from Western modes of thought, particularly that which is reinforced by universities. First, Indigenous African philosophies are based on a fundamental appreciation for the interconnectedness of all life, whereas Western philosophy tends to segment out various factions of life into different compartments (Asante, 1988; Oruka, 1990; Santos, 2014). The very idea of religion and education as separate from other aspects of life is incongruous within many Indigenous African philosophies (Goduka, 1999). Second, Indigenous African philosophies privilege communal orientations as opposed to individualistic notions centred on the self that dominates Western thought (Asante, 1988; Boaventura de Sousa, 2014; Falola, 2003). Consequently, notions of citizenship prioritise demonstrating concern for others above upholding one's own inherent rights (Gyekye, 2011). Third, Indigenous African philosophies emphasise respect for the wisdom of the elders, many of whom still transmit knowledge to younger generations through oral traditions and circumstances (Oruka, 1990). The difficulty of decolonising conceptualisations of Indigenous African philosophies lies in the fact that most of the published work in this field have been written in English (or French, Italian, Dutch, etc.), viewed through Western philosophical conceptual frameworks, and limited to the privileged few in academia (Wiredu, 1998). Part of the challenge of Indigenising African philosophy is to disentangle Western frameworks that fail to capture the totality of African thought and way of life despite the colonial leanings that have already been infused in African philosophers through their own education and training (Wiredu, 1998).

In applying decoloniality to education, Maldonado-Torres (2007) reiterates that coloniality is 'maintained alive in books, in the criteria for academic performance, in cultural patterns, in common sense, in the self-image of peoples, in aspirations of self, and so many other aspects of our modern experience' (p. 243). Decolonisation of higher education must then recentre Indigenous African life at the core, rather than Western orientations to thinking about others. While the decolonisation of higher education has been debated at length since the 1960s, few educational structures have been conceptualised or implemented to make such decoloniality and centring of Indigenous Africa a reality. And this highly political process of Africanisation has often turned out to reproduce inequalities in a different way. Even among Indigenous languages, linguicide continues; in Tanzania, where an estimated 156 languages are spoken, Kiswahili was the only African language to be selected as one of the official languages of the country along with English (Muzale & Rugemalira, 2008). Even though Tanzania has been applauded for its successful propagation of Kiswahili, many other languages of smaller marginalised ethnic groups are endangered and dying (Legère, 2006). Decolonising is not limited to Africanisation; decoloniality requires re-examining any and all oppressive structures and norms put in place by former colonisers that continue to privilege certain Indigenous groups over others. Because this systematic oppression is reflected across institutions, even administrations committed to decolonisation maintain and promote the colonial oppression of Indigenous knowledge and epistemologies by simply continuing to operate.

Critical Issues in Higher Education Decoloniality

Several guiding questions inform our approach to decolonising African higher education. First, how do collective movements ensure decolonising processes model anti-oppressive approaches? Given that decolonial movements are not currently coordinated across institutions, communities, or countries, what ongoing efforts must be in place to ensure efforts to Indigenise curricula, pedagogy, research, service, and structures do not reimpose dehumanising norms? While Indigenous philosophies have often been romanticised as creating perfectly harmonious communities, just like any other society, some aspects were biased against certain groups. For instance, many Indigenous groups in Africa retain patriarchal limits on women's freedom: Some traditions and proverbs paint women as inferior to men, essentially relegating women to servanthood or property (Ssetuba, 2002). Some African cultures traditionalised practices such as female genital mutilation to ensure the fidelity of women to their partner whereas such restrictions were not imposed on men. We are not suggesting a return to such, and indeed, safeguards must be in place to continually assert basic rights to self- and collective-determination. Thus, we take a stance to remain critical and humane when applying Indigenous philosophies to the decolonial process. The opportunity for Indigenous philosophies to grow and expand a human rights-based foundation has, in essence, been stripped away by coloniality. What is needed is not a return to the imagined Africa of old but to revitalise by drawing inspiration from roots that have been previously stripped away.

A second guiding question centres expectations: Can we transform higher education within un-transformed societies? Since colonisation maintains its influence across the continent, simultaneously engaging in multiple Indigenous African recentring processes across sectors may be required. For instance, while Mandela strove for a bloodless revolution that ushered out apartheid systems, he was unable to shift white ownership of wealth. We too recognise that colonial infrastructures outside the realm of higher education directly shape primary and secondary school systems, housing, economies, health care, and all related public and private sectors. The outcomes of any systemic transformation towards decoloniality could still favor specific racial groups that collaborate most closely with colonising influences, maintaining and/or gaining dominance over other Indigenous groups. Any processes thus require tremendous Ubuntu-framed engagement committed to ongoing processes that heighten previously silenced people, languages, and knowledges as well as a commitment to transferring tangible wealth and resources from coloniser contexts. This will no doubt be painful; no one wants to give up privileges. Yet in a world of drastic inequalities, wherein higher education has been built to sustain and justify inequities, higher education as a public good must directly lead to tangible land, wealth, and intellectual reparations.

The third guiding question extends these safeguards with a focus on hope: How do we collectively imagine and create Indigenous African-centric higher education to operate in a global system of white-defined higher education? For example, if Indigenous African philosophies are integrated across African universities in ways that honor multiple and interconnected notions of faith, how will the world's university systems react? Indigenous African philosophies are holistic and fundamentally spiritual, transcending the barriers of the mind and body, often with no separation between the physical and spiritual worlds (Mosha, 1999). At the same time, Christianity strongly influences Western thinking, and many of the premiere universities in the world were founded—and sustain—as seminaries. Much Indigenous African religion has been labelled as fetish or backwards due to Western anthropologist depictions of Africans as primitive and less complex compared to Western familiarities. Studying African philosophies as more than a tangential area of study is necessary to centre Indigeneity, and to understand multiple visions of African ways of life and thinking. Infusing multiple faith-based organising into the fabric of higher education will change institutional values, which, in turn, will impact ranking systems and funding metrics. How to transform to include important aspects of Indigenous African spirituality while the rest of the world continues to invest in secularism and whiteness-centred science becomes an ongoing discussion of purpose. Such spiritual aspects will make many current academics extremely uncomfortable, yet a decolonial university must diligently model intellectual, social, and cultural engagement with multiple worldviews, in tandem with ensuring that classrooms reflect the continent's multifaceted people, in spite of the world's pressures to silence difference.

While we recognise the daunting challenges, the chapters herein convey a sense of urgency; we are beyond late, and the world continues to melt, just as we continue to lose people, languages, cultures, and the very essences that sustain life on Earth. Higher education is uniquely situated to lead societal collaborations to address and remedy the many crises facing the continent. In short, the world cannot survive without dramatic expansion of investments into Indigenous African-led decolonial higher educations. In this book, then, we engage numerous authors to highlight decolonial approaches to specific aspects of higher education, examining current efforts to offer directions forward. We centre higher education practitioners across the continent who spend much of their day-to-day professional activities attempting to dismantle colonial infrastructures that impede Indigenous African knowledges.

In what comes next, Indigenous African higher education practitioners reimagine African universities as leading local, regional, and continental decolonial movements. These scholar-practitioners examine foundational aspects of higher education in order to envision transformation from contemporary towards a survivable future. In Chapter 2, Mishack T. Gumbo, Velisiwe Gasa, and Christopher B. Knaus, writing from South African contexts, challenge universities to centre African epistemologies in transforming the purpose of higher education towards a decolonising mission. In Chapter 3, Ngepathimo Kadhila and John Nyambe, writing from Namibia, clarify African curricular decolonisation, offering a vision for transformation across higher education infrastructures. In Chapter 4, Khazamula J. Maluleka presents findings from a qualitative study of South Africa-based decolonial student activists, suggesting student alignment with, and leadership of, decolonial movements. In Chapter 5, Ferdinand Chipindi, Ane Turner Johnson, and Marcellus

Forh Mbah clarify Zambian higher education, arguing for localised learning systems that can boost multiple ways of knowing and expressing human experiences. In Chapter 6, James Isabirye engages Indigenous framed music education within Uganda, offering a community-aligned curriculum to challenge coloniality

In Chapter 7, Abdirachid Ismail, in an interview discussion with Christopher B. Knaus, clarifies the complexities of colonially enforced linguistic dominance, offering a model of Indigenous language development to transform Djibouti's education system. In Chapter 8, Bella Bello Bitugu and Austin Wontepaga Luguterah situate Ghanaian physical education within a colonial lens, presenting a national approach to holistic Indigenous framed sport and activity. With Chapter 9, Takako Mino and Elaine Alowo-Matovu conclude our offering with hope, sharing a localised framework for reassimilating Indigeneity at an upcoming university in Uganda. Taken collectively, the contributors align with a commitment to strengthen and invest in Indigeneity, to align regionally and across the continent to transform higher education systems, and to ultimately elevate Indigeneity as a systemic, sustainable solution to our global problems.

References

Adeyemi, M., & Agboluaje, R. (2020). Why Nigeria's research institutions are passive in providing COVID-19 solutions. *The Guardian*, Interview, July 18. https://guardian.ng/interview/why-nigerias-research-institutes-are-passive-in-providing-covid-19-solutions/

Asante, M. (1988). *Afrocentricity*. Africa World Press.

Azumah, J.A. (2014). *The legacy of Arab-Islam in Africa: A quest for inter-religious dialogue.* Simon and Schuster.

Behari-Leak, K., Josephy, S., Potts, M.A., Muresherwa, G., Corbishley, J., Petersen, T.A., & Gove, B. (2019). Using vulnerability as a decolonial catalyst to re-cast the teacher as human(e). *Teaching in Higher Education, 26*(4), 1–16. doi:10.1080/13562517.2019.1661376

Belluigi, D.Z., & Thondhlana, G. (2019). 'Why mouth all the pieties?' Black and women academics' revelations about discourses of 'transformation' at an historically white South African university. *Higher Education, 78*(6), 947–963. doi:10.1007/s10734-019-00380-w

Benyere, E. (2020). How and why is colonialism a contract? In E. Benyere (Ed.), *Breaking the colonial contract: From oppression to autonomous decolonial futures* (pp. 1–28). Lexington Books.

Boonzaier, F., & Mhkize, L. (2018). Bodies out of place: Black Queer students negotiating identity at the University of Cape Town. *South African Journal of Higher Education, 32*(3), 81–100. doi:10.20853/32-3-2514

Bornman, E., Álvarez-Mosquera, P., & Seti, V. (2018). Language, urbanisation and identity: Young Black residents from Pretoria in South Africa. *Language Matters, 49*(1), 25–44. doi:10.1080/10228195.2018.1440318

Brown, R.L. (2020). An ocean apart, similar stories: US protests hit home in South Africa. *The Christian Science Monitor*, June 8. https://www.csmonitor.com/World/Africa/2020/0608/An-ocean-apart-similar-stories-US-protests-hit-home-in-South-Africa

Buckley, S. (2012). Higher education and knowledge sharing: From ivory tower to twenty-first century. *Innovations in Education and Teaching International*, *49*(3), 333–344. doi:10.1080/14703297.2012.703015

Carter, P. (2012). *Stubborn roots: Race, culture, and inequality in U.S. and South African schools*. Oxford University Press.

Césaire, A. (2000). *Discourse on colonialism* (Translated by Joan Pinkham). Monthly Review Press.

Chantiluke, R., Kwoba, B., & Nkopo, A. (2018). *Rhodes must fall: The struggle to decolonise the racist heart of empire*. Zed Books.

Chilisa, B. (2020). *Indigenous research methodologies* (2nd ed.). Sage.

CIA. (2020). *South Africa*. The World Factbook. https://www.cia.gov/library/publications/the-world-factbook/geos/sf.html#People

De Bruijn, M., van Dijk, R. A., & Foeken, D. (Eds.). (2001). *Mobile Africa: Changing patterns of movement in Africa and beyond* (Vol. 1). Brill.

Du Bois, W. E. B. (1925). Worlds of color. *Foreign Affairs*, *3*(3), 423–444.

Duermeijer, C., Amir, M., & Schoombee, L. (2018). *Africa generates less than 1% of the world's research; Data analytics can change that*. Elsevier Connect. https://www.elsevier.com/connect/africa-generates-less-than-1-of-the-worlds-research-data-analytics-can-change-that

Fadiji, A. W., & Reddy, V. (2020). Learners' educational aspirations in South Africa: The role of the home and the school. *South African Journal of Education*, *40*(2), 1–13. doi:10.15700/saje.v40n2a1712

Falola, T. (2003). *The power of African cultures*. University of Rochester Press.

Fanon, F. (1963). *The Wretched of the Earth*. Grove Press.

Faraclas, N. (2013). *Nigerian Pidgin*. Routledge.

Fourie, M. (2003). Beyond the ivory tower: Service learning for sustainable community development: Perspectives on higher education. *South African Journal of Higher Education* *17*(1), 31–38. doi:10.4314/SAJHE.V17I1.25189

Freire, P. (1970). *Pedagogy of the oppressed*. Herder and Herder.

Giles, C., & Mwai, P. (2020, July 13). *How Africa is responding to a coronavirus surge*. https://www.bbc.com/news/world-africa-52395976

Goduka, I. N. (1999). Indigenous epistemologies-ways of knowing: Affirming a legacy. *South African Journal of Higher Education*, *13*(3), 26–35.

Gouws, A. (2017). Feminist intersectionality and the matrix of domination in South Africa. *Agenda*, *31*(1), 19–27. doi:10.1080/10130950.2017.1338871

Gyekye, K. (2011). African ethics. In E. N. Zalta (Ed.), *The Stanford encyclopedia of philosophy* (Fall 2011). Stanford University. https://plato.stanford.edu/archives/fall2011/entries/african-ethics/

Knaus, C. B., & Brown, M. C. II. (2016). *Whiteness is the new South Africa: Research on post-apartheid racism*. Peter Lang.

Kopytoff, I. (Ed.). (1987). *The African frontier: The reproduction of traditional African societies*. Indiana University Press.

Lakner, C., Mahler, D. G., Negre, M., & Prydz, E. B. (2020). *How much does reducing inequality matter for global poverty?* World Bank.

Laurencin, C., & McClinton, A. (2020). The COVID-19 pandemic: A call to action to identify and address racial and ethnic disparities. *Journal of Racial and Ethnic Health Disparities*, *7*(3), 398–402.

Legère, K. (2006). Language endangerment in Tanzania: Identifying and maintaining endangered languages. *South African Journal of African Languages*, *26*(3), 99–112. doi:10.1080/02572117.2006.10587273

Lentz, C. (2006). First-comers and late-comers: Indigenous theories of landownership in West Africa. In R. Kuba & C. Lentz (Eds.), *Land and the politics of belonging in West Africa*. Brill.
Lodhi, A.Y. (1994). Muslims in Eastern Africa: Their past and present. *Nordic Journal of African Studies*, 3(1), 88–99.
Lulat, Y. G-M. (2003). Confronting the burden of the past: The historical antecedents of the present predicament of African universities. In J.C. Smart (Ed.), *Higher education: Handbook of theory and research* (Vol. 18, pp. 595–667). Springer. doi:10.1007/978-94-010-0137-3_11
Lulat, Y. G-M. (2005). *A history of African higher education from antiquity to the present: A critical synthesis*. Praeger.
Makhubela, M. (2018). 'Decolonise, don't diversify': Discounting diversity in the South African academe as a tool for 'ideological pacification.' *Education as Change*, 22(1), Article 2965, 1–21.
Makoni, M. (2020). Sparks fly over study on black students and biological sciences. *University World News*, Africa Edition. https://www.universityworldnews.com/post.php?story=20200609201341525
Maldonado-Torres, N. (2007). On coloniality of being: Contributions to the development of a concept. *Cultural Studies*, 21(2–3), 240–270. doi:10.1080/09502380601162548
Maluleke, T.S. (2004). African Christianity as African religion: Beyond the Contextualisation Paradigm. In E. Conradie (Ed.), *African theologies in transformation* (pp. 181–191). EFSA.
Manthalu, C., & Waghid, Y. (2019). *Education for decoloniality and decolonisation in Africa*. Palgrave Macmillan.
Marginson, S. (2016). The worldwide trend to high participation higher education: Dynamics of social stratification in inclusive systems. *Higher Education*, 72(4), 413–434. doi:10.1007/s10734-016-0016-x
Marley, B. (1976). War. *Rastaman vibration* [CD]. Island Records.
Marx, A. (1998). *Making race and nation: A comparison of South Africa, the United States, and Brazil*. Cambridge University Press.
Mbembe, A.J. (2016). Decolonizing the university: New directions. *Arts and Humanities in Higher Education*, 15(1), 29–45. doi:10.1177/1474022215618513
McCoy, D.L., Luedke, C.L., & Winkle-Wagner, R. (2017). Encouraged or weeded out: Perspectives of students of color in the STEM disciplines on faculty interactions. *Journal of College Student Development*, 58(5), 657–673. doi:10.1353/csd.2017.0052
McEvoy, J. (2020, June 15). Here's how statues across the world look after a week of reckoning. *Forbes*. https://www.forbes.com/sites/jemimamcevoy/2020/06/15/heres-how-statues-across-the-world-look-after-a-week-of-reckoning-photos/#4e6ffb436658
McKay, J., & Devlin, M. (2016). Low income doesn't mean stupid and destined for failure: Challenging the deficit discourse around students from low SES backgrounds in higher education. *International Journal of Inclusive Education*, 20(4), 347–363. doi:10.1080/13603116.2015.1079273
Mignolo, W.D. (2000). *Local histories/global designs: Essays on the coloniality of power, subaltern knowledges and border thinking*. Princeton University Press.
Mignolo, W.D. (2011). *The darker side of Western modernity: Global futures, decolonial options*. Duke University Press.
Mignolo, W.D. (2017). Coloniality is far from over, and so must be decoloniality. *Afterall: A Journal of Art, Context and Enquiry*, 43, 39–45. doi:10.1086/692552
Morreira, S. (2017). Steps towards decolonial higher education in Southern Africa? Epistemic disobedience in the humanities. *Journal of Asian and African Studies*, 52(3), 287–301. doi:10.1177/0021909615577499

Morreira, S., Taru, J., & Truyts, C. (2020). Place and pedagogy: Using space and materiality in teaching social science in Southern Africa. *Third World Thematics: A TWQ Journal, 5*(1), 1–17.

Mosha, R.S. (1999). *The heartbeat of Indigenous Africa: A study of the Chagga educational system.* Routledge.

Moyo, D. (2009). *Dead aid: Why aid is not working and how there is a better way for Africa.* Farrar, Straus and Giroux.

Mpofu, W.J. (2013). Coloniality in the scramble for African knowledge: A decolonial political perspective. *Africanus, 43*(2), 105–117.

Muzale, H.R., & Rugemalira, J.M. (2008). Researching and documenting the languages of Tanzania. *Language Documentation & Conservation, 2*(1), 68–108.

Nattrass, N. (2020). Why are black South African students less likely to consider studying biological sciences? *South African Journal of Science, 116*(5/6), Art. 7864. doi:10.17159/sajs.2020/7864

Ndlovu-Gatsheni, S.J. (2013). The entrapment of Africa within the global colonial matrices of power: Eurocentrism, coloniality, and deimperialization in the twenty-first century. *Journal of Developing Societies, 29*(4), 331–353. doi:10.1177/0169796X13503195

Ndlovu-Gatsheni, S.J. (2015a). Decoloniality as the future of Africa. *History Compass, 13*(10), 485–496.

Ndlovu-Gatsheni, S.J. (2015b). Decoloniality in Africa: A continuing search for a New World Order. *ARAS, 36*, 22–50.

Nkrumah, K. (1963). *Africa must unite.* Frederick A. Praeger.

Nyerere, J.K. (1987). Ujamaa: The basis of African socialism. *The Journal of Pan African Studies, 1*(1), 4–11.

O'Shea, S., Lysaght, P., Roberts, J., & Harwood, V. (2016). Shifting the blame in higher education – social inclusion and deficit discourses. *Higher Education Research & Development, 35*(2), 322–336. doi:10.1080/07294360.2015.1087388

Oruka, H.O. (1990). *Sage philosophy: Indigenous thinkers and modern debate on African philosophy.* Brill.

Quijano, A. (2000a). Coloniality of power and social classification. *Journal of World Systems, 6*(2), 342–386.

Quijano, A. (2000b). Coloniality of power, Eurocentrism and Latin America. *Nepantla: Views from the South, 1*(3), 533–579.

Quijano, A. (2007). Coloniality and modernity/rationality. *Cultural Studies, 21*(2–3), 168–178.

Ramoupi, N.L.L. (2014). African research and scholarship: 20 years of lost opportunities to transform higher education in South Africa. *Ufahamu: A Journal of African Studies, 38*(1), 269–286.

Rautenbach, S., & Mitchell, C. (2005). Questioning service learning in South Africa: Problematising partnerships in the South African context. A case study from the University of KwaZulu-Natal. *South African Journal of Higher Education, 19*(1), 101–112.

Rodney, W. (2018). *How Europe underdeveloped Africa.* Verso Trade.

Rosenberg, M.Y. (2020). Is America's future South Africa's past? *Foreign Policy*, June 10. https://foreignpolicy.com/2020/06/10/race-apartheid-united-states-george-floyd-protests/

Said, E.W. (1978). *Orientalism.* Pantheon Books.

Santiago-Ortiz, J.D. (2019). From critical to decolonizing service-learning: Limits and possibilities to social justice-based approaches to community service learning. *Michigan Journal of Community Service Learning, 25*(1), 43–54.

Santos, B. de S. (2014). *Epistemologies of the South: Justice against epistemicide.* Routledge. doi:10.4324/9781315634876

Shah, M., Sachdeva, M., & Dodiuk-Gad, R. (2020). COVID-19 and racial disparities. *Journal of the American Academy of Dermatology, 83*(1), E35.

Shepard, T. (2015). *Voices of decolonization: A brief history with documents.* Bedford/St. Martin's.

Ssetuba, I. (2002). The hold of patriarchy: An appraisal of the Ganda proverb in the light of modern gender relations. In *Cairo Gender Symposium Organized by CODESRIA/ARC, Cairo 7th–10th.*

Taylor, A. (2020). The statues brought down since the George Floyd protests began. *The Atlantic.* https://www.theatlantic.com/photo/2020/07/photos-statues-removed-george-floyd-protests-began/613774/

Teferra, D., & Altbach, P.G. (2003). *African higher education: An international reference handbook.* Indiana University Press.

Tuck, E., McKenzie, M., & McCoy, K. (2014). Land education: Indigenous, post-colonial, and decolonizing perspectives on place and environmental education research. *Environmental Education Research, 20*(1), 1–23. doi:10.1080/13504622.2013.877708

Tuck, E., & Yang, K.W. (2012). Decolonization is not a metaphor. *Decolonization: Indigeneity, Education & Society, 1*(1), 1–40.

wa Thiong'o, N. (1986). *Decolonising the mind: The politics of language in African literature.* James Currey.

wa Thiong'o, N. (2005). Europhone or African memory: The challenge of the pan-Africanist intellectual in the era of globalization. In *African Intellectuals: Rethinking Politics, Language, Gender and Development* (pp. 155–164). CODESRIA/Zed.

Walker, M. (2005). Rainbow nation or new racism? Theorizing race and identity formation in South African higher education. *Race, Ethnicity and Education, 8*(2), 129–146. doi:10.1080/13613320500110501

Walker, M. (2018). Aspirations and equality in higher education: Gender in a South African university. *Cambridge Journal of Education, 48*(1), 123–139. doi:10.1080/0305764X.2016.1254159

Washington, H.A. (2008). *Medical apartheid: The dark history of medical experimentation on Black Americans from colonial times to the present.* Anchor.

Wilson-Strydom, M. (2017). Disrupting structural inequalities of higher education opportunity: 'Grit,' resilience and capabilities at a South African university. *Journal of Human Development and Capabilities, 18*(3), 384–398. doi:10.1080/19452829.2016.1270919

Wiredu, K. (1998). Toward decolonizing African philosophy and religion. *African Studies Quarterly, 1*(4), 17–46.

World Bank. (2018). School enrollment, tertiary (% gross) – Sub-Saharan Africa. https://data.worldbank.org/indicator/SE.TER.ENRR?locations=ZG

Wright, R. (1957). *White man, listen!* Harper Perennial.

2
CENTRING AFRICAN KNOWLEDGES TO DECOLONISE HIGHER EDUCATION

Mishack T. Gumbo, Velisiwe Gasa, and Christopher B. Knaus

Universities in Africa predominantly serve Black and Indigenous students, yet the education that such universities engage represents Western epistemologies. This claim is backed by Mutekwe (2015), who states that the advent of modern Western education, enforced throughout the African continent, has compromised Indigenous knowledge systems, resulting in the dismissal of Indigenous knowledge as non-knowledge. This dismissal remains a systemic barrier, designed to structure African inferiority to the West, forcing generations of Indigenous communities from pursuing Indigenous knowledges endemic to localised circumstances. Indeed, African people were forced to conform to the cultures and traditions of the colonisers, which were imposed through slavery, dominance, oppression, and control of Africa's resources (Jensen, 1984). Colonising governments used education as they realised that the most important strategy to gain strength is through mental control (Mart, 2011; Serequeeberhan, 2010). School systems were identified as the central intellectual location whereby Western hegemony was implemented and justified, as schools extended foreign domination through economic exploitation of the colony (Kelly & Altbach, 1984). Students were equipped with skills, knowledge, and attitudes designed to drive Western countries' various sectors of economy, including the creation of a class of interpreters to communicate their needs to the millions that they govern in Africa (Akena, 2012; Khapoya, 2012). In essence, coloniality implemented schools to create a pool of persons who may be African in blood and colour but Westernised in speech, accent, actions, opinions, morals, and intellect.

Post-colonial syndrome continues to distance Indigenes from Indigenous knowledges, leaving contemporary Africans with a limited and/or distorted sense of their past. Coloniality through schools affects cultural self-confidence, while creating a desire to disassociate oneself with Indigenous heritages. The roots of post-colonial syndrome rest with the educational approach of taking away original forms of knowledge, systems of classification, technologies, and codes of social life, which, ironically, were recorded as 'new discoveries' around the seventeenth century (Smith, 2012). Many children who were born in subsequent eras grew up not knowing the difference between enforced ideas of the colonisers and their accepted native practices. They were indoctrinated into accepting the distorted information. This affected their identities as they crossed into a phase of hybridity whereby multiple cultural forms, practices, and beliefs emerged. Ngũgĩ wa Thiong'o (1986) documented the damage that colonial education caused in Africa, clarifying how people's belief in their names, languages, environment, heritage, capacities, and ultimately in themselves were crushed. They were made to glorify the very Westernisation processes that had enslaved and killed their ancestors, thereby creating systemic, impossible to reconcile multi-generational, emotional, physical, intellectual, and spiritual dismissals.

This chapter thus argues that Indigenous African epistemologies offer unique localised solutions to globally imported societal problems and should therefore be at the foundation of African higher education. We proffer this argument as central to the decolonisation agenda. Indeed, to foster a local, regional, and continental decolonisation agenda, universities must be sites where African students can flourish and develop as a 'well-rounded person with unhu or ubuntu, youths and adults who are loyal, responsible, productive and respectful of the laws, rules, customs and traditions of their societies' (Mutekwe, 2015, p. 1295). This notion of Ubuntu, wherein students are encouraged to learn and know who they are within a context of others around them, transforms from a self-thinking, me-first Western approach and towards a collective vision of human sustainability.

Such education must therefore liberate Africans from Western-based training, which continues to extend the centuries-long Western tradition of enslaving Africans in the interests of corporate profits. Slavery, we contend, was never only about forced Black labour; educational systems, including the Western church, were specifically adapted to intellectually, socially, and spiritually enslave Africans (Lulat, 2005; Ndlovu-Gatsheni, 2013). According to Chivaura (2014), the aim of Bantu education trained Africans for lower levels of work in industry. These industries remain focused on resource extraction, taking Africa's wealth, further retrenching white supremacies, and limiting the role and presence of African-affirming employment and community development models. Instead, we argue for Indigenous African-centric higher education that fosters independent thinkers who liberate themselves and others from the global Western approach to life as a commodity. An Indigenous higher education that helps students develop who and how they are, individually and in collective with others in their local and regional communities, will recentre African Ubuntu, which we frame as necessary to sustain life on this abused, over-taxed, colonised planet.

African Epistemologies

African epistemology is a foundational tenet of African philosophical worldviews. Philosophy is the love of wisdom which manifests in the reason for the wholeness of unfolding human experience (Ramose, 2004). According to Ramose (2004), the manifestation of reason may mainly be a tradition or codified and formally institutionalised as a written word pertaining to a field of learning. 'Tradition,' in the context of this chapter, inspired us to advance African perspectives of philosophy. In that sense, philosophy involves a constant reflection upon oneself (Marumo & Chakale, 2018; Oyeshile, 2008). African philosophy is directly related to history and culture, and the African intelligentsia upon the beingness of an African is significant and responds to the challenges of Western civilisation, including underlying white supremacies (Oyeshile, 2008). Oyeshile's (2008) argument is supported by Marumo and Chakale (2018), who state that African philosophy is 'concerned with defining the ethnophilosophical parameters of African philosophy and what differentiates it from other philosophical traditions' (p. 11696). Africa is endowed with rich legacies contained in our cultural material—works of antiquity, abundant arts and religion, as well as cultural expressions such as parables, folktales, myths, and proverbs sustain daily life (Anakwue, 2017). We therefore situate African epistemology within the African concept of philosophy; the two cannot be separated on a practical level.

A fundamental question that confronts the discussion on African philosophy, reflecting ongoing impacts of coloniality, remains basic: 'Is there an African philosophy and if there is one, what is it?' (Bodunrin in Etta & Asukwo, 2019, p. 280). Although Ozumba (2003) and Iroegbu (2005) state that no author is opposed to the idea of African philosophy, Western education, by design, has been implemented to oppose African philosophy, hence the need to centre African epistemologies in African higher education. African traditional philosophy is based on the epistemological attitude that is both African and locally tribal (Etta & Asukwo, 2019). African philosophy accords African epistemology a highly metaphysical (reality) conception (Etta & Asukwo, 2019). According to Anakwue (2017), people seek to interpret reality (metaphysics) in terms of the significant symbols of culture—culture is the totality of the way of people's life and the acquisition of knowledge of their proximate world over time. Apart from the arts, songs, and dance, culture means the investigation of nature and application of its possibilities in practice, through values, virtues, and people's interpretation of themselves in nature (Anakwue, 2017). Anakwue (2017) observes that 'philosophers argue that culture, like nature, was basically at the core of philosophy' (p. 170). Osuagwu (2005) uses the term *philosopheme* to refer to culture as a basic raw material of philosophy, and therefore, life.

As indicated above, African epistemology is embedded in African metaphysics (Etta & Asukwo, 2019) which cannot be separated from knowledge, which can be seen as knowingness of reality. Thus, Etta and Asukwo (2019) contend that 'African philosophy touches on epistemological matters' (p. 281). An African epistemological attitude stems from how Africans conceive reality, 'which is wholistic, ontological and features a perspective from oral tradition' (p. 281); this tradition embraces spirituality as well. Spirituality, a bedrock of African epistemology, transcends the empirical world of space and time based on the belief that 'everything which exists is charged with life forces or spirits, that is, all beings possess a spiritual backing' (p. 281). According to Etta and Asukwo, life forces are hierarchically presented as 'god, divinities, ancestors, man, animals, plants and minerals.'

Etta and Asukwo (2019) cite Aja's (1993) dimensions of knowledge which guide African epistemological knowledge. The first is *self/subject*, as the knower, who plays a critical role in translating ideas from the mind to the material reality. Perceptions and things known exist in the mind of self. The subject and object are inseparable compared to Western epistemology which splits the two into rationalism and empiricism, subjectivism and objectivism; the West sees people as separated from nature according to scientific reasoning. The second (in no particular order) is *object*, the manifestation of the phenomenal and noumenal world, refers to studies about being (material, mind, persons, etc.). As African epistemology remains highly spiritual, knowing requires the self to spiritually penetrate ontology. Etta and Asukwo (2019) offer five categories of predominantly anthropocentric ontology which can be used in this regard:

(1) God, who is perceived as the ultimate explanation of the genesis and substance of all things, including humans;
(2) Spirit being which includes super-human beings and the spirits of man who died a long time ago;
(3) Man, who include human beings who are alike and those who are about to be born (as authors, we recognise that in the West, man is a highly gendered term reflecting the West's binary construction of sex and gender. African Indigeneity rejects these binaries);
(4) Fauna and flora/remainder/biological life; and
(5) Phenomena and objects which do not possess biological life.

(p. 292)

The third dimension is *oral tradition/spoken word/human voice*. Oral communication is the most powerful way to pass on history, stories, folktales, religious beliefs, and meaning from one generation to another. Oral traditions are a way of life through which morals and values are taught; the spoken word unifies the family, clan, and community. Through oral traditions, music, song, myths, and ways of framing ideas, Africans use diverse means of knowing and imagination, with intuition and emotion playing key roles in expression. Thus, oral literacy is a platform for collective activity. Oral tradition needs to be defended as some scholars think that the spoken word cannot attain a philosophical status (Ramose, 2004), further reflecting Western binary thinking. Ramose (2004) dismisses this thinking, claiming that such thinking is a question of power, not science.

These dimensions of knowing are sourced from holistic, intuitive, perceptual, mystical, rational, ancestral, communal, God's, ontological, and individual knowledges (Etta & Asukwo, 2019). The multifaceted African epistemological attitude thus presents knowledge as a form of togetherness (Etta & Asukwo, 2019). Hence, African epistemology cannot be thought of without *Ubuntu*, and cannot be conceptualised without a comprehensive engagement of multiple ways of knowing, being, and expressing.

Towards *Ubuntu*

Viewed from a togetherness perspective, knowledge in African tradition is social. According to Hamminga (2005), this implies that 'we' know, not 'I' know. According to Etta and Asukwo (2019), knowledge depends on human and social factors, as opposed to a notion of objectivity that is codified in impersonal relations between an object and knower. Self-detachment, which scientific knowledge imposes on humanity, is unaccommodated in African epistemological attitude, as instead African epistemology situates self as the centre of the world and this unfolds the self's experience (feeling, living with, and grasping relations) of the personal world.

Hamminga (2005) centres African epistemology on ancestors as critical knowledge holders, and thus claims that knowledge is not acquired by labour but given by the ancestors. Hamminga uses a tree metaphor to facilitate understanding of the ramification of knowledge from ancestors—ancestors are roots which give energy to the tree trunk, which refers to the adults. The trunk supplies branches, leaves, and flowers, which are children. The notion of ancestors being knowledge libraries means that knowledge flows from the spiritual to the physical realms; divine forces revealing knowledge to humans (Etta & Asukwo, 2019). Togetherness presupposes that much of this knowledge resides in the community which is expressed through this tree metaphor. This is illustrated through *Dumelang* (Tswana), *Sanibona* (isiZulu), and *Molweni* (isiXhosa) when greeting an elderly person: *Ubuntu* of respect. The plural form of greetings denotes the respect accorded to the elder, and in most instances the greeter will bow or sit down before greeting the elder.

Etta and Asukwo (2019) add another layer to the tree metaphor in accordance with African conceptions of reality, God Himself, whom they regard as the highest Being (Force) and Wisdom from whom knowledge flows. It is God who releases knowledge to other human forces (Etta & Asukwo, 2019), the metaphysical significance subdues the material aspect. This attests to the pronouncement of the Bible: 'The fear of the Lord is the beginning of wisdom, and knowledge of the Holy One is understanding' (Proverbs 9:10). According to Etta and Asukwo, 'man's knowledge is limited without a divine source' (p. 285). We subscribe to this notion of interconnected divinity and acknowledge the legacy of knowledge that the ancestors left for the current generations. The respect of the Supreme Being of knowledge opposes the sophistic teachings of Protagoras which has shaped colonial thinking, which claims that 'man is the measure of all things, of the things that are, that they are end of the things that are not, that they are not' (Uduigwomen & Ozumba, 1995 in Etta & Asukwo, 2019, p. 285). The claim that Africans were pagan upon the arrival of the Westerners on African soil is thus an ontological impossibility; each African knew God long before the arrival of Westerners (Anczyk, 2013; Mahoso, 2014; Mutekwe, 2015).

In our view and in alignment with African Indigenous thinking, lingering coloniality is not about belief in God, but the distortion of Western interpretations of Christianity, particularly in reference to justifying African enslavement. Missionaries who started the Western type of education in Southern Africa did not follow a Biblical philosophy of education but that of a settler imperialist (Mahoso, 2013). Mutekwe (2015) highlights the importance of such clarification as he argues that 'much of the bible is African in origin and the approach to learning is implied.' To illustrate this learning-centric approach, the author cites Luke Chapter 2: 41–52 where Jesus and his parents went to the feast in Jerusalem when he was 12 years old to fulfil their customary duties. Jesus stayed behind as they were returning, but they did not initially notice him missing. They went back to look for him, and after 3 days, found him sitting with teachers, listening and asking questions. When they found him, his mother asked, 'Son, why have you done this to us? Look, your father and I have sought You anxiously.' According to Mutekwe, Jesus's response to his parents—that he had to prioritise his father's business—attests to African educational philosophy implicit in the Bible.

Mutekwe (2015) further argues that Western education advances modernisation paradigms to increase levels of Western-based schooling and mass media, fostering Western-based definitions of democratic political institutions at the expense of traditional African practices and communal values. Modernisation, according to Mutekwe, is linked to globalisation, characterised by economic expansion of capitalism, forcing the world into one integrated economic system reliant on the West; the cultural spread and integration of ideas, values, norms, behaviours, and ways of life across the globe; and the political development of forms of governance whose policies and rules all nations should abide by. Technological development as practised by the West intend to globally integrate communication technologies and distribute media in ways that exclude African Indigenous technologies and inventions.

What the world is experiencing is the increased sophistication of transportation and communication with concomitant urbanisation and mobility, trends that are attributed to the decline of extended family ties (Mutekwe, 2015). This decline extends the impact of slavery, further decimating family structures, leading to African aspirations to convert to Westernisation (Wright, 1956). In essence, the West has enforced a definition of development, modernisation, and globalisation that directly supports Western cultural practices and values that align with white supremacy (Knaus, 2018). Adoption of these approaches by Africans, while providing intentionally limited access into the global marketplace, reinforces the exploitation of African resources. Thus, the modernisation model is a direct cause of under-developing Africa, as efforts are based on the colonial system of education as teaching Africans to exploit each other. Such systemic miseducation fosters anti-Blackness while dismissing historic African curricula, which had been taught formally in initiation schools and in higher education institutions dating back thousands of years (Lulat, 2005). This miseducation also structurally denies informal education conducted through ceremony, family, and community functions.

An Indigenous African-centric Ubuntu-based education attempts to counter these colonial manifestations through socialising children into local, regional, and continental cultural heritage frameworks that maintain political and social cohesion (Mutekwe, 2015). Mutekwe further clarifies the aim of what we frame here as Ubuntu-based education, including: (a) Orientating children into performing activities and occasional rituals in the household and village; (b) teaching children the body of traditional lore about natural phenomena, custom, and traditional history; (c) condemning the subjugation of nature and general oppressiveness, non-Indigenous rationality, science and technology; (d) promoting development as self- and collective-determination, including as protection against colonisation, exploitation, appropriation, and commercialisation; and (e) legitimating and validating Indigenous practices and worldviews. Such approaches integrated relatively non-competitive, localised societies, transmitting common cultures across generations.

Western Academia in Resistance to African Epistemologies

As we strive to clarify, implement, and extend Ubuntu-framed educational systems, we recognise the ongoing need to define colonial schooling models, the details of their implementations, their ongoing impacts, and ways in which they adapt to maintain coloniality. Derrick Bell, the U.S.-based scholar often attributed to founding critical race theory, identified a key theme, which he referred to as *interest convergence*, in legal and policy approaches that maintain the structures of white supremacy. Bell (2004) dismissed racial justice efforts within the United States as failing because, at their core, they never aimed to disrupt white supremacy. Indeed, writing on the eve of the end of South Africa's apartheid system, Bell (1991) challenges that the very goals of equity were problematic and white-centric, arguing that 'the goal of racial equality is, while comforting to many whites, more illusory than real for blacks' (p. 13). This illusion rests in the reality that the West has infiltrated the very structures of society, across countries and continents, such that every effort to improve society brings hope; this hope, however, is soon dashed by the sustaining power of white supremacy. Indeed, just as Black South Africans put their faith in the overthrow of apartheid (and the overthrow of coloniality before that):

> ... blacks discover all too soon that the new relationship, while seeming better than the one they risked so much to escape, has placed them in a

different but still subordinate posture. Each time, the symbol of the new relationship ends up behind a new and more imposing door, constructed of current economic needs and secured with a racism that is no less efficient because some blacks are able to slip by the barriers of class, wealth and bigotry.

(Bell, 1998, p. 160)

Bell (1991) might as well have been writing about the overthrow of Western rulers across the continent when he clarifies that 'even those herculean efforts we hail as successful will provide no more than temporary "peaks of progress," short-lived victories that slide into irrelevance as racial patterns adapt in ways that maintain white dominance' (p. 12).

Furthermore, applying Bell to decolonial and transformation efforts across Africa reinforces that the very structures of educational coloniality remain staunchly intact. Indeed, while numerous programmes and departments focused on Indigenous knowledge systems and African languages exist across institutions, languages of instruction, especially at elite institutions, remain colonial. Even the creation of Indigenous-focused departments reflects what Banks (2006) refers to as additive approaches, wherein the structures of coloniality remain embedded across the curriculum, teaching approaches, and infrastructures of learning. Indigenous-centred departments remain under the framework of the university, where tenure and rank, teaching approaches, research orientations, and even curriculum details—including what counts as a course, as academic credit, as a degree, and who counts as an instructor—remain undeniably imposed by the West.

We argue that higher education approaches across the continent retain the infrastructures of white supremacy, silencing Indigenous knowledge systems and limiting implementation of African orientations. The basic infrastructure of learning, including approaches to teaching, definitions of curriculum, and physical infrastructures, were designed as colonial tools (Knaus, 2018). While early universities existed across the continent, these were largely dismantled by colonising powers, who supported the establishment of missionary schools and higher education institutions. Later, many of these merged or operated in parallel with state-supported institutions linked and supported directly with institutions located in Europe, with the explicit purpose of taking students deemed worthy into the machinery of elite Western universities. This preparation was designed to teach colonial rule, where graduates would return to implement Western-based institutions. Thus, early purposes of higher education were intended to teach coloniality to Africans, and structures, including funding models, buildings and classrooms, and ideas of learning, all reflected white supremacist, colonial approaches aligned with exploiting African resources (Lulat, 2005).

These structures are based on notions of teaching that reinforce Freire's (1970/2006) notion of banking approaches, wherein instructors hold knowledge, and students are essentially customers withdrawing such knowledge. Lecturing, as teaching is often referred to at the collegiate level, by design limits collaboration, shared learning, and collective responsibility across learning opportunities. While certainly lecturing can be one of many tools for sharing knowledge, African traditional learnings centre oral sharing of stories, language, and experience only in conjunction with learner responsibility and engagement. But the very nature of classrooms, be they physical or digital, remains aligned with Western-oriented banking systems.

Similarly, texts remain exclusive by virtue of U.S. and European publisher preferences for already established literature bases that result in economic monopolies and exclusion of African authors (wa Thiong'o, 1986). This literary exclusion parallels library systems that remain limited by economic reality and digital firewalls that exclude most African college students and faculties who simply cannot afford Western-based fees to access knowledge repositories. This reality is exacerbated by the historical context of the West stealing African archives; many African works of antiquity are thus only accessible to Western audiences, just as many Western audiences omitted, obliterated, and otherwise mis-interpreted African epistemologies, even as they are now situated as knowledge experts (Depelchin, 2005).

These structures and designs further reinforce pedagogical and curricular theories that reinforce the binary thinking of Western philosophies. The reliance on teaching objectivity, distance from social problems and contexts, and preference for European languages of instruction further the commitment to individualise grading and evaluations, rejecting the collectivist approaches to learning that traditional African knowledges engage. Indeed, the penalisation of Indigenous African languages mirrors the classroom perpetuation of linguistic domination, as future generations continue to be excluded from learning and developing academic-oriented Indigenous language systems. Indeed, as Brock-Utne (2010) argues, 'no university in sub-Saharan Africa has an Indigenous African language as the language of instruction' (p. 94). While this is slowly changing, such linguistic coloniality remains the violent norm.

White supremacy additionally remains structured through the ways in which higher education defines, measures, and calculates knowledge. Academic reward systems remain largely based on publishing in Western channels, just as research funding is largely determined by Western interests, steering the researcher to conform to fulfilling Western orientation towards research. These channels continue the colonial purpose of research endeavours, as knowledge is framed as something to be extracted from Indigenous communities, rather than collaborative processes leading to sustainable collective impact (Chilisa, 2020; Smith, 2012). Research, aligned with higher education structures, thus reinforces an individualistic approach to knowledge, as dissemination reflects one (or several) authors, rather than collective communities. The push for globalisation of knowledge further cements a monolingual Western hegemony of experts who continue to dismiss those writing from within Indigenous African communities, using perhaps their third, fourth, or fifth languages.

These structures exist to maintain white supremacy and the global domination by the West, functioning to ensure that the purpose of higher education for students is to strengthen individualised capitalistic access. For our purposes, centring an African Indigenous higher education means intentional disruption of the historic and continued colonial purpose, and that means overthrowing the operational structures upon which current African higher education is built. We recognise that this task is extremely difficult, as our faculties are built upon a global network of training that reinforces and rewards Western assumptions, yet the need for sustainable, healing, African-centric systems cannot be more pressing.

Towards an African Higher Education

Western education remains a central concern for policy makers, academic leaders, and scholars across Africa. Blumberga (2012), Nyamnjoh (2012), Ndlovu-Gatsheni (2014), Ndofirepi (2014), Mamdani (2016), Mbembe (2016), and Zembylas (2018) have documented how the demands to decolonise universities by transforming curriculum have recently intensified. Cossa (2009) postulates that Africans have increasingly been reconsidering our place in the world, rethinking and redefining through the 'reformulation of practical strategies and solutions for the future benefit of the Africans' (p. 1). This is in line with African Union Commission's (2014) 'Agenda 2063: The Africa we want,' which calls for action: 'We are deeply conscious that Africa in 2015 stands at a crossroads and we are determined to transform the continent and ensure irreversible and universal change of the African condition' (p. 14).

As African leaders, students, and communities call for Africanisation of universities, whereby African contextual realities are placed at the epicentre, we note the need for relevant, timely responsiveness to the priorities, challenges, and realities of African people. We echo the calls for epistemological emancipation, re-imagining, re-thinking, and re-inventing the limited definitions and processes surrounding knowledge at universities. In short, the world continues to struggle to disrupt settler coloniality, to dismantle capitalistic systems designed to extract and exploit, and ultimately to decolonise the very educational systems that prepare subservience to whiteness, to Western ideologies. We thus recognise and extend those who have come before, echoing the call to decolonise African higher education through transformation of the purpose, scope, and structure of what we call the university.

We argue that decolonising African higher education requires not just a transformed purpose, but an alignment of the way in which higher education is conceptualised. This means reshaping the goals towards collective impact, wherein students strengthen who they are, their cultural, tribal, linguistic, social identities, and Indigenous knowledges. In honouring ancestor knowledges and a reflection of being on this earth to bring individual strengths to collective struggles, decolonial education means students learn for an explicit purpose of strengthening personal capacity to, in turn, strengthen collective capacity.

Nabudere (2003) echoes this decolonial purpose to strengthen Indigeneity, arguing that the construction of new African epistemology and methodology in the university would shrink existing dominant interests, as well as question Eurocentric paradigms and Western 'scientistic' epistemologies of knowledge. Transforming the purpose of university to strengthen and invest in Indigeneity—including language, knowledge, and all engagement practices—essentially centres Africa and Africanism as foundational knowledge. Wahyudi (2014) engages the concept 'glocalise' in order to give primacy to local languages, adaptive technology, and social practices. A glocal approach ensures contextualisation of education so that Indigenous African students can participate in the global space by contributing to and strengthening African epistemologies.

On an organisational level, decolonising African higher education towards collective impact shifts the three tenets of the university from research, teaching, and service to collective community impact, Indigenous-centric teaching, and research to decolonise. Thus, the entire framework of the university must be transformed to prepare students to address social problems from within glocalised Indigenous-centric approaches (Wahyudi, 2014). This glocal shift also requires transformation from an atmosphere of competition and individual performance to collective freedom, where students are supported to engage, challenge, and further the knowledge processes they learn. This engagement places responsibility on students to learn from an ubuntu perspective, enriching other's knowledges as part of the process of self-learning.

Service to others, then, becomes the first goal of the university. This notion of service rejects Western approaches of outside-in solutions (Knaus & Brown, 2016), instead arguing for a localised Africanism, with a focus on students addressing problems they, and their communities, face. Waghid (2017) proposes a locally relevant education that promotes Ubuntu into university cultures and develops a humane and just society. Odora-Hoppers (2005) suggests that African knowledge systems must reflect African ownership and needs of African society and people. Lumumba-Kasongo (2017) further argues for an infusion of pan-African approaches and ideologies in the curriculum of university systems. Ndofirepi (2014) reiterates that for university knowledge to be referred to as African 'it must be done the African way, by African authors in Africa, on African issues within the African context of time and space, to generate African doctrines' (p. 157). Enacting this African centrism integrates the university into and with local Indigenous communities, transforming notions of partnership to glocal commitments with shared responsibility for ongoing societal problems. Service with, as a structural goal, situates local elders and related Indigenous knowledge holders and practitioners as essential contributors of knowledge for sustainable development and for doing the day-to-day work of the university.

Within the context of Africanising the scope of the university, teaching then becomes the secondary goal, in support of, and as a process to, prepare students for glocal service. Recent scholars have highlighted home-grown teaching strategies spearheaded by Africans that reflect this service-with mission. For example, the Culturo-Techno-Contextual Approach or CTCA unveiled by Professor Peter Akinsola Okebukola of Nigeria's Lagos State University has been promoted during training sessions of graduate students in Lagos State University and the University of Burundi Doctoral School. The inventor of the model proposes that students' cultural background, available technology, and the context of the environment of the learner and the teacher must be recognised through situational learning and teaching (Awaah, 2020). This recognition honours student identities, languages, and contexts, while ensuring students engage with others. Gumbo (2016) suggests aligning teaching principles across programs and institutions, where pedagogy reflects glocal contexts as a way to prepare students for local and global realities. Similarly, Fataar (2016) and Zembylas (2018) call for humanising pedagogy that can foster transformation and liberation of the oppressed. Thus, Africanising higher education teaching honours students in their contexts, supports intellectual liberation, and prepares students to in turn foster societal liberation, specifically from Western oppressive structures.

While service and teaching provide the framework for an Africanising education, research as active praxis becomes the foundation. The weave between knowledge research, its production and dissemination are regarded as an important factor for societal change in Africa (Adjei, 2007; Akena, 2012). Maringe (2017) emphasised the need to accelerate the efforts to emancipate the academy in Africa. He pointed out the critical issues that urgently need to be transformed to ensure that they serve not only the universities as institutions, but also the societies they are expected to change. These critical issues include decolonising knowledge production, research processes, knowledge in relationship with curriculum, knowledge in relation with teaching and learning, and ongoing training of postgraduates. All of these require a deepened commitment to the decolonial research agenda (Chilisa, 2020).

A decolonial research agenda requires transformation of graduate programmes as well so that students can initiate and carry forward relevant research processes with Indigenous communities. Tillmann and Salas (2011) describe how Sichuan University in China decolonised the master's coursework to reflect the Tibetan, Qiang, and Yi cultures. Over 10 days, the lecturers and graduate students conducted a curriculum design workshop. They incorporated the theory and methods of Indigenous knowledge and cultural affirmation in the curriculum and an alternative for students to be applied research specialists. They selected content from cultural studies which included ecology, history, and anthropology, which were also translated into Chinese. The course was framed in the general philosophical-theoretical lens. The workshop caused the participants to self-reflect in terms of their own knowledge to acknowledge alternative ways of thinking reality. The designed curriculum covered Indigenous knowledge concepts, methods, rights and ethics, pedagogical approaches, and methods. Active participation, non-compliance to conventional teaching, epistemological foundations were ensured during the workshop, including a foundational commitment to chronicle Indigenous knowledges for the purpose of future integration across the curriculum. Such projects help apply Indigenous research methods for the purpose of transforming the institution's teaching approaches, relying upon the local knowledges of ethnic minorities (in China). As a parallel, numerous glocal models exist across universities on every continent, and a decolonising research university sees, as its purpose, the role of research as leveraging ancestral knowledges to transform universities and communities (Smith, 2012). Such decolonial research requires, at minimum, a transformation of research funding models, wherein investments are made to support glocal process-based engagement with ancestral knowledges, localised communities, and student learning.

Conclusion

If the purpose of an African higher education is to decentre the imposition of Western knowledges and the violent impacts such bring, the mission of individual universities then must be transformed to reflect African notions of justice. Thus service to communities, transformed teaching rooted in student social identities and orientations, and a decolonial research agenda must be reflected in the everyday structures of what constitutes 'campus.'

In South Africa, higher education's role of promoting and developing social responsibility and awareness amongst students was endorsed through Education White Paper 3, published just after the end of apartheid. Osman and Petersen (2013) further argue for higher education's need to be in service of society and its needs. Publishing such calls for action does not, however, initiate the decolonial turn that was hoped for by the newly liberated educational community, just as legislating transformation does not ensure Indigeneity. Rather, we argue that higher education institutions alone hold the key to responding to ongoing historical injustices such as colonisation, apartheid, racism, inequalities, and structured violence, but that the work must be shared across communities, states, and international organisations. Higher education can and must transform to processes centred on graduates who contribute to earth-sustainable approaches to addressing each individual society's locally oppressive structures. In committing to the development of a more just and humane glocal society, African universities should strengthen our collective responses to social, political, economic, and cultural struggles. This can be done through prioritisation of service to and with, through a teaching commitment to glocal contexts, and through decolonial research processes with historically excluded knowledge holders.

References

Adjei, P.B. (2007). Decolonising knowledge production: The pedagogic relevance of Gandhian Satyagraha to schooling and education in Ghana. *Canadian Journal of Education, 30*(4), 1046–1067. doi:10.2307/20466678
African Union Commission. (2014). *Agenda 2063: The Africa we want*. African Union Commission.
Aja, E. (1993). *Element of theory of knowledge*. Auto-Century Publisher.

Akena, F.A. (2012). Critical analysis of the production of Western knowledge and its implications for Indigenous knowledge and decolonization. *Journal of Black Studies*, *43*(6), 599–619. doi:10.1177/0021934712440448

Anakwue, N.C. (2017). The African origins of Greek philosophy: Ancient Egypt in retrospect. *Phronimon*, *18*, 167–180. doi:10.17159/2413-3086/2361

Anczyk, A. (2013). Coming home to paganism: Theory of religious conversion or a theological principle? *Studia Religiologica*, *46*(3), 161–171. doi:10.4467/20844077SR.13.013.1601

Awaah, F. (2020). Towards an Afrocentric teaching model. https://www.universityworldnews.com/post.php?story=20200414083021396

Banks, J.A. (2006). *Cultural diversity and education: Foundations, curriculum, and teaching*. Pearson.

Bell, D. (1991). *Faces at the bottom of the well: The permanence of racism*. Basic Books.

Bell, D. (1998). *Afrolantica legacies*. Third World Books.

Bell, D. (2004). *Silent covenants: Brown v. Board of Education and the unfulfilled hopes for racial reform*. Oxford University Press.

Blumberga, S. (2012). Dimensions of epistemic authority of university professors. *Social and Natural Sciences Journal*, *5*, 1–5. doi:10.12955/snsj.v5i0.299

Brock-Utne, B. (2010). English as the language of instruction or destruction: How do teachers and students in Tanzania cope? In B. Brock-Utne, Z. Desai, M.A.S. Qorro, & A. Pitman (Eds.), *Language of instruction in Tanzania and South Africa: Highlights from a project* (pp. 77–98). Sense Publishers.

Chilisa, B. (2020). *Indigenous research methodologies* (2nd ed.). Sage.

Chivaura, V.G. (2014). Progress on meeting SADC education targets. *Zimbabwe*, *4*, 19–25.

Cossa, J.A. (2009). African renaissance and globalization: A conceptual analysis. *Ufahamu: A Journal of African Studies*, *36*(1), 1–25. doi:10.5070/F7361009576

Depelchin, J. (2005). *Silences in African history: Between the syndromes of discovery and abolition*. Mkuki na Nyota Publishers.

Etta, E.E., & Asukwo, O.O. (2019). The reality of African epistemology. *International Journal of Innovative Science, Engineering & Technology*, *6*(10), 279–305.

Fataar, A. (2016). Towards a humanising pedagogy through an engagement with the social–subjective in educational theorising in South Africa. *Educational Research for Social Change*, *5*(1), 10–21. doi:10.17159/2221-4070/2016/v5i1a1

Freire, P. (1970/2006). *Pedagogy of the oppressed*. Continuum.

Gumbo, M.T. (2016). Pedagogical principles in technology education: An Indigenous perspective. In G. Emeagwali & E. Shizha (Eds.), *African Indigenous knowledge and the sciences: Journeys into the past and present* (pp. 13–32). Sense Publishers.

Hamminga, B. (2005). Epistemology from the African point of view. In J. Brzezinski, A. Klawiter, A. Kupracz, K. Lastowski, T. Maruszewski, L. Nowak, & R. Stachowski (Eds.), *Poznan studies in the philosophy of the sciences and the humanities* (pp. 57–84). Rodopi B.V.

Iroegbu, P. (2005). Philosophy of education: Ethics of teaching profession. In P. Iroegbu & A. Echekube (Eds.), *Kpim of morality: General, special & professional*. Heinemann Educational Books.

Jensen, K. (1984). Civilization and assimilation in the colonized schooling of Native Americans. In G.P. Kelly & P.G. Altbach (Eds.), *Education and the colonial experience* (pp. 117–136). Transaction.

Kelly, G.P., & Altbach, P.G. (1984). Introduction: The four faces of colonialism. In G.P. Kelly & P.G. Altbach (Eds.), *Education and the colonial experience* (pp. 1–5). Transaction.

Khapoya, V. (2012). *The African experience: Colonialism and the African experience*. Routledge.

Knaus, C.B. (2018). 'If everyone would just act White': Education as a global investment in whiteness. In J. Brooks & G. Theoharis (Eds.), *Whiteucation: Privilege, power, and prejudice in schools* (pp. 1–21). Routledge.

Knaus, C.B., & Brown, M.C.B. II. (2016). *Whiteness is the new South Africa: Qualitative research on post-apartheid racism*. Peter Lang.

Lulat, Y. G-M. (2005). *A history of African higher education from Antiquity to the present: A critical synthesis*. Praeger.

Lumumba-Kasongo, T. (2017). Pan-African curriculum in higher education: A reflection. In M. Cross & A. Ndofirepi (Eds.), *Knowledge and change in African universities*. Sense Publishers.

Mahoso, T. (2013). The death of the dollar. *Zimbabwe, 3*, 13–17.

Mahoso, T. (2014). Towards an African philosophy of education. *Zimbabwe, 5*, 4–5.

Mamdani, M. (2016). Between the public intellectual and the scholar: Decolonisation and some post-independence initiatives in African higher education. *Inter-Asia Cultural Studies, 17*(1), 68–83. doi:10.1080/14649373.2016.1140260

Maringe, F. (2017). Transforming knowledge production systems in the new African university. In M. Cross & A. Ndofirepi (Eds.), *Knowledge and change in African universities*. Sense Publishers.

Mart, Ç.T. (2011). British colonial education policy in Africa. *Internal Journal of English and Literature, 2*(9), 190–194. doi:10.5897/IJEL11.050

Marumo, P.O., & Chakale, M.V. (2018). Understanding African philosophy and African spirituality: Challenges and prospects. *Gender & Behaviour, 6*(2), 11695–11704.

Mbembe, A.J. (2016). Decolonising the university: New directions. *Arts and Humanities in Higher Education, 15*(1), 29–45. doi:10.1177/1474022215618513

Mutekwe, E. (2015). Towards an Africa philosophy of education for Indigenous knowledge systems in Africa. *Creative Education, 6*(12), 1294–1305. doi:10.4236/ce.2015.612129

Nabudere, D.W. (2003). Towards the establishment of a Pan-African university: A strategic concept paper. *African Journal of Political Science, 8*(1), 1–29.

Ndlovu-Gatsheni, S.J. (2013). *Coloniality of power in postcolonial Africa: Myths of decolonization*. Council for the Development of Social Science Research in Africa.

Ndlovu-Gatsheni, S.J. (2014). Global coloniality and the challenges of creating African futures. *Strategic Review for Southern Africa, 36*(2), 181–202.

Ndofirepi, A.P. (2014). Africanisation of epistemology in the 21st century university in Africa. In E. Shizha (Ed.), *Remapping Africa in the global space: Propositions for change* (pp. 151–166). Sense Publishers.

Nyamnjoh, F.B. (2012). 'Potted plants in greenhouses': A critical reflection on the resilience of colonial education in Africa. *Journal of Asian and African Studies, 47*(2), 129–154. doi:10.1177/0021909611417240

Odora-Hoppers, C.A. (2005). *Culture, Indigenous knowledge and development: The role of the university*. Centre for Education Policy Development (CEPD).

Osman, R., & Petersen, N. (2013). *Service learning in South Africa*. Oxford University Press Southern Africa.

Osuagwu, M.I. (2005). Philosophy of non-philosophy: Okere's trilogy on African philosophy. In J.O. Oguejiofor & G.I. Onah (Eds.), *African philosophy and the hermeneutics of culture*. Transaction Publishers.

Oyeshile, O.A. (2008). On defining African philosophy: History, challenges and perspectives. *Humanity & Social Sciences Journal, 3*(1), 57–64.

Ozumba, G.O. (2003). *A colloquium on African philosophy* (Vol. 1). Pyramid Publication.

Ramose, M.B. (2004). In search of an African philosophy of education. *South African Journal of Higher Education*, *18*(3), 138–160. doi:10.4314/SAJHE.V18I3.25487

Serequeeberhan, T. (2010). Africa in a changing world: An inventory. *Monthly Review. Independent Social Mag*, *61*(8), 26–38. doi:10.14452/MR-061-08-2010-01_3

Smith, L.T. (2012). *Decolonizing methodologies: Research and Indigenous peoples* (2nd ed.). Zed Books.

Tillmann, H.J., & Salas, M.A. (2011). Intercultural dialogue in support of Indigenous cultures: Indigenous knowledge curriculum design at Sichuan University. http://www.bioculturaldiversity.net/Downloads/Papers%20participants/Tillman_et_al.pdf

Uduigwomen, A., & Ozumba. (1995). *The place of oral tradition in African epistemology: Footmarks on African philosophy*. O.O.P.

wa Thiong'o, N. (1986). *Decolonising the mind: The politics of language in African literature*. James Currey.

Waghid, Y. (2017). Ubuntu: African philosophy of education and pedagogical encounters. In M. Cross & A. Ndofirepi (Eds.), *Knowledge and change in African universities*. Sense Publishers.

Wahyudi, R. (2014). 'Democratic' online courses as 'glocalized communication' in English language teaching and applied linguistics: A proposal. *Journal of Global Literacies, Technologies, and Emerging Pedagogies*, *2*(3), 248–260.

Wright, R. (1956). *The color curtain: A report on the Bandung Conference*. University of Mississippi Press.

Zembylas, M. (2018). Decolonial possibilities in South African higher education: Reconfiguring humanising pedagogies as/with decolonising pedagogies. *South African Journal of Education*, *38*(4), 1–11. doi:10.15700/saje.v38n4a1699

3
CURRICULUM TRANSFORMATION TO DECOLONISE AFRICAN HIGHER EDUCATION

Ngepathimo Kadhila and John Nyambe

Decolonisation and transformation of higher education systems has long been recognised by post-colonial African governments as a potentially powerful lever for improved societal well-being, redressing past inequalities, meeting pressing national and international needs, and responding to new realities and opportunities (Mullet, 2018). Higher education is seen as a catalyst for equity, meritocracy, employability, economic performance, quality of life and sustainable development (MacGregor, 2009; Padayachee, Matimolane, & Ganas, 2018). Indeed, the role of higher education in Africa's sustainable social, political, and economic development cannot be overemphasised (Badat, 2011; Castells, 2009; D'Andrea & Gosling, 2005; MacGregor, 2009). However, with few resources, inadequate capacity and a history of neglect, higher education as a sector has been struggling to meet the growing demands, offering instead an outdated, colonial curriculum. In particular, curricular decolonisation and transformation has proved challenging, as evidenced in actions and calls by higher education pundits and commentators in recent years for a responsive curriculum addressing the real African social and economic development needs. This is more so because some of the key pillars of colonisation such as economic exploitation and disfigurement of African communities and cultures are still prevalent in most of African communities, well after the end of political decolonisation (Luckett, 2016).

This chapter analyses curriculum decolonisation and transformation agendas implemented in African higher education, including successes and challenges for implementation of such broad-reaching initiatives. We clarify tangible ways to make African higher education more relevant and responsive to pressing social and economic development needs. This includes a focus on decolonising and transforming higher education structures, curricula, pedagogy, research, and community relationships. Decolonisation and transformation discourses are intentionally discussed together in this chapter as these two notions are seen as interrelated, as curriculum decolonisation may be achieved through a process of curriculum transformation. We argue that higher education can only go so far as our curriculum; thus, the decolonisation of the curricular infrastructure is paramount to transforming the entire system of higher education.

Within the context of African higher education, the status quo of the colonial foundation continues colonial conditions, including anti-Black and anti-Indigenous violence, resource disparities, and a higher education system that remains unprepared and unresourced to address these daily concerns. Thus, the African higher education sector reflects national and continental social inequalities, reduced public funding, insufficient infrastructural development, lack of qualified academic staff largely due to brain drain, disastrous effect of HIV/AIDS and related pandemics (e.g., the recent COVID-19 outbreak), poor governance, political interference, poor internal efficiency, mismatch between graduate output and employment, and resource constraints that pose serious challenges to curriculum transformation in African higher education (Shabani, Okebukola, & Oyewole, 2014). This chapter recognises the current context, arguing for a reconceptualisation of the purpose of higher education as fundamentally about sustaining life, transforming learning into processes that foster locally sustaining knowledge, and working to solve local and continental African problems. In this chapter, curriculum can be viewed in a broad sense to include decolonising the higher education landscape as a whole. This is due to the understanding that decolonisation must include all aspects of the higher education system, as one cannot only decolonise the curriculum without also addressing structures, faculty, scholarship and research, teaching, fees and funding, localised politics, and institutional concerns. Some of the drivers of African curriculum transformation include calls to decolonise, responsiveness to social context, epistemological diversity, renewal of pedagogy and classroom practices, and institutional cultures of openness and critical reflection (Nkoane, 2006). Accordingly, transformation discourse is associated with terms like equity, access, opportunity, eradication of all forms of discrimination, redress, democratic ethos, human rights, a fostering of critical public discourse, a humane, non-racist, non-sexist social order, and advancement of all forms of life-sustaining knowledge and scholarship (Mullet, 2018). These broad calls unite a transformative and decolonial agenda, reflecting a changing higher education landscape across the continent, urging a prioritisation of purpose in order to align efforts to the current condition.

Globalisation of African Higher Education

Globalisation is characterised by continued exploitation of the global poor, which continue to be concentrated across the continent. There has been 'an expansion of economic activities across national boundaries' as manifested by 'international trade, international investment and international finance,' and the 'flows of services, technology, information and ideas across national boundaries' (Badat, 2011, p. 5) as well as the global organisation of production through transnational corporations. In addition to the growing marketisation and commodification of higher education, there has also been an increasing internationalisation and trans-nationalisation of higher education (Badat, 2011). An understanding of these factors and the broader role of higher education in Africa is the first step to dealing constructively with the challenges that inevitably affect curriculum transformation and decoloniality.

Higher education in Africa has undergone a significant transformation in recent years. The key drivers of the twenty-first-century academic revolution in higher education include the massification of higher education, a debate on the public versus private good, the impact of information and communication technologies (ICTs), the rise of the knowledge economy, and increasing globalisation. We term this an academic revolution because this series of transformations have influenced higher education more than ever before; in addition, these revolutions are global in nature. These transformations affect numerous higher education institutions as well as the broader population. All these factors, coupled with other powerful forces such as the shift to an emphasis on graduate employability attributes, online pedagogies, lifelong learning, qualification articulation, student mobility, credit transfer systems, and cross border recognition of qualifications, have forced African higher education institutions to develop meaningful and responsive curricula that meet local needs and respond to global demands (Badat, 2003; Barnett, 1999). Although many higher education institutions have become more mobile and internationally oriented as a result of this global emphasis, most remain structured and unfortunately limited to national circumstances.

The central reality of the twenty-first century has been the massification of higher education, due primarily to the call for mass access to higher education across the continent. Although less than 10% of the post-school age group participate in higher education in the majority of African countries, the participation rate in higher education has, in the main, increased dramatically at the global level (UNESCO, 2021). The massification of higher education has been inevitable, with growing societal needs that can only be met through higher education's potential as a tool to cultivate political, social, and economic transformation. In addition, higher education has been acknowledged as having the potential to improve the well-being of modern society and enhance quality of life; thus, higher education growth has been fuelled by Western philanthropies and nations (MacGregor, 2009). However, with mass participation in higher education comes a loss of public trust in higher education, accompanied by a fear of a decline in standards (Badat, 2011). Underneath these fears rests a pressing need for, and related lack of continental commitment to, decoloniality.

A further reality of the twenty-first century is the knowledge economy. Information communication technologies comprise a global force and one of the most powerful influences on higher education in Africa. Such economic growth is dependent on the quantity, quality, and accessibility of information available, rather than the means of production (MacGregor, 2009). According to MacGregor (2009), growing segments of the workforce require advanced education offered in higher education institutions in Africa. The impact of such technological growth on science and scholarship, teaching and learning in traditionalist universities, possibilities for distance education, and even the internal management of universities has been particularly profound. However, there is also little doubt that deep inequalities persist with regard to access, use, and influence, particularly in countries with whom the higher education sector excludes all but the wealthiest or politically connected (Badat, 2011; MacGregor, 2009). African higher education thus faces structural fragmentation, poor quality of education, high drop-out and low completion rates, and graduate unemployment or under-employment (Mohamedbhai, 2020). With poor-quality higher education offered in most African higher education institutions, Africa is also missing out on gains that arise from the growth of artificial intelligence, the Internet of things, big data ecosystems, digitalisation, greening for sustainable development, and the development of smart cities.

Furthermore, Africa is a continent with abundant natural resources. However, despite these resources, the continent continues to be the poorest on the globe. Africa still faces development challenges which have perennially threatened the socio-economic well-being of its people and stifled most facets of growth. Over the past years, poverty reduction has been accelerating in the poorest countries of the world, but not fast enough in the so-called continent of wealth. According to recent estimates, the number of deprived people in the region has grown from 278 million to 413 million in the last 25 years, while the average skyrocketing poverty rate of 41% makes Africa the poorest of all time (AfroEuro Foundation, 2020). The ongoing impacts of COVID-19 simply exacerbate what is already failing. What is more disheartening is that the continent is blessed with the rarest minerals required to build new technologies, but still more than 300 million Africans are living in extreme conditions with daily wages less than US$1.90 (AfroEuro Foundation, 2020).

Meanwhile, colonial relationships continue to shape the economic reality of nations across the continent. Africa's abundant natural resources continue to be exploited and exported at the hands of the former colonial masters without value addition locally. Millions of tons of raw natural resources continue to be exported out of Africa without building local infrastructures, continuing wealth extraction from Africa. Instead of manufacturing products that have the potential to grow economies, create jobs, and improve livelihood, Africa remains the end user of products made from its own natural resources. Many African countries rely on the sale of commodities in the form of raw minerals and materials to drive their economies. The African continent, for example, has dominated the production of raw platinum, used extensively in electronics, for many years. However, very little of the mineral refinement or component production happens on the continent. Similarly, despite huge demand, diamond mines are operated by unskilled personnel, which results in low-quality final products to be refined off continent (AfroEuro Foundation, 2020). The ability to benefit more widely from the rich resources found on African soil is dependent on the knowledge and resources that can be used to add value, to refine, to use materials in manufacture, and, then, to market and distribute finished products across the world (Boughey & McKenna, 2021; Kromydas, 2017).

Boughey and McKenna (2021) point out that knowledge is the driver of productivity and economic growth, and achieving these goals requires building human capital through more accessible, equitable, and better-quality higher education systems. However, Africa continues to experience the prevailing lack of a critical mass of educated professionals who can innovate, build cutting edge manufacturing industries, turn natural resources into value-added products, and hence grow local economies (MacGregor, 2009; Shabani et al., 2014). Daniel, Robert, and Samuel (2019) argue that African higher education graduates are weak in problem-solving, business understanding, computer use, and communication skills. This points to the lack of capacity for African higher education curriculum to grow quality graduates with requisite graduate employability attributes such as entrepreneurship for sustainable social and economic development of the continent (Boughey & McKenna, 2021; Mohamedbhai, 2020).

Research activities have also expanded in scope and relevance and the knowledge economy is enhancing the mobility of highly trained professionals. Inadequate and undiversified funding regimes, however, remain a major challenge to the development of more vibrant research and innovation infrastructure in higher education in Africa (Iqbal, 2015). In the absence of private-sector funding and competitive grants, public higher education institutions and research institutes in Africa predominantly depend on dwindling public subsidies as well as unpredictable international donor support. This narrow funding base suggests that research and innovation systems in African countries face severe financial deficits and lack the capacity to formulate and drive their own domestic research agendas. Research output from higher education institutions is extremely poor when compared to other world regions, partly because of lack of resources such as up-to-date journals and good Internet connectivity, but equally due to the absence of research-strong academics. For example, Africa is one of the continents with the lowest number of patents. Few papers by African researchers are published in internationally acclaimed premier journals. Indeed, acute shortage of high calibre academics is one of the greatest challenges facing African higher education institutions (Mohamedbhai, 2013). National policy makers and higher education institutions leadership need to be encouraged to work in closer partnership and to prioritise the strategic importance of research and innovation in national economic growth and competitiveness by investing more significantly in strengthening research capacity, infrastructure, and research opportunities in higher education institutions.

Curriculum Transformation

Within these dire global contexts, curriculum transformation has been gaining traction across Africa, in large part due to student activism, but also governments and related stakeholders. Most higher education systems in Africa have implemented curriculum transformation agendas as a response to these pressures. These efforts have led to small but significant steps towards progress in terms of addressing the imbalances inherited from the past colonial regimes, which include race, gender, social, and educational inequalities and related complex, intractable challenges (Mkwanazi & Bojabotseha, 2014). Despite these continued colonial contexts, there have been a number of achievements for higher education in Africa, including recently developed and implemented policy frameworks for higher education. The progressive realisation of this agenda has the potential to create a higher education system that is congruent with the core principles of social equity and redress, social justice, democracy, and development (Lotz-Sisitka, 2017; Lumadi, 2021; Mullet, 2018). Related policy efforts include higher education reform, strengthening quality assurance systems, harmonisation of higher education across the continent, construction of modern higher education systems, and marketisation and internationalisation. These efforts, while perhaps not transformative in and of themselves, build towards a unified structured approach to invest in higher education systems.

These infrastructure improvements come at a time when the current African higher education gross enrolment rate remains the lowest in the world. Indeed, on average, Africa enrols just over 12% of the population, well below the global average of 32% (UNESCO, 2021). While these numbers reflect coloniality and disparity, access to higher education in Africa has generally improved over the last two decades, and there has been increased and broadened participation in higher education. That much of this broadening reflects an explicit commitment to advance social equity and meet economic and social development needs on the continent is of direct significance; the continent has largely recognised the need to expand access while at the same time developing infrastructures, enhancing relevance, and transforming. Towards that end, quality assurance frameworks and related structures have also been established, with policies, mechanisms, and initiatives driving institutional audits, programme accreditation, quality promotion, and capacity development across African higher education systems (Iqbal, 2015). While not all utilise a transformed or decolonial approach, these amount to drastic infrastructure improvements at a continental level.

Thus, African higher education displays considerable strengths and much promise with respect to knowledge production and dissemination, to contributing to social equity, to economic and social development and democracy, and to the development needs of African continent. However, transformation remains a difficult process to implement, and where transformation has been implemented as a policy approach, those higher education systems have not, in the end, yielded tangible results. National transformation policy machinery, it seems, has proven to be insufficient to ensure implementation (Soudien, 2010). Nonetheless, these failures to implement suggest a need to re-prioritise and refocus efforts to use curriculum as a lever for higher education transformation and decoloniality.

Decolonising African Higher Education

Decolonisation and Africanisation processes are not new in Africa, as the call to decolonise higher education and curricula could be traced back to the late 1950s in countries such as Tanzania, Nigeria, and Senegal. Many of these initial efforts involved replacing foreign staff and Eurocentric curricula. These processes led to the establishment of centres of excellence of African knowledge production, including the Ibadan School, the Dar es Salaam School of Political Economy, and the Dakar School of Culture (Dell, 2018). According to Le Grange (2021), the term decolonisation is variously used in the literature, most often referring to insurrections and uprisings against colonisation, which eventually resulted in the removal of colonial administrative rule.

Decolonisation as a concept and as a process has been extensively interrogated in the South African higher education system, particularly in relation to the curriculum mostly through #FeesMustFall, #RhodesMustFall, and #DecoloniseTheCurriculum movements that were initiated in 2015. However, although almost all African countries have gone through some form of colonialism, not much has been widely written about curriculum decolonisation discourse at the continental level. Le Grange (2016) posits that Africa has gone through two phases of colonialism, namely the first-generation colonialism which was the conquering of the physical spaces and bodies of the colonised; and second-generation colonialism which was the colonisation of the mind through disciplines such as education, science, economics, and laws (wa Thiong'o, 1986). Decolonisation discussed in this chapter focuses on the latter phase, as many of the first generation have indeed been overthrown and/or replaced. The coloniality of the mind, however, remains the foundational challenge of higher education in Africa.

Decolonisation remains a highly contested, complex and subjective sociocultural phenomenon. Decolonisation refers to processes of mourning the loss of knowledges, cultures, and languages, discovering and recovering histories, cultures, and identities; and correcting the deficit ways in which colonised peoples have been defined and theorised. Decolonisation invokes Indigenous histories, knowledges, and worldviews to imagine alternative futures, seeks self-determination, internationalises common experiences, struggles, and hopes, and protects the knowledges of colonised peoples (MacGregor, 2009; Padayachee et al., 2018). Decolonising the curriculum is about embedding liberation and equality in all aspects of higher education from changing course content, changing the language of teaching, changing the way courses are taught, updating assessment techniques, developing research and publication practices, supporting training, resources, and funding, and modifying recruitment criteria (Ameyaw, Turnhout, Arts, & Wals, 2019). A decolonised curriculum would challenge Eurocentric approaches, provide different perspectives on topics, encourage critical thinking, and discuss issues that are important to marginalised groups across local, national, and global communities (Lumadi, 2021).

Le Grange (2016) argues that decolonisation of the curriculum entails a shift from Western/Eurocentric individualism and universalism to an Ubuntu-infused curriculum, which acknowledges the independence of humans and the more-than-human world. An Ubuntu-infused African-centred curriculum does not necessitate the destruction of dominant knowledge systems, but rather demands a recentring or integration of African knowledge systems into dominant epistemological discourses. According to Lumadi (2021), knowledge does not necessarily have to emanate from Africa, but must address African realities. The work of decolonisation theorists such as Fanon (2004), Spivak (1988), and wa Thiong'o (1986) clearly illustrates that the decolonisation process is complex and multidimensional, replete with conflicts, contradictions, and paradoxes. Mbembe (2016) draws attention to the fact that the decolonisation process encompasses all aspects of being in the higher education space. These aspects include the predominantly colonial architecture of higher education institutions and the Eurocentric academic models that still exist, the authoritative systems of control and management, both of students (through the standardised assessment processes) and, increasingly, of lecturers. Mbembe also pointed out the injustice of the continued existence of syllabi created through epistemic violence and deliberately designed to meet the needs of African colonisers.

The Council on Higher Education (CHE) points out that the dominance of European culture, language, and theories in higher education has also been highlighted by other authors as problematic (CHE, 2017). wa Thiong'o (1993), for example, suggested a move away from current Eurocentric norms, towards the centring of African perspectives, that is, the need to place African culture, literature, and language at the centre of the educational project so that African students may learn about themselves first before learning about people and contexts further afield. There have been, however, counter arguments to wa Thiongo's notion of recentring African perspectives in higher education curricula, with suggestions that to recentre Africa would simply mean replacing one form of knowledge and one worldview with another, an approach that would accomplish little in terms of preparing graduates who can function in both local and global contexts. Thus, for graduates to be locally and globally responsive (as is required for a sustainable future), perhaps what is needed is higher education curricula that are epistemically diverse and both locally and globally relevant (Mbembe, 2016). This broader conception of an integrative decolonised curriculum thus bears striking similarity to the goals of education for sustainable development (CHE, 2017).

According to Lumadi (2021), the decolonisation of higher education should be viewed as a process of defying and dismantling the colonial systems that swayed education in the past and that are still perpetuated today. Decoloniality is a discourse geared towards total withdrawal from the influence of former colonial masters, to become socially, politically, and economically independent. Colonial practices were established during times when Western nations maintained supremacy over dependent territories. This implies that, although Africa has been politically independent, all aspects of higher education remain influenced by former colonial masters, including curriculum, pedagogy, and assessment (Mbembe, 2015). Moreover, decolonisation may involve deliberating the effects of colonisation on higher education, as well as examining the scope and frame of what a liberating curriculum entails. The foundational intent of decolonisation is to equip students with 'diverse academic learning environments, curricula and approaches to research within which Indigenous cultures, histories, and knowledge are embedded' (Waghid & Hibbert, 2018). Decolonisation calls for a proportional representation, advocating primarily for increased numbers of Indigenous, racialised, and low-income students and faculty, and the supplementation of existing curricula with non-Western perspectives (Lumadi, 2021).

Caution must be taken in the decolonial process, in part because Eurocentric epistemologies are still firmly entrenched in African higher education institutions (Badat, 2010). According to Mullet (2018), curriculum transformation is the process of creating new curricula to respond to the new realities. In the South African context, the Education White Paper 3 (1997) specifies that transformation '…requires that all existing practices, institutions and values are viewed anew and rethought in terms of their fitness for the new era' (p. 1.1). This Paper points out that a transformed higher education system that will:

- Promote equity of access and fair chances of success to all who are seeking to realise their potential through higher education, while eradicating all forms of unfair discrimination and advancing redress for past inequalities.
- Meet, through well-planned and coordinated teaching, learning, and research programmes, national development needs, including the high-skilled employment needs presented by a growing economy operating in a global environment.
- Support a democratic ethos and a culture of human rights by educational programmes and practices conducive to critical discourse and creative thinking, cultural tolerance, and a common commitment to a humane, non-racist, and non-sexist social order.
- Contribute to the advancement of all forms of knowledge and scholarship and, in particular, address the diverse problems and demands of the local, national, southern African and African contexts, and uphold rigorous standards of academic quality.

(p. 1.14)

Although these points were articulated in a South African context, this chapter contends that all African countries share a relatively common history of colonialism. According to Badat (2010), the higher education transformation agenda as pursued by the governments and higher education systems seems to be problematic in that its goals are in conflict with one another. For example, transformation goals such as social equity and redress allow for more students to access higher education while simultaneously most African governments have been reducing funding for higher education. Furthermore, Badat (2010) contends that most higher education systems in Africa have been also failing to provide effective academic development programmes for underprepared students to induct them into academic discourse so as to improve their chances of academic success. The result of encountering the tension between competing transformation goals is both poor quality and failure to graduate future generations prepared for the world they must transform.

This frame, operating within higher education systems that have yet to balance access, quality, and decoloniality, leads to the fundamental question of what does it mean to be a University in Africa? A decolonised curriculum to engage in the purpose of a specific African higher education institution should engage the following key questions: (a) How can what is being taught and how it is taught be legitimated? Taking into account calls for curriculum transformation for an African higher education institution, this question urges conversation about who legitimates knowledge and related teaching endeavours. (b) Have students and academics considered where knowledge for specific courses comes from? This question can become a guiding curricular orientation, ensuring students and lecturers consider the global contexts of knowledge bases (i.e., Europe, the U.S.A., Global North vs. Africa/Global South). If the purpose is to help students conceptualise decolonisation projects, the curriculum must be a lever for such knowledge-based conversations.

Additional course-based questions can be leveraged as a structural approach to teaching. Making transparent what knowledge comes from the Global South, how that engages within a localised context, and how that differs from Eurocentric approaches can provide a foundation of criticality. Examples of how knowledge is used in local/African Global South contexts can be infused across the curriculum, while students can also be tasked with identifying, justifying, and legitimating such local knowledges. Relatedly, lecturers can engage questions about how specific curricular knowledge is linked to the histories of different students within specific class, programmes, departments, and faculties. In essence, if the purpose of decolonising the curriculum is to integrate localised knowledges, lecturers must make explicit how knowledge is created within disciplines, and indeed, how disciplines have been created and maintained within a critical lens towards coloniality.

As African higher education is influenced by colonial education systems, academic disciplines are not linked to African cultures and realities; yet higher education institutions continue to replicate these colonial structures. Asking the above questions may help to unearth hidden practices which can make African students feel distanced, excluded from, and silenced by academic disciplines and classroom interactions. Asking such questions also allows lecturers to become active learners within their own classroom, while creating more hospitable environments for learning. Such approaches also empower students to see themselves in the curriculum, and when they do not, to engage and, in part, to take on responsibility for dialogue about missing knowledges.

This calls for the need for higher education curricula to be adapted to better prepare graduates for current and future uncertainties by including more explicitly the critical issue of sustainable development (Lumadi, 2021). Lotz-Sisitka (2017) provides a convincing interpretation of decolonisation theory and practice as a frame for education for sustainable development, to reorient the purpose of higher education towards the common good. Similarly, Maringe and Ojo (2017) also highlight the interconnection between notions of decolonisation of higher education in Africa and those of sustainable development in their exploration of the meaning, rationale, and approaches for decolonised, sustainable development in African higher education.

Nkoane (2006), for example, speaks to the need for 'the re-invigorating of Africa's intellectuals, and the production of knowledge which is relevant, effective and empowering for the people of the African continent, and more particularly, the immediate African societies the universities serve' (p. 49). To counter the Eurocentrism of higher education institutions, Africanised education

> maintains African awareness of the social order and rules by which culture evolves; fosters the understanding of African consciousness; facilitates a critical emancipatory approach to solve the problems of their lives; and produces the material and capacities for Africans to determine their own future(s).
>
> *(Nkoane, 2006, p. 51)*

In this view, Africanising higher education means relating curricula to African experiences and the societal needs which have emanated and continue to emanate from such experience (MacGregor, 2009). Underlying this view is discourse about the African Renaissance, which was about a rebirth or reawakening, a 'reconstituting of that which has decayed or disintegrated' (Nkoane, 2006, p. 59). The main issue identified with respect to curriculum at African institutions of higher learning is that most modules and/or academic programmes (such as education, science, law, psychology, sociology, and political science) are not linked to African cultures and realities (Le Grange, 2016). The disciplinary problematisations, classifications, examples, illustrations, comparisons, models, social systems and structures, institutions, interpretations and misinterpretations, mistakes, and solutions all come from Western realities and socio-cultural constructs. African students are trained in these systems but expected to work and follow a career in African environments, setting up a long-term disjoint between lived experience, college learning, and professional context.

Shay (2013) argues that the challenge of relevance to real-world problems implies, certainly in the professional areas of study, asking such questions as 'In an African medical curriculum, should higher education institutions prepare students for the problems of first-world specialists or those of doctors working in poor rural areas?' This relates to the question of whether African higher education institutions are producing people who can help alleviate poverty and inequality, and whether what universities teach is adequate to the needs of the society in which they are located (Le Grange, 2016). A decolonised curriculum must include local context and content, especially when connecting theory to practice (Le Grange, 2021). To the authors, decolonising the curriculum of the twenty-first century should consider the Fourth and Fifth Industrial Revolutions (4th/5th IRs) to effectively respond to the current social and economic development needs of Africa. In short, decolonisation of the curriculum could involve a range of possibilities such as the radical rethinking of Western disciplines and exploring ways of developing and designing locally and regionally relevant curricula to replace Western epistemologies that continue to dominate and justify unequal power relations.

Reimagining African Higher Education

Given the extensive challenges that continue to confront African higher education, the entire sector needs to rethink higher education. In particular, African higher education must cultivate the knowledge, competencies, and skills that enable graduates to contribute to grow local economic sustainability in ways that foster greater social equality and culturally aligned development. However, we cannot assume that if a country's higher education sector produces high-quality graduates, especially in natural science, engineering, and technology fields, that this will automatically have a profound effect on the economy. Indeed, efforts to address local societal inequalities, as well as environmental sustainability, must be integrated across fields. Additionally, the formation of professionals through higher education is a necessary condition for economic growth and development, innovation, and global competitiveness, but is not a sufficient condition. The contribution of graduates is also dependent on the economic environment outside of higher education—in particular, industrial policy, the availability of investment capital and venture capital, and the openness and receptivity of state enterprises and business sectors. There should also be no pretence that, in terms of a higher education response to labour market needs, it is a simple matter to establish the knowledge, skills, competencies, and attitudes that are required by the economy, constituent parts, and society more generally. An instrumental approach to higher education which reduces value to economic growth, and calls that higher education should prioritise professional, vocational, and career-focused qualifications and programmes and emphasise skill development is to denude higher education of our considerably wider social value and functions.

Furthermore, the task of educators is to enable students to gain what Lumadi (2021) termed epistemological access to the disciplines. This means that curricula, teaching, and assessment should be designed in ways that induct students into the knowledge of the field, including the ways of knowing that will contribute to academic success. This integration must occur in tandem with decoloniality of that field, such that the field transforms to reflect African contexts, cultures, languages, and realities. Therefore, curriculum decolonisation and transformation should consider all dimensions in totality, including curriculum content, pedagogy, assessment practices, research and innovation, and community engagement.

This totality involves placing African identity, knowledge, history, society, and ideals on an equal footing with foreign (Western, European, American) values, ideals, approaches, and content in academic programmes. This decolonial approach exposes students to an African-centred worldview, while acknowledging the existence of other worldviews and perspectives, without assuming a uniform, monolithic or one-dimensional African world view, undifferentiated and uncritical. Such a decoloniality should include, but not be limited to, studying works by African authors, scientists and artists, Western theorists, academics, thinkers and philosophical pioneers, and ground-breakers that do not necessarily have their origins in Africa. Recognition of the scholarly perspectives from refugees, migrants, and others who represent the Global South's diaspora should also integrate across and decolonise within notions of the West. The voice of both the student and the broader society, irrespective of culture, language, gender, religion, and background, must be heard and examined in such module content and outcomes with a view to recognising and developing new Africanised and other alternative knowledge types and their underlying assumptions as relevant to the area of study (North-West University, 2018).

Relatedly, a specific focus on translation of a decolonised African curriculum into pedagogy must accompany all transformative efforts. Fomunyam (2013) defines pedagogy as the art and science of how teaching and learning is practised, or how it unfolds, and how students learn what is taught. How students experience the curriculum is essential, as education is both an epistemological and an ontological project. In other words, as students engage with knowledge, they become different kinds of people. However, traditionalised Western teaching practices emphasise on didactic instruction, which focuses on classroom management, discipline, and 'how to' skill development, hence the need to decolonise and transform pedagogy to localised African contexts. Decolonising pedagogical approaches is essential to ensuring that teaching and learning reflects localised languages, cultures, and contexts. According to Vorster (2016), decolonised teaching and learning practices inspire students to think critically on and engage with issues such as discrimination, racism, inequality, poverty, colonialism, alienation, inclusion, and ethical conduct. Furthermore, decolonised teaching and learning encourages students to interpret curriculum content based on their own experiences, according to their cultural norms, personal belief systems, preferences, and backgrounds, and to share their interpretations with fellow students as valid and valued real-life experiences.

We thus contend that curriculum transformation must include transformative pedagogies that will produce transformational graduates who are critical thinkers and problem solvers with entrepreneurial mindset as agents for social justice able to transform society and economy. These graduates will be able to create local investments on the continent rather than the current slogan of attracting foreign investment, which continues to impoverish Africa as huge profits are shipped out of Africa in the name of foreign investment. Some critical questions that need to be asked at the institutional level include (Boughey, 2015): What needs to change and what approaches are, in the main, effective with regard to teaching? What values, beliefs, and ideas underpin our teaching? How do these reflect, engage, and further African Indigenous knowledge systems? What is our view of the student regarding teaching and learning? What is our view of teaching? To what extent is our teaching emancipatory (critical pedagogy, transformative pedagogy, criticality, reflectivity, praxis, etc.)? How do these questions centre student experiences, perspectives, while addressing the material and psychological conditions of poverty? We suggest these questions become tangible guides to transparent decolonial restructuring.

Relatedly, we cannot transform curriculum and teaching approaches without a commitment to transparent assessment systems. How institutions know which knowledges are being taught effectively, with which students, is central to transformation agendas. Decolonising assessment practices is about engaging assessment practices that move beyond determining competence to understand individual areas of strength and growth to ensure that knowledge gaps can be addressed the future development of individual students. Some critical questions that must be asked about decolonisation and transformation of assessment practices include (Boughey, 2015): What values, beliefs, and ideas underpin our assessment metrics? Who has access to power and control, and how do we flatten hierarchical power relations in alignment with Ubuntu? To what extent do we use assessment strategies that empower students, including self-assessments, peer-assessments, and community assessments? How do we balance assessment of lecturers versus students as we consider learning? How do institutions commit to transparent definitions of decoloniality that can be woven throughout assessment metrics? Such questions intend to guide institutional transformation at a concrete level.

Higher education institutions are resource rich and inextricably linked with their communities (Vorster, 2016). Therefore, to be beneficial to democracy and development, it is imperative to establish and maintain honest mutualistic, respectful partnerships with specific localised communities. This demands that higher education institutions become more vigorous partners when searching for answers to moral, civic, social, and economic challenges. This also requires higher education institutions to build strong linkages, collaboration, and partnership with industry and society in all facets including programme development, delivery, research, innovation, and development. The transformation of community engagement, aligned with a decolonial agenda, ensures that higher education institutions specifically focus on partnering with localised efforts to address the material impacts of long-term colonial relations as well as current disparities. Integration of community across the curriculum is essential for such efforts, such that disciplinary boundaries include mitigating impacts while challenging the structures of oppression.

Related to service, research and scholarship must be reconceptualised, across the curriculum, to have tangible application to real-world problems. Research outputs and knowledge production are vital for Africa's sustainable socio-economic development through innovation and development (Vorster, 2016). However, Africa is still lagging far behind in terms of public expenditure on research and development. On average, the continent contributes less than 1% of the world's research outputs. In addition, a report on patent filings by the World Intellectual Property Organisation (WIPO, 2020) found many African countries ranked poorly in this category. It is, therefore, not surprising that Africa accounts for less than 1.5% of the total global publications in international scientific journals and has been declining steeply in recent decades. Therefore, there is a need for Africa to acknowledge that research is important for innovation and development as research output can be used in industry and manufacturing, as well as in public sectors. To realise the potential of science and innovation, Africa must recommit to ensuring that scientists in African universities and research institutions have access to well-equipped laboratories and related social science resources to invest in decolonial sciences. Industrialisation is important in lifting Africa out of poverty, in generating local investments, local economies, and improvements to the daily quality of life, especially for those with limited water, housing, sanitation, and school facilities.

Decolonising research requires more than increasing productivity and must be integrated across the curriculum so that the entire higher education community sees research as service to, and with, African communities. Thus, research cannot be divorced from the praxis of learning and teaching. Research manifests across bodies of knowledge, constituting a critical engagement between lecturers and students in a decolonised curriculum. This encompasses what is both taught and learnt and the resultant social and personal impact thereof. Neither do these processes stand in isolation from community engagement. Decoloniality goes beyond doing research *on* society and includes generating knowledge with community, industry, and societal partners that contribute to different types of knowledge by using established participatory research methodologies such as action research and appreciative enquiry. These efforts are difficult, but the stakes cannot be higher—African higher education must transform, with a decolonial lens, across each and every endeavour.

Conclusion

This chapter concludes that higher education in Africa plays a significant role in equipping the next generation of leaders with knowledge and essential skills for sustainable environmental, economic, and social development. However, although there has been some degree of improvements in African higher education, challenges remain considerable, with perhaps the largest challenge being the need to align higher education across goals of access, quality, sustainability, localised knowledges and languages, and ultimately, relevance to Africans. Therefore, Africa must recognise the importance of transforming higher education through prioritisation of curriculum transformation, including teaching and learning, curricular assessment, community engagement, research, and related infrastructures. Curriculum decolonisation and transformation must develop competent graduates who are critical thinkers, with an entrepreneurial mindset, able to meaningfully grow an economy rooted within Eurocentric exploitation, and who can leverage local social justice agendas. Furthermore, African governments need to acknowledge that nothing is possible without substantial investment. For an African Renaissance, rooted in Ubuntu, to occur, there must be an alignment of support for higher education to transform while addressing quality challenges, limited institutional capacities, inadequate funding, and pressing social issues. Therefore, there is an urgent need for African governments to invest in higher education research, innovation, strong linkages, collaboration, and partnership between higher education institutions, industry, and society, creating centres of excellence and in the development of the new generation of scholars, based on a foundation of a transformed, decolonial curricular frameworks.

References

AfroEuro Foundation. (2020). Why Africa is poor despite having the most diamonds. https://afroeuro.org/magazine/why-africa-is-poor-despite-having-the-most-diamonds/

Ameyaw, J., Turnhout, E., Arts, B., & Wals, A. (2019). Creating a responsive curriculum for postgraduates: Lessons from a case in Ghana. *Journal of Further and Higher Education*, 43(4), 573–588. doi:10.1080/0309877X.2017.1386285

Badat, S. (2003). *Transforming South African higher education, 1990–2003: Goals, policy initiatives and critical challenges and issues.* CHET.

Badat, S. (2010). *The challenges of transformation in higher education and training institutions in South Africa.* Paper Commissioned by the Development Bank of Southern Africa.

Badat, S. (2011). The context of higher education. CHERTL PGDHE Programme.

Barnett, R. (1999). Power, enlightenment and quality evaluation. In CHEPS (Ed.), *Quality management in higher education* (pp. 73–88). LEMMA.

Boughey, C. (2015). *Unpublished presentation to new lecturers at the 2015 Academic Orientation Programme.* Rhodes University.

Boughey, C., & McKenna, S. (2021). *Understanding higher education: Alternative perspectives.* African Minds.

Castells, M. (2009). The role of universities in development, the economy and society. http://www.chet.org.za/papers/role-universities-development-economy-and-society

Council on Higher Education (CHE). (2017). *Decolonising the curriculum: Stimulating debate.* Council on Higher Education.

D'Andrea, V., & Gosling, D. (2005). *Improving teaching and learning in higher education: A whole institutional approach.* Society for Research into Higher Education/Open University Press/Bell and Brain.

Daniel, D., Robert, O., & Samuel, A. (2019). A philosophical outlook on Africa's higher education in the twenty-first century: Challenges and prospects, pedagogy in basic and higher education – current developments and challenges. https://www.intechopen.

com/books/pedagogy-in-basic-and-higher-education-current-developments-and-challenges/a-philosophical-outlook-on-africa-s-higher-education-in-the-twenty-first-century-challenges-and-pros

Dell, S. (2018). Curriculum transformation - A long and tortuous battle. *University World News*. https://www.universityworldnews.com/post.php?story=20180926115231110

Education White Paper 3. (1997). *A Programme for the transformation of higher education*. Department of Education.

Fanon, F. (2004). *Wretched of earth*. (Translated by P. Philcox). Grove Press.

Fomunyam, K.G. (2013). *Student teachers experiences of teachers' professional identity within the context of curriculum change in a university in KwaZulu-Natal*. University of KwaZulu-Natal.

Iqbal, M. (2015). Africa's higher education landscape. https://www.qs.com/africas-higher-education-landscape/

Kromydas, K. (2017). Rethinking higher education and its relationship with social inequalities: Past knowledge, present state and future potential. *Palgrave Communications*, *3*(1), 1–12. doi:10.1057/s41599-017-0001-8

Le Grange, L. (2016). Decolonising the university curriculum. *South African Journal of Higher Education*, *30*(2), 1–12. doi:10.20853/30-2-709

Le Grange, L. (2021). (Individual) responsibility in decolonising the university curriculum. *South African Journal of Higher Education*, *35*(1), 4–20. doi:10.20853/35-1-4416

Lotz-Sisitka, H.B. (2017). Decolonising as future frame for environment and sustainability education. In P. Corcoran & J. Weakland (Eds.), *Envisioning futures for environment and sustainability education* (pp. 45–62). Wageningen Academic Publishers.

Luckett, K. (2016). Curriculum contestation in a post-colonial context: A view from the South. *Teaching in Higher Education*, *21*(4), 415–428. doi:10.4324/9781351171441-4

Lumadi, M.W. (2021). The pursuit of decolonising and transforming curriculum in higher education. *South African Journal of Higher Education*, *35*(1), 1–3.

MacGregor, K. (2009, July 5). Trends in global higher education. *University World News*, 83. University World News. http://www.universityworldnews.com/article.php?story=20090705083940943

Maringe, F., & Ojo, E. (2017). Sustainable transformation in a rapidly globalizing and decolonising world: African higher education on the brink. In F. Maringe & E. Ojo (Eds.), *Sustainable transformation in African higher education* (pp. 25–39). Sense.

Mbembe, A.J. (2015). Decolonizing knowledge and the question of the archive. https://wiser.wits.ac.za/system/files/Achille%20Mbembe%20-%20Decolonizing%20Knowledge%20and%20the%20Question%20of%20the%20Archive.pdf

Mbembe, A.J. (2016). Decolonizing the university: New directions. *Arts and Humanities in Higher Education*, *15*(1), 29–45.

Mkwanazi, T.S., & Bojabotseha, T.P. (2014). Higher education in South Africa at the crossroads. *Mediterranean Journal of Social Sciences*, *5*(2), 469–475.

Mohamedbhai, G. (2013). *Towards an African Higher Education and Research Space (AHERS)*. Working Group on Higher Education (WGHE): Association for Development of Education in Africa.

Mohamedbhai, G. (2020). India's new national education policy: Lessons for Africa. *University World News*. https://www.universityworldnews.com/post.php?story=20200921085451102

Mullet, D.R. (2018). A general critical discourse analysis framework for educational research. *Journal of Advanced Academics*. doi:10.1177/1932202X18758260

Nkoane, M.N. (2006). The Africanisation of the university in Africa. *Alternation*, *13*(1), 49–69.

North-West University. (2018). *North-West University's Declaration on the Decolonisation of University Education: The imperative to transform teaching and learning, the research agenda and community engagement*. North-West University.

Padayachee, K., Matimolane, M., & Ganas, R. (2018). Addressing curriculum decolonisation and education for sustainable development through epistemically diverse curricula. *South African Journal of Higher Education*, *32*(6), 288–304. doi:10.20853/32-6-2986

Shabani, J., Okebukola, P., & Oyewole, O. (2014). Quality assurance in Africa: Towards a continental higher education and research space. *International Journal of African Higher Education*, *1*(1), 139–171. doi:10.6017/ijahe.v1i1.5646

Shay, S. (2013). Conceptualising curriculum differentiation in higher education: A sociology of knowledge point of view. *British Journal of Sociology of Education*, *34*(4), 563–582. doi:10.1080/01425692.2012.722285

Soudien, C. (2010). *Transformation in higher education: A briefing paper*. Development Bank of Southern Africa. https://www.dhet.gov.za/summit/Docs/2010Docs/Transformation

Spivak, G.C. (1988). Can the subaltern speak? In C. Nelson & L. Grossberg (Eds.), *Marxism and the interpretation of culture* (pp. 271–313). University of Illinois Press.

UNESCO. (2021). Sustainable Development goals 1-4 national monitoring. http://data.uis.unesco.org/?queryid=142

Vorster, J. (2016). *Curriculum in the context of transformation: Reframing traditional understanding and practices*. Rhodes University.

wa Thiong'o, N. (1986). *Decolonising the mind: The politics of language in African literature*. James Currey.

wa Thiong'o, N. (1993). *Moving the centre: The struggle for cultural freedoms*. James Currey.

Waghid, Z., & Hibbert, L. (2018). Decolonising preservice teachers' colonialist thoughts in higher education through defamiliarisation as a pedagogy. *Educational Research for Social Change*, *7*(1), 60–77.

World Intellectual Property Organisation (WIPO). (2020). *The geography of innovation: Local hotspots, global networks*. https://www.wipo.int/edocs/pubdocs/en/wipo_pub_944_2019.pdf

4
REMOVING AND RECENTRING

Student Activist Perceptions of Curricular Decolonisation

Khazamula J. Maluleka

> Ours now is to focus on the decolonial project in its entirety … Our identity starts as black people, and that is where we must centralise it. Go to Langa. Go to Khayelitsha. Go to Mutubatuba. Go to Alexandra. Go to Soweto, and fight with the people.
>
> *(Rehad, 2019)*

The debate on knowledge in African universities has witnessed extensive recent disagreements. The call to decolonise education was a cornerstone of student protests (#FeesMustFall and #RhodesMustFall) at various South African universities in the middle of October 2015 (Costandius et al., 2018). The demand for free education across the higher education sector was accompanied by a call for changes in the knowledge systems and curricula, in the light of what students described as forced exposure to Eurocentrism at untransformed institutions (Fataar, 2018). During the protests, South African students indicated that they were still taught irrelevant and oppressive knowledge after many years of independence. The decolonisation of the curriculum was thus one of the key demands during the #FeesMustFall protests (Griffiths, 2019). Student demands were critical of Western mono-conceptualisations of modernity and democracy and the role modern universities play in imposing these ideals on Indigenous communities. This decolonial critique insists that modernity and coloniality be understood as mutually constitutive concepts. These demands indicate student recognition of the complexities of decolonising higher education curricula. Morreira, Luckett, Kumalo, and Ramgotra (2020) submit that there is no one single way of implementing decolonial thought and practice in the classroom. Thus, student protesters appear to be arguing for multifaceted approaches that expand traditionalised higher education scopes, suggesting processes for curricula to become both pluriverse and contextually situated.

The Gap Identified

Researchers that have proposed the topic of decolonisation include Gumbo and Williams (2014), who wrote extensively on the decolonisation of technology education (TE); Maluleka and Themane (2020), who argued for the decolonisation of TE through culturally responsive methods; and Msila (2009) and Kamwendo (2014), who deliberated on Africanisation of education. The 2015 student protests, however, indicated a gap between research and the implementation of the decolonisation idea (Mampane, Omidire, & Aluko, 2018). The protests further triggered a renewed interest in the decolonisation of university curriculum in South Africa. The decolonisation of the curriculum has been an ongoing conversation since well before the overthrow of apartheid (Mampane et al., 2018); however, implementation remains long overdue, given that the Western model of academic organisation, on which the South African university is based, remains largely unchanged.

When considering the impact of the apartheid era on the institutional culture at higher learning institutions, it is not surprising that transformation is slow, even after some years of democracy (Mampane et al., 2018). This slow pace is despite South Africa's mandate to advance the goals of transformation in higher education. Since the idea of decolonisation attracted the attention of African-focused scholars, a lot has been written, but the challenge that remains is implementation. The question is, who is responsible for such decolonial implementation? While researchers and policy makers discuss and debate responsibility, there is a growing dissatisfaction with the state of education, despite the progress that has been recorded over the last decades (Mampane et al., 2018). Students are becoming impatient with the pace at which decolonisation is taking place, particularly given ongoing racial disparities across school systems (Knaus & Brown, 2016). Student movements have long been advocating for the urgency of decolonisation. The South African History Online [SAHO] (2020) clarifies how the South African Students Movement (SASM), an organisation of mainly high school students, came to national fame when members organised the boycotts against Bantu Education and especially against the imposition of Afrikaans as a medium of instruction, which resulted in the June 1976 uprising. The 1976 students were supported by Steve Biko's Black Consciousness Movement (SAHO, 2020).

With an intention of contributing to the implementation of curricular decolonisation, the main question addressed in this study is: How can the convolutions (difficulties) of decolonising the curricula in higher education be confronted? The following sub-questions were devised: What are students' understanding of the decolonisation of the curriculum? How did #FeesMustFall contribute to revealing the need for decolonisation? Why did some student activists consider violence as a lever for change? What are the challenges of the process of decolonisation of the higher education curriculum? How can curricular decolonisation be implemented in higher education? To answer these questions, I interviewed 13 male and female Black students who identified as activists during the #FeesMustFall protests between 2015 and 2019. These students noted the decolonisation of the curricula as their highest priority.

Theoretical Framework

The theory underpinning this study is transformative learning theory (TLT), which was promulgated by Mezirow in 1975 (Mezirow, 1997). TLT's roots are in Habermas's theory of communicative action, which suggests that different kinds of actions are inspired by different kinds of reason (Christie, Carey, Robertson, & Grainger, 2015, p. 10). Thus, life experiences contribute to knowledge and the determination of who we are (Mezirow, 1997). TLT is based on the idea that individuals learn how to make effective judgements and isolate themselves from things that have not been tested before. Mezirow's theory maintains that every individual has a particular worldview. The worldview may or may not be well articulated, but is derived from individual upbringing, life experiences, culture, and education (Christie et al., 2015). An essential element of Mezirow's theory is the need to develop communicative skills so that internal and external conflicts, which result from changes in perspective, can be resolved via rational discourse, rather than force. The insistence on rationality as a key to 'communicative action' and eventual transformation has been a contested aspect of the transformation theory (Christie et al., 2015).

TLT is important in this study, which deals with students impatient with higher education authorities and the slow pace of change, and whom, in some cases, resorted to violence as a means to bring about change in education (Mbiza, 2018). According to this theory, communicative skills should be strengthened in students so that internal and external conflicts, which result from changes in perspective, can be resolved via rational discourse rather than force. Based on this theory, the argument is that for students to embrace communication, institutions should acknowledge that every individual has a particular worldview, derived from their cultural context and upbringing, that needs to be respected. It is essential to note that the conflicts between worldview can also be exacerbated by social conditions, which, in turn, can be exacerbated by higher education coloniality and denial of specific cultural communities, languages, and ancestral knowledges. The historic context of South Africa suggests continuation of student protests against irrational state policies, such as coloniality and apartheid, and in particular, that higher education institutions have not fully repudiated, much less transformed from, these irrational policies. Indeed, the continuation of higher education coloniality continues to cause aggressively enforced concrete inequalities (Knaus & Brown, 2016).

Decolonisation

In addition to the theoretical frameworks provided previously, this section clarifies the concept of 'decolonising curricula.' Colonisation and decolonisation are concepts with historical and ideological origins from the phenomenon of colony (Mampane et al., 2018; Sommer, 2011). Colonialism is a system of domination and subjugation of people from another culture, including all forms of imperial rule and cultural differences that exist between the government and the governed. Colonisation is when a group of people impose their own culture over the land and people. Decolonisation, on the other hand, consists of the conscious rejection of values, norms, customs, and worldviews imposed by the colonialists (Mampane et al., 2018). Decolonisation seeks to reverse and remedy such violent imposition through direct action (O'Dowd & Heckenberg, 2020). Decolonisation is the attempted change that colonised countries go through when they become politically independent from their former colonisers (Oelofsen, 2015). But complicating independence movements, decolonisation is a set of processes, not just one-time actions or policies.

Chilisa (2020) suggests five phases in the process of decolonisation: *Rediscovery and recovery*; *mourning*; *dreaming*; *commitment*; and *action*. *Rediscovery and recovery* refer to the process whereby colonised peoples rediscover and recover their own history, culture, language, and identity. *Mourning* refers to the process of lamenting the continued assault on the world's colonised and oppressed peoples' identities and social realities. It is an important part of healing that enables more creative efforts encapsulated through dreaming. *Dreaming* is when colonised peoples invoke their histories, worldviews, and Indigenous knowledge systems, to theorise and imagine alternative possibilities—in this instance, a different curriculum. *Commitment* is when academics and students become political activists, who work to include the voices of the colonised, in this case, through the university curriculum. *Action* is the phase where dreams and commitments translate into strategies for social transformation. Those who see decolonisation as a way to transform higher education curriculum often follow this suggested process. Student leaders, for example, have argued for curriculum that facilitates recovery of Indigenous worldviews, histories, cultures, languages, and identities (Costandius et al., 2018).

As higher education in South Africa was a tool of coloniality, students continue to demand the fall of the image and infrastructure envisioned by the British imperialist and coloniser, Cecil Rhodes (Mgqwashu, 2016). Muldoon (2019) maintains that it has been 4 (now 6) years since the first #RhodesMustFall protest took a global stage, yet both protesters and institutionalists misunderstand what decolonisation means in practice. While many have recently come out in support of a decolonial campaign, not all academics are on board. Muldoon (2019), a lecturer at the University of Exeter, claimed that calls to decolonise the curriculum is a big mistake, since the last thing that universities need is to have male, pale, and stale voices side-lined. Mgqwashu (2016) argues that these critics neglect to mention that decolonising universities is not about completely eliminating whites from the curriculum; it is about challenging the longstanding biases and omissions that limit how people understand society. Charles (2019) maintains that decolonising the curriculum thus means creating spaces and resources for a dialogue among all members of the university on how to imagine and envision all cultures and knowledge systems in the curriculum.

Student Movements to Decolonise Curricula

The year 2015 witnessed the rise of student protests at various higher education institutions across South Africa, including the #FeesMustFall and #RhodesMustFall (RMF) protests. #FeesMustFall was a student protest movement that began in South Africa (Costandius et al., 2018). Costandius et al. (2018) further explain that the initial demand made by the students was the 'fall' of university fees that were based on historic access to wealth. Thus, given colonial legacies and apartheid wealth distribution, students protested for equal access to institutions that had maintained racial and economic exclusivity as if wealth had been redistributed. The #RhodesMustFall movement sharpened the #FeesMustFall protests towards the decolonisation of higher education. Sparked by the continued presence of Cecil John Rhodes's statue at the centre of the University of Cape Town campus (Ndlovu-Gatsheni, 2015), students argued that higher education's racial segregation in essence proves the incompleteness of decolonisation, especially 30 years after the overthrow of apartheid. At the heart of these movements lies the quest for a decolonial curriculum that will reflect the ethos of the people higher education is meant to serve. The calls for a decolonised curriculum from student movements have refuelled a quest to reassess and develop a curriculum that will be relevant to the current challenges faced by a country and region still affected by colonisation and apartheid.

The 1976 student uprising in South Africa was triggered by the announcement that Afrikaans, alongside English, was to be made the compulsory medium of instruction in all Black schools (Educational Policy Consortium, 2015). Black students who saw this as a continuation of colonisation began mobilising to fight for the full integration of Indigenous languages across all educational infrastructures. This linguistic removal and structural silencing have been one of the most crucial aspects of colonisation (Maluleka & Themane, 2020). On June 16, 1976, estimates of up to 10,000 students, mobilised by the South African Students Movement's Action Committee, supported by Steve Biko's Black Consciousness Movement (BCM), marched peacefully to demonstrate against the government's directive (SAHO, 2020). These uprisings, started by secondary students from Orlando High, soon spread to include students from primary schools to universities.

Paralleling this history, the #FeesMustFall protests were also a response to an announcement issued by the Minister of Higher Education and Training. The Minister announced that the country's universities were facing serious funding challenges at the same time South Africans were having trouble affording tuition; thus the Minister proposed that universities set their own fee increases for 2017, with a recommendation to not increase beyond eight per cent (Hauser, 2016). According to the announcement, student funding, debts, and the National Student Financial Aid Scheme [NSFAS] were to be affected (Bitzer & de Jager, 2018). The announcement was not well-received, since the South African democratic dispensation was based on the Freedom Charter, whose guidelines the governing party, the African National Congress (ANC), promised would form the basis to build the new South Africa. The Freedom Charter provides that education shall be free, compulsory, universal, and equal for all children (Educational Policy Consortium, 2015). Thus, the ANC's comments as a response to the protests came as a surprise, and #FeesMustFall argued that free higher education was promised by the ANC. The ANC maintains that the Freedom Charter has been misquoted in this regard (Educational Policy Consortium, 2015).

The placards carried by students during their marches illustrated the demands made by the #FeesMustFall and #RhodesMustFall (RMF) movements, suggesting a clear linkage between the two campaigns. The demands were put forth by a multiracial coalition advocating for transformation. Initially students were concerned with fees; however, as support for the protests spread to other campuses nationally and gained broader public support, the demands changed to include decolonisation. South African students were supported by solidarity protests, particularly in the United Kingdom, as students there saw the linkage between U.K.-supported institutions and Oxford-trained colonial administrators such as Rhodes.

Towards a Curricular Decolonial Framework

Decolonisation has been a buzz word for some years. However, the practicality of the implementation of a decolonised curriculum in higher education remains an unrealised dream (Dastile & Ndlovu-Gatsheni, 2013, p. 24). Student demands for a relevant education was an indication that decolonisation remains elusive. This further demonstrates the significant challenges that hamper the implementation of decolonisation. One primary challenge is structural: South Africa's democratic government inherited 36 institutions of higher learning from the apartheid government in 1994. Resources at the different institutions were inequitably distributed. The division into various races (Black, white, Indian, and so-called Coloured)—forged by colonialism and then apartheid—intentionally created inequities in resource distribution that persist today (Mampane et al., 2018). For the South African government and institutional authorities, undoing programmes that have been implemented by the colonialist and apartheid regimes has been tremendously difficult. When considering the depth of the institutional culture of the apartheid era in higher learning institutions (e.g., sustained racial division), it is not surprising that transformation has been slow, even after years of democratic rule. Thus, racial inequities remain despite the government's mandate to advance the goals of transformation in higher education (Department of Education, 1997; Mampane et al., 2018).

Dastile and Ndlovu-Gatsheni (2013) maintain that students indicated that, since the introduction of the democratic dispensation (almost three decades ago), they are still being taught irrelevant content. In addition, Ngũgĩ wa Thiong'o has long argued for the restoration of African languages and cultures as a first step in reversing cultural imperialism, psychological rehabilitation, African relevance, and identity reconstruction (Ndlovu-Gatsheni, 2015). Long ago challenging coloniality in language of instruction, wa Thiong'o (1986) suggests that language be at the centre of people's explanation of themselves in relation to their natural and social environment and the world at large. Yet Mawere (2010) realised that the implementation of decolonisation in education is made difficult by some who still see Western knowledges as superior to African knowledges (Oelofsen, 2015). Wa Thiong'o (1986) specifically emphasises the importance of local languages in decolonising the mind of African people. Maluleka and Themane (2020) further argue that decolonisation has to start with language.

Yet in addition to linguistic racism, Eurocentric epistemologies are still firmly entrenched in South African universities and, thus, the call for intellectual spaces must be decolonised, de-racialised, de-masculinised, and de-gendered (Joseph, 2017). The Eurocentric epistemological and ontological coloniality permeating university campuses partially explains why students during the #RhodesMustFall and #FMF campaigns expressed their frustration thus:

> Getting a degree here [referring to UCT] is a form of mental slavery and colonization. We can no longer breath! We want to breathe! We must exorcise the colonial ghost from the curriculum. We want relevant knowledge, we want to study African history, we want to reclaim our black history.
> *(Luckett, 2016, p. 416)*

Le Grange (2016) proposes various approaches to decolonise the curriculum: (a) The radical rethinking of Western disciplines described as, 'distant, antiseptic and removed from the experiences of the lived world [that] comes from recognising the pain, anger and anguish being experienced in society.' (b) A possibility is through emerging transdisciplinary knowledge, not based on a socially distributed knowledge system that only comprises those produced by the university, but one expanded to include ordinary citizens (including Indigenous communities). The decolonised curriculum is based on the 4Rs central to an emergent Indigenous paradigm. The 4Rs are relational accountability, respectful representation, reciprocal appropriation, and rights and regulation. (c) The approach would be to explore ways of developing and designing locally and regionally relevant curricula [in those places] where Western epistemologies continue to dominate, and unequal power relations remain prevalent. (d) The approach, in the African context, is for students to learn together about the origin of human beings, and the epistemologies that emerged from the Cradle of Humankind. (e) A possibility is to draw inspiration from the approach used by the Intercultural University of the Indigenous Nations and Peoples, Amawtay Wasi, in Ecuador. The curriculum pathway comprises three cycles: Cycle in the formation of ancestral sciences (doing community, learning to learn); cycle of Western sciences (learning to unlearn and then relearn); cycle of interculturality (learning to unlearn and relearn and going from learning to undertaking (Le Grange, 2016)).

According to Moncrieffe, Asare, and Dunford (2019), a critical multicultural education can be applied to challenge Eurocentrism within the national curriculum. The understanding is that reflection on the lives and shared histories of majority and minority groups in societies and communities can produce innovation and advancement in teaching and learning. They further allude that critical multicultural education can be applied to teaching and learning through the nation's multicultural history. Specifically, this lens can be applied to how South Africa learns and relearns the meaning of tolerance and mutual respect of those with different faiths and beliefs.

Joseph (2017) argues that to decolonise the curriculum, people are required to view anew all existing practices, institutions, and values, which should be reconsidered in terms of their fitness for the new era. The intention should be to create an anti-racist and anti-sexist system of higher education that will promote equity of access and fair chances of success to all who are seeking to realise their potential, while eradicating all forms of discrimination and advancing redress for past inequalities. One should also acknowledge that although this sounds ideal, we are still having a long and winding road to go when one considers the dominant influence of Western institutions that continue to shape what South Africans experience as schooling and education (Knaus & Brown, 2016). This indicates that the alternative is to start with changing the mindset of people [the decolonisation of the minds] (wa Thiong'o, 1986).

Ndlovu-Gatsheni (2015) echoes this focus, calling for 'understanding a deeper meaning of the concept of transformation of higher education in Africa [and in South Africa] in pursuit of an elusive African university' (p. 21). Soudien (2010) reminds that institutions of higher education are faced with three enormous challenges regarding such transformation: They fail to engage sufficiently with new students entering the institution; the staff profile and make-up does not reflect these new students and, lastly, the curriculum remains colonial (Joseph, 2017). Clearly institutions of higher education are struggling to transform, and the national transformation policy machinery has proven to be insufficient to ensure implementation. As Soudien argues, and as student protests suggest, racism as everyday reality remains the most pressing issue (University World News, 2010). This further demonstrates that the decolonisation of the mind is also necessary for non-Indigenous communities. At some institutions, transformation is completely invisible, with no transformation office or staff. Thus, it is not surprising that the #FeesMustFall and #RhodesMustFall student movements did not make a call for transformation; instead, they demanded decoloniality, together with free education. The challenge to decolonise remains seemingly impossible, especially to Black youth who still attend apartheid-era schools in woefully under-resourced townships (Knaus & Brown, 2016; Soudien, 2010).

Methodology

In order to explore what students committed to decolonising higher education think about barriers to decoloniality, this qualitative study used qualitative interviews to directly solicit student responses. Phenomenology was used to clarify participant lived experience (Creswell, 2013), focusing interview questions on experiences with decolonising the curricula while enrolled at a higher education institution in South Africa. Due to COVID-19 conditions, a dual technique of telephonic interviews and email-distributed open-ended questionnaires was used to collect data. Students who were telephonically interviewed were those who participated in the #FeesMustFall protests. There was a standing agreement with these students that whenever a need for more information on certain issues arises, the researcher may conduct telephonic conversation to clarify the issue. Students who identified as the missing middle (below the threshold needed to afford university enrolments, but with parental incomes too high to be awarded university bursaries) were given an opportunity to complete open-ended questionnaires. Students whose questionnaires demonstrated more valuable information were telephonically consulted to provide more information or seek additional clarity. These techniques were chosen to avoid the spread of the coronavirus as well as to ensure that the participants were most comfortable when providing information. Participants agreed to be recorded, and pseudonyms are used to report participant data.

Interviews and questionnaires were based on the following questions, with additional clarifying questions raised during interviews. What does the concept of 'decolonisation of the curriculum' mean? What influences student worldviews? Initially the #FeesMustFall student movement demanded the 'fall' of university fees; why there was a demand for decolonisation? Why did some #FeesMustFall protests turn to violence to bring change to education instead of negotiations? What are the challenges of the decolonisation of higher education curriculum? How can the decolonising of the curricula be implemented in higher education?

Sample

The sample consisted of 13 Black male and female honours degree students from five universities located in Gauteng, South Africa. Each university officially designated English as the language of instruction. Students were of various ages (between 20 and 25 years) and languages (see Table 4.1) who are however taught in English. Seven had participated in the #FeesMustFall and #RhodesMustFall protests as members of student representative councils (SRCs) who were at the forefront of the protest in their various institutions. The remaining six represented the *missing middle*—students who, due to their parents' financial status, could not qualify for National Student Financial Aid Scheme (NSFAS) and, on the other hand, their parents could not afford to pay for them to register. Although this

TABLE 4.1 Participants

Pseudonym	Age	Home Language
Bongani	20	IsiZulu
Rhulani	21	Xitsonga
Nyiko	25	Xitsonga
Tshepo	23	Setswana
Rhuzani	21	Xevenda
Bhekani	24	IsiZulu
Ntswaki	23	Setswana
Venolia	21	Xevenda
Moremi	23	Sesotho
Naum	25	IsiZulu
Moserwa	23	Setswana
Morwesi	24	Setswana
Lerato	25	Setswana

study selected only Black participants, non-Black students also supported during the protests. Selection criteria thus included student protestors and those who were directly impacted by current funding schemes that specifically have a racialised impact on Black students living in township communities. All participants were thus purposefully selected as students with in-depth experiences focused on increasing access to and decolonising higher education.

Data Analysis

Thematic analysis was used for systematically identifying, organising, and offering insight into patterns of meaning across interview data (Braun & Clarke, 2012, p. 2). During the first phase, the researcher read and re-read the textual data (transcripts). In the second phase, the researcher generated initial codes from the data. Once the code was identified and extracted, the associated text was marked. After generating the first code, the researcher reviewed data until the next potentially relevant excerpt was identified. This process was repeated throughout the entire dataset. The third phase focused on shifting from codes to themes. According to Braun and Clarke (2012), a theme 'captures something important about the data in relation to the research question and represents some level of patterned response and meaning within the dataset.' Coded data were reviewed to identify areas of similarity and overlapping between codes. The fourth phase was characterised by reviewing developing themes in relation to the coded data and the entire dataset. A final re-reading of all data confirmed all themes, and the fifth phase, associated themes with specific quotes. The sixth phase involved crafting of main findings for each research participant to engage sub-questions. The results of the inductive thematic analysis revealed two themes, as presented in the next section.

Findings

Two themes, defining decolonial curriculum and student protest movement, clarified that in addition to removing fees, students were deeply concerned with decolonisation efforts.

Moving towards a Decolonial Curriculum

Participating students viewed decolonisation of the curriculum as a series of adjustments to remove the suppression of cultures imposed by the colonialists. According to students, decolonisation required a centring of the cultural context of Black communities, but also a full withdrawal of political control over the everyday way of life. Ntswaki, for example, clarified that 'the decolonisation of the curriculum is when the amendments are also made in the curriculum.' Bongani went further in arguing for a theoretical framework:

> Decolonisation is viewed as a removal of domination and suppression of people culture, including values, norms, customs and world views, imposed by the colonialists. Decolonisation of the curriculum is when the culture, values, norms, customs and world views of the previously suppressed people are included into the curriculum.

Rhuzani also saw the decolonial process as when the curriculum reflects 'the way of life of the indigenous people.' Thabo suggested that this reflection had to also place specific attention to 'the aspects that were ignored by colonisers.' Venolia added that 'decolonisation is when colonisers withdrew their political control of their conquered territories,' noting the importance of settler-coloniality that South Africa's ruling Black political party had not fully engaged. Moserwa suggested that this withdrawal meant 'creating spaces and resources for a dialogue among all members of the university on how to imagine and envision all cultures and knowledge systems in the curriculum.'

To clarify how students came to see decoloniality in these ways, participants suggested that their very way of thinking was not included in current higher education contexts. Lerato summarised the official curriculum, suggesting that 'we are taught an irrelevant education.' Nyiko clarified this irrelevance: '[Our] worldviews are derived from the knowledge that we have accumulated from home. [But] even at tertiary level, we are still considered as blank sheet (tabula rasa).' Nyiko's point suggests that their personal, cultural, and linguistic knowledge are simply not considered in current conceptions of higher education. Rhulani continued this point: '[Our] indigenous knowledge was considered as nothing. Efforts have not gone that far to decolonise the curriculum in higher education.' Naum suggested that there was an intentional conflict between her daily realities and the ways universities operate: '[Our] upbringing was based on a particular way of life or economic activities that are not supported by the education we receive.' Venolia similarly argued that: '[Our] view of life was not acknowledged by westerners who occupied our countries,' suggesting that this occupation continues through higher education systems. Bongani, using language that recognises higher education as a process of colonisation, clarified that '[Our] worldview which represent our culture was considered as barbaric and backwardness.'

These quotes indicate that students recognised that their worldviews were suppressed and felt a clear devaluation of knowledge they accrue from home. Their very worldviews, referenced here as Indigenous knowledge, continue to be regarded as invalid, just as their daily experiences have been, and continue to be, excluded from the formal curriculum. In addition to being framed within racial stereotypes (barbaric and backwardness), these students were clear that their ways of life and even the way they earn income were not only not supported, but instead, directly challenged by university curriculum.

Given what was framed as a colonial higher education curriculum that seemed intent on challenging (versus expanding) their worldviews, students recognised concrete challenges to their involvement in shaping how decoloniality should be occurring. Nyiko remarked: 'There are some of the Indigenous people who argue that the African languages are not adequately developed, and Indigenous education are not capable or ready for inclusion in the curriculum.' Ntswaki also recognised internalised oppression: 'Some of the previously colonised people are comfortable with the Western education system, because they associate it with progress.' Bongani further suggested an embrace of Western ideas, stating that 'many people become proud when their children speak English and cannot read or write their own languages.' Rhulani stated that, because of these internalised Western superiorities, 'there are people who do not understand decolonisation.' This limited understanding suggested a need for a more thoughtful decolonial movement to educate younger generations as to the promises of decoloniality.

Students were clear that many of the challenges to curriculum decolonisation rest within Indigenous Africans themselves. While many of the protests target Western infrastructures, these students also suggest the need for efforts to challenge Indigenous African commitments to Western approaches. Some Indigenous people still oppose the inclusion of their cultures, values, norms, and customs into the curriculum, in part as they see these knowledge bases as relics of the past. Students saw such people as representing a challenge since, in theory, Indigenous Africans would benefit from decolonisation; instead, many seem comfortable with the Western education system.

Given what was framed largely as resistance within Black South African communities, students suggested pathways forward to transform the daily experience at universities. Underneath these efforts rested a commitment to decentring and removing white and Western knowledges. Moremi suggested that universities must 'get rid of western staff from our library shelves.' To facilitate this replacement, Tshepo suggested that 'all modules/courses must be rewritten with an intention of decolonising the curriculum.' Moserwa was of the view that 'it is the responsibility of the affected people to work hard to produce literature that will include the indigenous perspective.' Thabo wanted Indigenous people 'to replace the western knowledge with an Indigenous one,' recognising that such efforts required Indigenous Black scholars to elevate their decolonial works. Moremi echoed this reliance on Indigenous scholars: 'Those with writing expertise must do their best because we cannot get rid of western knowledge and expertise without replacement.' Most students saw replacement as a foundational goal of decoloniality.

Lerato, on the other hand, argued for an integration of multiple systems: 'I honestly want to see what is best from Indigenous and western knowledge be adopted into the new education system for all … it is important to bring balance that will suit the multicultural classroom.' Bhekani also spoke in favour of a compromised curriculum that was based on what is best from both Indigenous and Western knowledge. While Lerato and Bhekani were the only students to advocate for a balance of knowledges, the others first recognised that removal was essential to achieve such a balance. Indeed, given that all participants saw the official curriculum as promoting a Western-only approach, Lerato and Bhekani's notion of balance was seen as unachievable without initial decentring, as suggested by the rest of the participants. What a colonial curriculum should be replaced with remains a key tension, though students agreed that Indigenous Africans must be at the core of any decolonial curricular effort, particularly in terms of rewriting modules and courses. Students specifically saw Indigenous Africans taking on the leading role of this rewriting and replacing, agreeing that people who were colonised must work hard to produce literature that reflects decolonisation.

Student Protest Movements

The second theme reflected the escalation of decolonial protests, which on many campuses turned violent after sustained protest. While initial #FeesMustFall protests started non-violently, as protests shifted towards decoloniality, students adopted anti-colonial approaches, including removing physical symbols of coloniality (e.g., statue of Rhodes). Ntswaki clarified how these initial protests efforts were met with silence from campus administrators: 'We tried to negotiate with the institution not to increase the fees. However, our request was not given attention.' Similarly, Morwesi reported that 'through our student body, we confronted the Minister of Education for a fair distribution of student funding by removing the concept of the "missing middle." Our request was ignored, and we were left with an option of protesting.' Naum, who had been part of a student negotiating team at one of the universities, recognised an intentional dismissal of student perspectives, clarifying 'it does not mean that we do not have the communicative skills or negotiation skill, we are not taken serious by people in power.' Bongani saw this dismissal as leaving students no other option than to elevate methods:

'We really want to bring change to our education and we will use whatever means to achieve that. Negotiation did not bear any fruits.' Tshepo summarised: 'There are students who demonstrate good leadership among us. They tried their best to negotiate on our behalves. Nothing came out of such negotiations. Protest was the answer. There are areas where our peaceful marches turned into violence.' Lerato further noted that while initial protests were 'peaceful, it turns into violence when police ordered us to disperse.'

The framing of protest as violence was clearly seen as a last resort, with Lerato arguing that this shift was only in response to police-initiated violence. This contradicts many of the more mainstream narratives of student protests. Indeed, students demonstrated intentional strategies designed to decolonise, including negotiations within institutions and with the minister of higher education and training. Students argued that their leadership demonstrated good communication skills and required thoughtful negotiation skills. Despite clear documentation of student demands issued to university leadership, though, students felt their demands were dismissed. This dismissal ultimately led to rethinking strategy, leading students to elevate protests. Students further claimed that these elevated protests remained peaceful, and that police-initiated violence when they ordered students to disperse. This resulted in the arrest of student protestors and a larger media context that blamed student protests without recognition of failed negotiations.

Students also noted that, in part because they were being systematically silenced by administrators, protests deepened to incorporate decoloniality. Nyiko, one of the students who participated in protests, remarked: 'Initially our #FeesMustFall movement was to demand the "fall" of university fees. In the process, we started to demand the decolonisation of higher education.' Moremi showed dissatisfaction by saying: 'We are more than 26 years in our democracy, but we are still paying high fees for irrelevant education. We want free education that was promised African National Congress through their working document called Freedom Charter.' Moremi here tied protest efforts to the ANC's struggle for freedom, arguing that official documents should be used to support transformative agendas. Moserwa, as one of the missing middle, was denied financial support and remarked that 'the announcement issued by the Department of Higher Education and Training, about student funding, made life difficult for us and this is one reason that made us to be violent and further demand the decolonisation of education.' Lerato summarised that '#FeesMustFall protest created a platform for the demand of the decolonisation of higher education.' Bongani clarified how being structurally excluded from higher education combined with colonial curriculum to force students into protests:

> As a person who was denied financial assistance [I] support the protest that we lead to free education… in addition our life experiences we acquired from our homes are not part of what we learn. We realised that without force a change cannot be reached.

Participants indicated that the #FeesMustFall protests created opportunities for students to demand the decolonisation of higher education. The ongoing structural dismissal of students, through both the curriculum and administrative silencing, laid the foundation for student efforts to decolonise the curriculum.

Students were clear that their demands—for both a free and a decolonial education—were promised through the Freedom Charter. To their frustration, however, the Minister of the Department of Higher Education and Training (whose party is in alliance with the ruling ANC party that has promised free and relevant education) announced that students must continue to pay. Students, most of whom still live within the impacts of apartheid-era policies and practices, recognised that funding inequitably excludes them from enrolment in South African higher education systems. This continued economic exclusion, coupled with colonial curricula, led them to demand the decolonisation of education and elevate their protest methods.

Recommendations

This research explored challenges of decolonising the curricula, with participants reiterating the need for systemic decolonisation. Through the #FeesMustFall and #RhodesMustFall protest movement, students have registered their concerns, elevated their strategies, and issued concrete demands. The students, South Africa's next generation of leaders, can no longer be ignored. Based on examination of student frustrations with a financially exclusive, colonial university curriculum, related protests and demands, recommendations for higher education practitioners must include a deeper recognition of student perspectives. Three recommendations for practice thus include (a) infusing student perspectives as policy practice within institutions, (b) engaging student worldviews, and (c) engaging Indigenous African knowledge to challenge prioritisation of Western approaches.

The first recommendation is to foster, recognise, and centre student perspectives as policy practice within institutions. This must begin with institutional listening to student demands. Through historic and contemporary student movements, from anti-apartheid protests to recent #FeesMustFall and #RhodesMustFall efforts, students have voiced perspectives on decolonisation of higher education. The sustained protest by youth, over decades, suggests both that students are very aware of the need for decoloniality, and that students do not see sufficient urgency regarding implementation. Thirty years into democracy, there are only minimal signs of making education relevant to higher education students. This should be an embarrassment to those who are in power, including at the national, local, and institutional levels, many of whom continue to support the impression that free education and decolonisation of the curriculum would be the priority.

Relatedly, policy makers and higher education administrators should ensure that there are transparent policies that guide the process of decolonisation. Students clearly want the cultures imposed by the colonialists to be removed. Students clearly want a curriculum that is not only relevant to their daily lives, but also that aligns with and expands their cultural values, norms, customs, worldviews, and languages. In addition, decolonisation must mean the withdrawal of colonisers' political control and the inclusion of the way of life of Indigenous communities. Regular, ongoing, accessible space and resources must be created for dialogue among all members of the university, with a prioritisation of those who are skilled in disrupting Western foundations and centring Indigenous knowledge systems in the curriculum. Students must be at the forefront of such processes.

The second recommendation is to centre the worldviews of all students but with a prioritised focus on Indigenous African students. Decolonising education is to contextualise what is taught in ways to tangibly benefit local people. Black student worldviews must be considered as important, since they are derived from the knowledge that was accumulated from home. From primary school to tertiary level, students should not be considered as empty vessels. The students' upbringing is based on specific ways of life, linguistic and cultural contexts, and economic activities resulting from ongoing apartheid conditions that must be supported within an educational curriculum that should be designed with these realities in mind. For example, Indigenous people's education was aimed at promoting agriculture, which was the common economic activity. Western education put more weight on the manufacturing industry than agriculture. Yet through subsistence farming, Indigenous people were able to survive, and such farming practices and related subsistence activities continue today.

Relatedly, it is important to consider the type of students who were elevating and demanding recognition of their worldview during recent protests. Many of these students live in un-resourced townships, living apartheid-era conditions that continue unabated. These circumstances are exacerbated by COVID-19 and dramatic lack of technological, economic, health, education, transportation, and housing infrastructure. Engaging higher education, let alone when it maintains irrelevance, becomes economically and intellectually expensive. This cost becomes even more substantial when financial support is provided only selectively, making the challenge worse for these students.

The third recommendation is designed to address these pressing challenges and to mitigate the intellectual cost by prioritising Indigenous African knowledge systems across higher education courses, curriculum, and structures. Such an integration would challenge the prioritisation of Western approaches, but also directly lead to removal of Western-based funding and structural considerations. Some of the challenges regarding the implementation of a decolonial higher education curriculum comes from Indigenous people who are expected to prioritise their own cultures. Yet administrators, often with little to no formal preparation in African Indigenous approaches, are tasked with spearheading or supporting the process of decolonisation. With limited knowledge and experience, and often no stated commitment to transformation, these administrators became stumbling blocks. This is the reason why wa Thiong'o (1986) advocated for the decolonisation of the mind. Higher education cannot continue to advocate for transformation without investing in decolonisation process, to challenge internalised Western superiorities and preferences, while also helping to centre African languages, knowledges, and approaches. The question must move from one of inclusion into Western systems and towards a decentring of Western ideologies and structures as the foundation. Such an effort must be collective: Institutions of learning at all levels, policy makers, parents and families, communities, and non-governmental organisations must align to advocate for this decolonisation mission.

Student participants suggested that the official curriculum be re-written to expel the system from the colonial experience. A critical multicultural education has to be applied to challenge Eurocentrism within the national curriculum. Transformation of the curriculum, or recurriculation, must take account of the various cultures, histories and multiple consciousnesses of Indigenous Africans. Student protestors have long argued that these processes must include elders and community leaders. Such a collaborative approach, engaged with ancestral knowledge and community elders, would explore ways to design locally and regionally relevant curricula, where Western epistemologies do not continue to dominate. Indeed, for South Africa to remain relevant within a continental perspective, national higher education must reflect the lives and shared histories of every group, including and beyond state-sanctioned official language and ethnic groups. Such an integration of lived cultural knowledge must be harnessed to produce innovation and advancement in teaching and learning that reflects the rainbow nation's lived experiences. Critical multicultural education must be applied to teaching and learning through the higher education curriculum and specifically, how the nation has come to learn and relearn the meaning of tolerance, mutual respect, and ultimately move towards a society based on freedom and democracy.

Conclusion

To be effective in the decolonisation of the curriculum, the people who are committed to this process must be required to understand what decoloniality entails. Understanding the meaning of Indigenous transformation of higher education in South Africa, Southern Africa, and indeed, across the continent, is essential to the pursuit of a truly African university. Due to ongoing coloniality, a systemic failure to transform at the societal level, and continued racial and class-based disparities, South African institutions of higher education face enormous challenges regarding transformation. We fail to engage sufficiently with students, with communities, with ancestral knowledges, with transformation agendas. While institutions of higher education are struggling to transform, the national transformation policy machinery has proven to be insufficient to ensure implementation. It is past time we listen, therefore, to Indigenous African students.

References

Bitzer & De Jager (2018). The views of commerce students regarding "free" higher education in South Arica. *South African Journal of Higher Education*, 32(4):12–36. doi:10.20853/32-4-2436.

Braun, V., & Clarke, V. (2012). Thematic analysis. In H. Cooper, P.M. Camic, D.L. Long, A.T. Panter, D. Rindskopf, & K.J. Sher (Eds.), *APA handbook of research methods in psychology, Vol. 2: Research designs: Quantitative, qualitative, neuropsychological, and biological* (pp. 57–71). American Psychological Association.

Charles, E. (2019). Decolonizing the curriculum. https://insights.uksg.org/chapters/10.1629/uksg.475

Chilisa, B. (2020). *Indigenous research methodologies* (2nd ed.). Sage.

Christie, M., Carey, M., Robertson, A., & Grainger, P. (2015). Putting transformative learning theory into practice. *Australian Journal of Adult Learning*, 55(1), 9–30.

Costandius, E., Blackie, M., Nell, I., Malgas, R., Alexander, N., Setati, E., & McKay, M. (2018). #Feesmustfall and decolonising the curriculum: Stellenbosch University students' and lecturers' reactions. *South African Journal of Higher Education*, 32(2), 65–85. doi:10.20853/32-2-2435

Creswell, J.W. (2013). *Qualitative inquiry & research design: Choosing among the five approaches*. Sage.

Dastile, P.N., & Ndlovu-Gatsheni, S.J. (2013). Power, knowledge and being: Decolonial combative discourse as a survival kit for Pan-Africanists in the 21st century. *Alternation*, 20(1), 105–134.

Educational Policy Consortium. (2015). Education and the Freedom Charter: A critical appraisal. www.educatiopolicyconsortium.org.za

Education White Paper 3. (1997). *A Programme for the transformation of higher education*. Department of Education.

Fataar, A. (2018). Decolonising education in South Africa: Perspectives and debates. *Educational Research for Social Change*, 7(SPE), vi–ix.

Griffiths, D. (2019). #FeesMustFall and the decolonised university in South Africa: Tensions and opportunities in a globalising world. *International Journal of Educational Research*, 94, 143–149. doi:10.1016/j.ijer.2019.01.004

Gumbo M.T., & Williams P.J. (2014). Discovering grade 8 technology teachers' pedagogical content knowledge in the Tshwane District of Gauteng Province. *International Journal Education Science*, 6(3), 479–488. doi:10.1080/09751122.2014.11890159

Hauser, C. (2016, September 23). 'Fees must fall': Anatomy of the student protests in South Africa. *New York Times*. https://www.nytimes.com/2016/09/23/world/africa/fees-must-fall-anatomy-of-the-student-protests-in-south-africa.html

Joseph, T.R. (2017). Decolonising the curriculum, transforming the university, a discursive perspective. www.dut.ac.za

Kamwendo, J. (2014). Indigenous knowledge systems and food security: Some examples in Malawi. *Journal of Human Ecology*, 48(1), 97–101. doi:10.1080/09709274.2014.11906778

Knaus, C.B., & Brown, M.C. II. (2016). *Whiteness is the new South Africa: Research on post-apartheid racism*. Peter Lang.

Le Grange, L. (2016). Decolonising the university curriculum. *South African Journal of Higher Education*, 30(2), 1–12. doi:10.20853/30-2-709

Luckett, K. (2016). Curriculum contestation in a post-colonial context: A view from the South. *Teaching in Higher Education*, 21(4), 415–428. doi:10.1080/13562517.2016.1155547

Maluleka, K., & Themane, M. (2020). A quest for a decolonised curriculum and the role of language of teaching as a decolonising tool. In C.C. Wolhuter, J. Seroto, & M.N. Davids (Eds.), *Decolonising education in the global south: Historical and comparative international perspectives*. Pearson Publishers.

Mampane, R.M., Omidire, M.F., & Aluko, F.R. (2018). Decolonising higher education in Africa: Arriving at a glocal solution. *South African Journal of Education*, *38*(4), 1–23. doi:10.15700/saje.v38n4a1636

Mawere, M. (2010). Indigenous knowledge systems' (IKSS) potential for establishing a moral, virtuous society: Lessons from selected IKSS in Zimbabwe and Mozambique. *Journal of Sustainable Development in Africa*, *12*(7), 209–222.

Mbiza, M. (2018). The issues with South Africa's education system. https://educonnect.co.za/the-issues-with-south-africas-education-system/

Mezirow, J. (1997). Transformative learning: Theory to practice. *New Directions for Adult and Continuing Education*, *1997*(74), 5–12. doi:10.1002/ace.7401

Mgqwashu, E. (2016). Universities can't decolonise the curriculum without defining it first. https://theconversation.com/universities-cant-decolonise-the-curriculum-without-defining-it-first-63948

Moncrieffe, M.L., Asare, Y., & Dunford, R. (2019). Decolonising the curriculum: Challenges and opportunities for teaching and learning. In G. Wisker, L. Marshall, J. Canning, & S. Greener (Eds.), *Navigating with practical wisdom*. doi:10.13140/RG.2.2.26574.72003

Morreira, S., Luckett, K., Kumalo, S.H., & Ramgotra, M. (2020). Confronting the complexities of decolonising curricula and pedagogy in higher education. *Third World Thematics: A TWQ Journal*, *5*(1–2), 1–18. doi:10.1080/23802014.2020.1798278

Msila, V. (2009). Africanisation of education and the search for relevance and context. *Educational Research and Review*, *4*(6), 310–315.

Muldoon, J. (2019). Academics: It's time to get behind decolonising the curriculum. *The Guardian*. https://www.theguardian.com/education/2019/mar/20/

Ndlovu-Gatsheni, S.J. (2015). Decoloniality in Africa: A continuing search for a new world order. *Australasian Review of African Studies*, *36*(2), 22–50.

O'Dowd, M.F., & Heckenberg, R. (2020). Explainer: What is decolonisation? https://theconversation.com/explainer-what-is-decolonisation-131455

Oelofsen, R. (2015). Decolonisation of the African mind and intellectual landscape. *Phronimon*, *16*(2), 130–146.

Rehad, D. (2019). Everything must fall. https://everythingmustfall.co.za/

Sommer, M. (2011). Colonies-Colonisation-Colonialism: A typological reappraisal. *AWE*, *10*, 183–193.

Soudien, C. (2010). *Transformation in higher education: A briefing paper*. Development Bank of Southern Africa. https://www.dhet.gov.za/summit/Docs/2010Docs/Transformation

South African History Online [SAHO] (2020). The South African Students Movement (SASM). https://www.sahistory.org.za/article/south-african-students-movement-sasm

University World News (2010). The Soudien Report: Deny racism at your peril. https://www.universityworldnews.com/post.php?story=20100424200305969

wa Thiong'o, N. (1986). *Decolonisation of the mind: The politics of language in African literature*. James Currey.

5
LOCALISING KNOWLEDGE SYSTEMS

Ferdinand Mwaka Chipindi, Ane Turner Johnson, and Marcellus Forh Mbah

The first school offering formal education in Zambia was established in 1883 at Kankoyo by Fredrick Arnot of the White Fathers Mission. Since then, thousands of schools modelled after that first missionary school have been established in Zambia. These schools aimed to teach basic English literacy and Western-based numeracy skills so that pupils could read the Bible. In addition, this civilisation mission was predicated on a need to spread the good word of 'God' to lands and people who were framed as living in darkness prior to the arrival of Europeans. Arnot is said to have once remarked, 'How we should rejoice and praise the Lord that even the ears of those who have for ages been in such a state should be opened to hear God's Word!' (Arnot, 1969, p. 58). As of 2017, it was estimated that there were approximately 10,000 primary and 1,400 secondary schools in Zambia. Such has been the colonial legacy of introducing formal education in Africa, which took place within the broader epistemic violence that accompanied the imperialist traffic of the sixteenth to the nineteenth century.

In elevating the status of his god above the gods of the Bulozi kingdom, including Nyambe, Arnot reflected the violent, binary nature of Western thinking. Derrida (1976) criticises Western thought, stating that this binary thinking produces meaning only through opposites such as good/evil, holy/heathen, and love/hate. In this binary thinking, Derrida surmises, the two sides are never equal. This thinking localises the gods of non-Western people, setting up a false opposite which is always less than, and secondary to, the first. 'When one of the terms is privileged, it is often articulated as the centre, marginalising and nearly eliminating the other term' (Meisenbach, 2004, p. 19). Indeed, as in any other part of Sub-Saharan Africa, formal education in Zambia persistently reflects colonially bequeathed epistemic systems. An increasingly versatile body of scholarship questions the global economy of knowledge production and dissemination, mainly about which knowledges are

DOI: 10.4324/9781003158271-5

privileged and assumed to be universal (e.g., Chakrabarty, 2000; Connell, 2018). This scholarship, which has gained enormous traction as the decolonial movement has expanded across the African continent and the West, raises critical questions about the blanket application of the canon of knowledge predicated on the Anglo-American epistemic system and then proposes several alternative directions towards a more localised 'sociological imagination' (Mills, 1959).

This chapter contributes to this scholarship by exploring how localised knowledge systems can be applied to the research agenda of African universities. Based on interviews with faculty members immersed in practical discussions of localising efforts at the University of Zambia (UNZA), we argue for a renegotiation of knowledge to reflect multiple ways of knowing and expressing the whole human experience. Our premise is that knowledge production is skewed towards the Global West, but African universities are more than extensions of the Western academy and need to serve localised development needs. We, therefore, call for the incorporation of localised knowledge into the character and purpose of knowledge generation in African universities.

Epistemic Violence and the Project of Formal Education

Applying localised knowledge systems in approaching research is critical for the African university to serve as a centre of excellence and seat of knowledge. Ajayi, Goma, and Johnson (1996) call for the university to 'educate itself to be development conscious and development-oriented' (p. 203). Dei (2014) similarly asserts that the African university should be contextually situated, reflexive, and epistemically Indigenous. Epistemological Indigeneity is an epistemic system that takes 'the learner to history, culture, tradition, past, and identity as both contested, concrete, and meaningful to how we come to decolonise the school/university curriculum and create social and academic excellence' (Dei, 2014, p. 165). Thus, our conceptualisation of localised knowledge transcends the mere appropriation of knowledge for its own sake but attempts to draw on a wide-ranging network of epistemic systems to advance the development of society and the social and physical environment (Barnett & Bengtsen, 2017; de Sousa Santos, 2007; Mbah, 2016).

As noted earlier, formal education was first introduced into the geopolitical space known as Zambia in the late nineteenth century through missionaries such as Frederick Arnot, David Livingstone, and Moffatt Stanley. Formal education in its present configurations is premised on the uncritical acceptance of the canon of knowledge produced and entrenched in these colonial encounters. The prioritisation of the Anglo-American epistemic system suggests that non-Western ways of knowing have very little to contribute to the canon of knowledge known as conventional science. This conceptualisation attempts to discard the sort of knowledge systems that can be considered too local to have any bearing on mainstream knowledge. During the imperialist traffic of the sixteenth to the twentieth century, Western forms of knowing obliterated and obscured the epistemic systems, cultural infrastructure, and the intellectual tapestry of the people and lands of Africa, Asia, and South and Central America. Spivak (1988) used the term epistemic violence to describe the process of othering in which the subaltern was 'excluded from being human, refused reciprocity and excluded from intelligibility' (Rawls & David, 2003, p. 494). This exclusion from intelligibility is predicated on the principles of universals, in which the colonised people become 'the other.' This encounter was characterised by subjugation (epistemologically and bodily) in Africa based on skin pigmentation (Mazrui, 2005). The imperial era orchestrated by Europe in the eighteenth century inaugurated a canon of knowledge that 'permeated the entire conceptual system of the social sciences from their inception' (Castro-Gómez, 2002, p. 277). Thus, epistemic violence obliterates the ability of colonised epistemic systems to speak or be heard (Spivak, 1988) and yet serves as the foundation of formal education in Zambia.

The Colonial History of Education

The history of colonial education in Zambia can be categorised into two broad epochs. During the first period, from 1885 to 1924, the territory was governed by the British South African Company (BSACo). Many of the first schools in Zambia were established in this era by Francis Coillard of the Paris Evangelical Mission Society. The affairs of education were administered with little or no involvement from the BSACo. Thus, the purpose of education tended to be very rudimentary, aimed chiefly at aiding the missionaries to spread the gospel. Young African converts to Christianity were given basic training in reading, literacy, and numeracy to interpret the Bible to their families and other community members. Accordingly, the character of this early formal education tended to reflect the need for converts. By the 1920s, 15 missions were working in the territory. Between them, these missionaries were operating approximately 1,688 schools, with an estimated enrolment of 922,000 pupils (Henkel, 1989). These institutions' education was erected almost entirely on a missionary epistemic system that intentionally removed local histories, traditions, and cultural infrastructures.

The second period commenced in 1925 when the British colonial office formally took over the administration of the territory from BSACo. In this era, various actors had different motivations and interests in the education given to Africans. White settlers, whose population was steadily growing, viewed education for the Africans as a recipe for political and economic turmoil. Thus, colonising settlers tended to view any developments in education for Africans with mistrust. They thus opposed any advancements that would improve schools (Kelly, 1991). Settlers' views on African education differed from those of the missionaries. The latter wanted literacy and skills training to be the bedrock of education. This inadvertently produced the African elite, whose values seldom corresponded with traditional leaders or even colonial authorities. Kelly (1991) notes that many 'local people increasingly wanted more education, of a higher standard and to a higher level...generally, they had to leave the country to get this' (p. 39). Similarly, the colonial administration ensured that African education was utilitarian and straightforward with very little academic rigour. Thus, education during the colonial period emphasised Christian-based religious teaching and moral instruction, to the effect of denying the very existence of localised religious and moral knowledges.

The Inception of Higher Education

Zambia gained independence from Britain on October 24, 1964. By then, the colonial education system and its motivations had gained nationwide traction. Colonial authorities had been opposed to the advancement of Africans through education. They had favoured a more diluted content and approach to prevent the emergence of Black consciousness. Thus, the colonially bequeathed education system was based on the desire to secure the subordination and exploitation of Africans. Education was designed to make Africans suitably compliant with the colonial administrative apparatus. Thus, the colonially bequeathed system was, in the words of Kelly (1991), '[a]n instrument of imperialist domination and economic exploitation, as a major source of economic inequalities and social stratification, as an instrument of intellectual and cultural servitude' (p. 39). Perceived as too local to be of any importance by colonial administrators, the mainstream academic infrastructure largely discarded and discounted Zambia's local knowledge systems.

However, Zambia faced an acute shortage of human resources at independence, with just 100 individuals with an undergraduate degree and just under 1,000 with a secondary school certificate. Thus, the newly independent country was in dire need of human resources to fill the positions of responsibility in the government from the departing British (Chipindi, 2018). To respond to the shortage of skilled human resources, the government embarked on a project to establish a university as a matter of great urgency (Chipindi, 2018). Accordingly, a commission was set up immediately after independence to consider this problem. The committee chairman was the distinguished academician from the United Kingdom, Sir John Lockwood, who had once served as the Vice-Chancellor of the University of London. The Lockwood Commission (1963), as it has come to be known, made several recommendations, chiefly that the new university was to be influenced by and responsive to the environment in which it was to be situated:

> The [new] university [to be established at Lusaka] should conceive its national responsibility to be more extensive and comprehensive than has sometimes been the case elsewhere. It should draw its inspiration from the environment in which its people live and function. It should be a vigorous and fruitful source of stimulus and encouragement to education and

training of all kinds… As an independent institution, it can be as inclusive as it wishes and experiments as it wishes without hindrance in desirable national fields.

(p. 2)

Furthermore, the Commission declared that the new university was to be 'responsive to the real needs of society' (p. 3). This meant that the institution was shaped by the context in which it was situated, namely, the newly independent country. This made the institution permeable to the dominant regional discourses such as liberation and decolonisation, specific to the Southern African region, and national discourses such as nation-building through human resource development and capacity-building in all sectors of the economy. This was to be achieved by extending the university's resources in the form of knowledge, expertise, and community service to the society that existed beyond the university's walls and recognising the influence of the political and socio-economic environment of the country on the university itself.

Goma, the first Indigenous Vice-Chancellor of UNZA, and Tembo (1984) opined that UNZA should 'take the lead in and play a prominent role in bringing about Africa's all-around development' (p. 20). They further envisaged the African university as an arbitrator of African civilisation. Tembo (1978) argues that 'unless African universities are transformed so that they reflect African conditions of life, they will never contribute effectively to social reform' (p. 31). Nor would UNZA hope to lead 'the reform of society…as the principal agent of social reform' (Chokani, 1984, p. 1). With its clearly articulated community service mission, UNZA has played a critical role in developing the country through the supply of expertise, scholarship, and knowledge production. However, the nature of this knowledge remains contested (Mbah, Johnson, & Chipindi, 2021).

The Nature of Localised Knowledge: Characterising a Debate

Conceptions of knowledge are complex and often contested, unbound by disciplinarity (Mawere, 2014). There is an implied debate in epistemological discussions regarding the differences and similarities between what can be considered local knowledge and Indigenous knowledge. Dei (2014) differentiated between localised knowledge and Indigenous knowledge when he asserted that 'while local knowledge addresses knowledge localised in a place, the question of land, connections with spirit and metaphysical realms of existence of a place, is central to a conception of Indigenous' (pp. 166–167). Emeagwali (2014), however, conflates these knowledges and states that Indigenous knowledge is 'the cumulative body of strategies, practices, techniques, tools, intellectual resources, explanations, beliefs, and values accumulated over time in a particular locality, without the interference and impositions of external hegemonic forces' (p. 1). So while Indigenous knowledge may form and evolve in a particular place and connect with the land, it also extends beyond place-bound community conceptions of reality. Indigenous knowledge may move with people via diaspora and continue to inform their connections to the world, despite no longer being in the place where the knowledge may have originated. Local knowledge, while often Indigenous, may be best understood and used in a particular context. Okere, Njoku, and Devisch (2005) assert that all knowledge is local knowledge, revealing 'any given culture's unique genius, and distinctive creativity which put a most characteristic stamp on what its members in their singular context and history meaningfully develop as knowledge, epistemology, metaphysics, worldview' (p. 3), underscoring that knowledge is more about a specific groups' 'organising principles' than their geographic location.

This discussion merely scratches the surface of a long history of intellectual engagement on Indigenous and local knowledges in Africa. Here we concern ourselves with localised knowledge, meaning knowledge specific to local communities in Zambia and Indigenous to Zambia. In the following section, we turn to the findings of a study that we undertook at UNZA to explore knowledge systems from the perspectives of those who create and disseminate knowledge: Academics.

On Localised Knowledge: Conversations with Academics

We used the case study approach to engage with faculty members' understandings of the phenomenon of localising knowledge (Stake, 1995). We sought insights into this single case (UNZA) while remaining cognisant of how this specific university may embody similar understandings in equivalent institutions and contexts. In tandem with our decolonisation posture, we tried to decolonise our conversations by not solely depending on theory (Chilisa, 2020). Thus, our study was driven by faculty members' conceptualisations of localised knowledge systems, specifically in answer to the question: What is the nature and role of different forms of knowledge in the Zambian academy?

Sampling

Criterion-based and snowball sampling techniques guided our selection of study participants. In selecting the participants, university faculty (N = 32), we first considered whether they could speak to our research questions. Thus, their knowledge of institutional policies and their role was the parameter for their inclusion in our study. Next, we pursued participants from various disciplines and academic units within the university, including the humanities and social sciences, natural sciences, medicine, and agricultural sciences. This multifaceted sampling approach enabled us to acquire a heterogeneous understanding of context. Finally, snowball sampling was used as a secondary approach, involving us asking participants we had selected through criterion-referenced sampling to nominate potential respondents (a) we could approach and (b) who met the criteria stated above. We then requested participants to identify additional faculty members (i.e., snowball) who could potentially speak to the foci of our research. Thus, the strategy enabled us to identify new potential participants as our study continued.

Data Collection

We engaged academics in relational dialogues (Chilisa, 2020). Our dialogues with academics were driven by questions regarding participants' work with the community, how they understood various forms of knowledge, how they could engage and represent Indigenous and localised voices/practices within their practice, and how the university has employed the knowledge produced by research. Depending on the nature and depth of the conversation, dialogues lasted between 30 minutes to 1 hour in duration.

Analysis

Our data analysis primarily focused on searching for patterns, consolidating meaning, and developing explanations (Saldaña, 2016). The first two phases of our analysis strategy used coding to parse the data or take the data corpus apart to make sense of the whole (Stake, 1995). Coding began with structural coding that captured conceptual phrases and participant-driven examples consistent with the research questions (Saldaña, 2016). The second phase of analysis entailed pattern coding that grouped the structural codes into smaller categories and identified emerging explanations of the case. Using categorical aggregation, we put the corpus parts deconstructed during coding back together to create an interpretation of the phenomenon under investigation (Stake, 1995). Finally, we focus on using participant stories and other descriptions—a method of validation of case study research—to illustrate aspects of the case in our work.

Localising Knowledge: The Practical Possibilities

Our conversations with the study participants came across some who outlined the differences between localised or Indigenous knowledge and Western or scientific knowledge. However, other participants identified a closer alignment between so-called conventional and localised knowledge systems. Others still emphasised the nature of localised knowledge, its production and application, its history, and the dissemination process. One faculty member stated the following:

> Okay, now, in the first place, these terms are terms that you also need to [be] very careful with them. Because, during the colonial system, the local knowledge was given very negative terms. When you call it native education, 'native' was taken in a very negative connotation, and so is

'Indigenous.' So, several times when you are using these terms, you are already [devaluing] that knowledge because of that history.

(Faculty member, Education)

According to these comments, a level of prejudice emerges when people are told about localised knowledge, reflecting the historic anti-Indigenous impact of colonial systems. Therefore, it is necessary to make localised knowledge relevant and attractive to today's society. Another participant averred that repackaging localised knowledge can increase its appeal to the students:

This knowledge is already there; it is not new knowledge. We have had it except that it was poorly packaged; let's [repackage] it and bring out certain concepts of knowledge…There is still negativity in some people who have not embraced Indigenous Knowledge… Nevertheless, most academics will separate two things: something else when they go back home from Indigenous Knowledge, which they live with every day. Very strange; it's a paradox, right?

(Faculty member, Agricultural Sciences)

In this dialogue, it becomes clear that faculty members were often complicit in rejecting localised knowledge even though they rely upon such knowledge in their households every day. One participant, a faculty member in religious studies, stated that: 'So you are looked down upon, and you are not taken seriously, and that's another challenge if you are into African Indigenous knowledge systems, and even you are publishing that… I don't think people will take you serious'.

Another faculty member asserted that he defined localised knowledge within his methodological pursuits by decentring 'conventional' design choices in research. He further noted that this interfered with how he related with community members in his research exploits.

First of all, the localised knowledge in my research has been a source of problem identification because localised knowledge is often not reflected in conventional knowledge and policies. The second part of localised knowledge has to do with the methodology…it has contributed to critical thinking such that when reading this textbook, which says a focus group discussion should have not more than eight people, and then you wondered and say, 'But this guy, does he know that actually in my rural area I cannot chase someone [away] who wants to add to the number [beyond 8]?' So I ended up trying to say, 'No, no, no.' In terms [of] methodological approach, there is something that conventional science can learn, which has motivated me to go much deeper into participatory research methods [and] action research-oriented approaches in research.

(Faculty member, Natural Sciences)

In this conversation, we see two primary issues standing out. Firstly, the faculty member grapples with how the consumers of knowledge view localised knowledge both within and beyond the university realm. Secondly, the faculty member considers ways of knowing and what would count as a credible way of arriving at such ways of knowing.

Meanwhile, another participant related her experience reflecting upon how members of the community adopt research outcomes. The following is what she said when we prompted her to elaborate:

> I learn a lot. Sometimes you go there, and you think that things work in a way. Still, when you go there, you listen to them... in Zambia, we have about 73 ethnic groups, some of them are matrilineal, some of them are patrilineal, and if you forget that then you will find that you are missing something... so now I pay attention to them. There is a reason why they have some of these systems. So, what happens to the widow when the husband dies? Does she still access land and whatever? Those are sort of insights I have learnt from Indigenous Knowledge, which I never used to think about before; before, I would go like, 'Why aren't they adopting this technology?' but then I realised you have to think about how the community is arranged traditionally and that will affect how they manage resources. So definitely, I've had real insights because of paying attention to Indigenous Knowledge.
>
> *(Faculty member, Natural Sciences)*

Another faculty member, whose research was in the realm of climate change, told us that he often found that community members would seldom take research outcomes seriously if such research did not adequately embrace localised concepts and contexts.

> So my contribution currently will be to see how to bridge the gaps between scientific Knowledge and Indigenous Knowledge because currently, it looks like that is the only way it will work; that is the only way people on the ground will accept even the working technology. They have to see it even being locally driven for them to adopt it.
>
> *(Faculty member, Environmental Science)*

Framing localised knowledge without drawing parallels with conventional science appeared to be a challenge for the faculty members. They clearly grappled with defining localised knowledge without invoking the binary logics that subjugated it to conventional science. One faculty member expressed their belief that using localised knowledge could advance a decolonisation agenda in the community if used within a localised context of dissemination.

> Throughout my own work myself... I have disseminated Indigenous Knowledge in various ways... So my plea and appeal for modern people

are to re-learn, rethink and unlearn what they have been carrying all these years because some of the knowledge they are carrying may not be entirely useful anymore. Hence there is a need to unlearn and re-learn knowledge.
(Faculty member, Environmental Education)

Ultimately, it appeared that using localised knowledge to address community-based challenges gave 18 (out of 32) faculty members a sense of empowerment. However, some respondents were less enthusiastic about the role of localised knowledge in the academy. For example, an academic from religious education study bewailed the 'packaging' of localised knowledge:

This knowledge is already there; it is not new knowledge. We have had it except that it was poorly packaged; let's [repackage] it and bring out certain concepts of knowledge…There is still negativity in some people who have not embraced Indigenous knowledge… But most academics will separate two things: something else when they go back home from Indigenous knowledge, which actually they live with every day. Very strange; it's a paradox, right?

Another participant expressed feelings of inferiority, stating that she felt 'looked down upon' and 'not taken seriously' by other academic peers because she had situated her research in African Indigenous Knowledge systems. Sentiments such as this highlight the pitfalls that could stand in the way of localising knowledge systems. Thus, validating localised knowledge would not be plain sailing.

Epistemological Possibilities

Interviewed faculty members demonstrated myriad ways of integrating localised knowledge in their academic pursuits. This integration occurs at a plethora of levels: personal, classroom, and institutional. In addition, faculty members related their efforts to expose students to localised epistemic systems through the content of their courses, as well as classroom-based events:

You see, we are training our students, our graduates, to impact the community, all right. So, we are not training them for export to Europe; we are training to impact the community… I think it's strongly important for our students to understand Indigenous knowledge contexts; we highlight this kind of knowledge as we teach.
(Faculty member, Veterinary Medicine)

Participants reported that the School of Education had instituted a degree programme in Zambian Cultures & Ceremonies. They also stated that the syllabi in the said programme attempted to incorporate localised knowledge systems. An assistant dean applauded the introduction of the programme in culture and ceremonies and stated that this heralded better times to come in future. She asserted that the School of Education had since instituted a research agenda that would bring localised ways of knowing into the mainstream academia:

> When I inherited this office, I found a very clearly tabulated research agenda and some cases of international work with South Africa, Namibia, Botswana, SADC [Southern African Development Community] countries…we have seen a lot of research and aspects of localised knowledge colleagues are researching on, but they are linked to other fields: Indigenous Knowledge and culture, Indigenous Knowledge with economics and Indigenous Knowledge and language; they are always linked to another discipline, so that's relevant.
>
> *(Faculty member, Education)*

This was but one of additional university-wide efforts to incorporate localised knowledge systems into the mainstream academic pursuits of the university.

Another faculty member clarified the need for larger national conversations to align scholarly resources.

> Intangible cultural heritage…funding was secured for that. It awakened the debate in the nation about intangible Knowledge or Indigenous Knowledge. Such a discussion made people understand that indeed you can have Indigenous Knowledge away from witchcraft. With every uproar last year, we were sure that there would be zero entry in this program. I think this is what UNESCO has brought about to say we can have a discussion, a national discussion, the national debate on what we believe is beneficial, from Indigenous Knowledge and how can we promote it and by introducing and reviewing curriculum like the university has done.
>
> *(Faculty member, Parasitology)*

In common parlance, anything that relates to traditional or local knowledge suffers from negative connotations in the academy, such as the stereotypical connection to witchcraft. Thus, when reports of intentions to introduce an intangible cultural heritage programme at UNZA became known, social media became awash with memes about how the institution intended to introduce witchcraft in its syllabi. In this conversation, the faculty member referred to a new academic programme, inspired in part by external financial support from the United Nations Scientific and Cultural Organisation (UNESCO).

The programme's primary focus was to promote and preserve intangible cultural heritage (ICH), which refers to 'experiences, skills, and techniques, remembered and accumulated' (Turner et al., 2008, p. 46). As the faculty member noted, the intention to introduce the programme sparked a nationwide debate, which illuminated the potential role of local ways of knowing in a conventional university. We sought out a faculty member teaching in the programme and struck up a conversation with him. He immediately tried to correct people's wrong perceptions about localised knowledge: 'People mistakenly...started saying, "You want to teach witchcraft." But that's Intangible Cultural Heritage, which we are doing in this course, which we have started with 16 people' (Faculty, Literature and Languages). These efforts and the nationwide dialogue elevated the value of localised knowledge systems and raised stakeholders' awareness of the epistemological possibilities inherent in the localised knowledge system. This view was summed up by a faculty member who clarified the impact such conversation had on their research:

> I will be frank with you about all these works that we have been doing [such as the ICH programme]...It has so made me think about this more differently...I realised that maybe when we are doing this research, we are not deliberate about understanding Indigenous Knowledge.
> *(Faculty member, Natural Sciences)*

By mainstreaming localised knowledge into academia, the university helped enhance the legitimacy of these localised ways of knowing its stakeholders and appears to have helped other faculty begin to reflect on how they can integrate Indigenous knowledges into their work.

Faculty members were clearly engaged in concrete attempts to mainstream localised knowledge into their academic pursuits. However, within the policy framework of the country and the university at large, the commitment to localised knowledge systems remained mostly rhetorical, unaccompanied by action or the creation of infrastructures to achieve concrete progress. Thus, in the following section, we advance several propositions that could help concretise and promote knowledge systems' localisation.

Recommendations

Institutional Level

Our conversations with faculty members uncovered increasingly deliberate efforts to incorporate localised ways of knowing into their teaching and research engagements. Institutional change emerged as a critical starting point in the furtherance of localised knowledge systems. It became evident that the institutional changes would help concretise actionable plans to incorporate localised knowledge systems into the mainstream academy. Therefore, the institution needed to institute the requisite policy framework to integrate localised knowledge systems into its core business. Thus, the further mainstreaming of localised knowledge systems needed to be accompanied by rule systems and norms that would demonstrate the epistemological parity between local knowledge systems and the so-called conventional sciences. These may include additional affordances such as inviting guest speakers who are conversant with localised epistemic systems and encouraging students to do obligatory coursework projects within specific communities, as well as faculty members sharing their lived experiences with these systems. This fundamentally requires a relevant curriculum that treats conventional science as equal in worth to localised knowledge. Since the university learning space remains captive to the vestiges of colonisation through, for instance, teaching, learning, and reference materials—which authors predominate, researchers, and dissemination channels monopolised from the Global North—there is a definite need to counteract these with Indigenous knowledge practices. The classroom remains a space where the remnants of the colonial encounter continue to get reproduced through the othering of knowledge systems that do not appear to conform to what is regarded as conventional science. By instituting locally relevant regulatory and policy frameworks, the university can help to decolonise these in-class transactions and make them more permeable to local ways of knowing.

We identified knowledge sharing as an acute bottleneck, in part due to the acceptability of localised knowledge. The faculty members we spoke to frequently bewailed the strong discipline-orientation of the academic space, a widespread trend in African universities (Maponya, 2005). For instance, making research contributions requires fitting into the existing Western-oriented theoretical frameworks. Contributions outside of the frameworks seldom receive the same respect and attention and are considered insufficiently scientific. Participants, however, intimated that they were well-aware that not incorporating localised knowledge systems in their academic space would ultimately impoverish their associated research outputs. Thus, we propose that acknowledging localised knowledge systems through teaching and scholarly outputs would enhance its legitimacy as a form of epistemology. This would require recognising these ways of knowing as valid bases for knowledge production. Furthermore, instituting regulations and policies that acknowledge localised knowledge would align with faculty members' academic pursuits. Ultimately this would energise the decolonisation of knowledge production. As Ndofirepi and Gwaravanda (2019) note, 'The advantage of this approach to decolonisation is that it recognises and respects other paradigms of knowledge while avoiding the fallacies committed by Eurocentric knowledge systems in silencing, dislocating and marginalising the African knowledge system' (p. 589). The harmonisation of localised knowledge systems can widen the university's epistemological diversity while validating localised Indigenous communities and revitalising outside-the-academy knowledge.

Researcher Level

At the researcher level, we propose an increased openness to embrace what Derrida (1976) defined as supplementarity, which means taking cognisance of multiple ways of knowing and treating each as no less or more than the other. In short, academic researchers must confer parity on localised and so-called conventional ways of knowing. This requires placing localised understandings and ways of knowing at the centre of teaching and research. Researchers must attempt to incorporate epistemic perspectives, knowledge, and thinking from local contexts into academic pursuits. These perspectives and epistemic systems must be placed on the same equal footing with the Western canon. Thus, researchers should recognise and act upon past and present epistemological domination and oppression, including recognition of language systems designed to exclude localised African communities. Researchers must undergird theoretical and conceptual dimensions of research and teaching undertakings with a plural approach to diverse canons, especially ones that have traditionally been othered and subjected through the colonially bequeathed systems of education. The researchers need to align their scholarship with Southern epistemologies. They need to contest the uneven intellectual terrain in which the Anglo-American episteme produces concepts and theory consumed without question on the African continent. Their research should avoid methodological approaches that homogenise the social experiences in a continent as culturally vast as Africa. Thus, the use of qualitative methodologies may help the researchers to entrench decolonial scholarship in their pursuits.

Community Level

A faculty member from Natural Sciences commented that 'the university's role is evident and very central, and if you look at Vice Chancellor's speeches when the ministers come for functions here, they always talk about engagement of the community.' Community engagement can be vital to document and disseminate knowledge through research collaboration with the custodians of localised knowledge. We thus recommend that to navigate the inaccessibility of local knowledge systems that have a history of being discounted, researchers and the custodians of localised knowledge must closely cooperate. This could be actualised through collaborative research between researchers and members of the specific cultural community. Often, custodians of Indigenous knowledge choose not to share their knowledge and technology with researchers because they suspect that they may be exploited, as Western academic systems encourage and reward researchers who take credit for the community's heritage (Johnson & Mbah, 2021). Re-energising collaborations between academics and community knowledge custodians are foundational to the transformation and decolonisation of the canon of knowledge (Shizha, 2010). This collaboration needs to be cemented by mutual trust; further incentivisation of community participation in and leadership of research may be achieved through a framework for patenting some dimensions to safeguard community knowledge while financially compensating the community for their intellectual contribution.

Conclusion

We conclude that there is a need to overhaul the Western epistemic canon that has continued to shape knowledge production across Zambia. The potential for mainstreaming localised knowledge has already gained traction but will need further entrenchment of this epistemological re-orientation. Our chapter has shown that the material history of imperial knowledge production has shaped the academic pursuits of the flagship university in Zambia, which has resulted in the dichotomisation of localised knowledge and conventional science. Moreover, the proliferation of this Eurocentric knowledge system has obliterated non-Western ways of knowing, resulting in an incomplete and inaccurate understanding of localised environments. Our conversations with faculty have highlighted various ways in which these epistemological colonialities can be reversed. We bookended this chapter by proposing concrete ways of embracing the plurality of epistemic systems in the character and purpose of higher education through integrated efforts at the institutional, researcher, and community levels.

References

Ajayi, J., Goma, L., & Johnson, G. (1996). *The African experience with higher education*. Ohio University Press.

Arnot, F. S. (1969). *Garenganze or, seven years' pioneer mission work in Central Africa*. Routledge.

Barnett, R., & Bengtsen, S. (2017). Universities and epistemology: From a dissolution of knowledge to the emergence of a new thinking. *Education Sciences*, 7(38), 1–12. doi:10.3390/educsci7010038

Castro-Gómez, S. (2002). The social sciences, epistemic violence, and the problem of the 'invention of the other.' *Nepantla: Views from South*, 3(2), 269–285.

Chakrabarty, D. (2000). *Provincializing Europe: Postcolonial thought and historical difference*. Princeton University Press.

Chilisa, B. (2020). *Indigenous research methodologies* (2nd ed.). Sage.

Chipindi, F.M. (2018). *Negotiating professional identities in a liberalised Sub-Saharan economy: A case of university of Zambia faculty* [Unpublished doctoral dissertation]. University of Minnesota. https://hdl.handle.net/11299/201064

Chokani, G.L. (1984). *The University of Zambia's response to the manpower needs of the country* [Unpublished master's thesis]. University of Zambia.

Connell, R. (2018). Decolonising sociology. *Contemporary Sociology*, 47(4), 399–407. doi:10.1177/0094306118779811

Dei, G.J.S. (2014). Indigenizing the school curriculum. In G. Emeagwali & G.J.S. Dei (Eds.), *African Indigenous knowledge and the disciplines* (pp. 165–180). Sense Publishers.

Derrida, J. (1976). *Of grammatology* (Translated by G.C. Spivak). Johns Hopkins University Press.

Emeagwali, G. (2014). Intersections between Africa's Indigenous knowledge systems and history. In G. Emeagwali & G.J.S. Dei (Eds.), *African Indigenous knowledge and the disciplines* (pp. 1–17). Sense Publishers.

Goma, L.H.K., & Tembo, L.P. (1984). *The African university: Issues and perspectives*. University of Zambia Press.

Henkel, R. (1989). *Christian missions in Africa*. Dietrich Reimar Verlag.

Johnson, A.T., & Mbah, M. (2021). (Un)subjugating Indigenous Knowledge for sustainable development: Considerations for community-based research in African higher education. *Journal of Comparative & International Higher Education*, 13(3). http://irep.ntu.ac.uk/id/eprint/43162/1/1447135_Mbah.pdf

Kelly, M.J. (1991). *The origins and development of education in Zambia*. Image Publishers.

Lockwood Commission. (1963). *The report on the development of a university in Northern Rhodesia (Zambia)*. Government Printer.

Maponya, P.M. (2005). Fostering the culture of knowledge sharing in higher education. *South African Journal of Higher Education*, 19(5), 900–911. doi:10.4314/sajhe.v19i5.25534

Mawere, M. (2014). *Culture, Indigenous knowledge and development in Africa: Reviving interconnections for sustainable development*. Langaa RPCIG.

Mazrui, A.A. (2005). The re-invention of Africa: Edward Said, V.Y. Mudimbe, and beyond. *Research in African Literatures*, 36(3), 68–82. doi:10.1353/ral.2005.0153

Mbah, M. (2016). Towards the idea of the interconnected university for sustainable community development. *Higher Education Research & Development*, 35(6), 1228–1241. doi:10.1080/07294360.2016.1144570

Mbah, M., Johnson, A.T., & Chipindi, F. (2021). Institutionalising the intangible through research and engagement: Indigenous knowledge and higher education for sustainable development in Zambia. *International Journal of Educational Development*, 82. doi:10.1016/j.ijedudev.2021.102355

Meisenbach, R.J. (2004). *Framing fundraising: A poststructuralist analysis of education fund raisers work and identity* [Unpublished doctoral dissertation]. Purdue University.

Mills, C.W. (1959). *The sociological imagination*. Oxford University Press.

Ndofirepi, A.P., & Gwaravanda, E.T. (2019). Epistemic (in)justice in African universities: A perspective of the politics of knowledge. *Educational Review*, 71(5), 581–594. doi:10.1080/00131911.2018.1459477.

Okere, T., Njoku, C., & Devisch, R. (2005). All knowledge is first of all local knowledge: An introduction. *Africa Development/Afrique Et Développement*, 30(3), 1–19. http://www.jstor.org/stable/24484617

Rawls, A.W., & David, G. (2003). Accountably other: Trust, reciprocity and exclusion in a context of situated practice. *Human Studies*, 28(4), 469–497. http://www.jstor.org/stable/27642729

Saldaña, J. (2016). *The coding manual for qualitative researchers* (3rd ed.). Thousand Oaks, CA: Sage.

Shizha, E. (2010). Rethinking and reconstituting Indigenous Knowledge and voices in the Academy in Zimbabwe: A decolonisation process. In D. Kapoor & E. Shiza (Eds.), *Indigenous knowledge and learning in Asia/Pacific and Africa* (pp. 115–129). Palgrave Macmillan.

de Sousa Santos, B. (2007). Beyond abyssal thinking: From global lines to ecologies of knowledges. *Review – Fernand Braudel Center for the Study of Economies, Historical Systems, and Civilisations*, 30(1), 45–89.

Spivak, G.C. (1988). Can the subaltern speak? In N. Carry & L. Grossberg (Eds.), *Marxism and the interpretation of culture* (pp. 271–313). University of Illinois Press.

Stake, R. (1995). *The art of case study research*. Sage.

Tembo, L.P. (1978). The African university and social reform. *African Social Research*, 25, 379–397.

Turner, N.J., Marshall, A., Thompson (Edōsdi), J.C., Hood, R.J., Hill, C., & Hill, E.-A. (2008). 'Ebb and flow': Transmitting knowledge in a contemporary Aboriginal community. In J.S. Lutz, & B. Neis (Eds.), *Making and moving knowledge: Interdisciplinary and community-based research in a world on the edge* (pp. 45–81). McGill-Queen's University Press.

6
RECLAIMING INDIGENOUS EPISTEMES

Entenga Drums Revival at Kyambogo University

James Isabirye

Entenga drum music of the Buganda kingdom, in Uganda, like other royal expressions, was prevented from being performed in 1967, following the illegalisation of cultural institutions and their associated cultural practices by the state. Therefore, no transfer of knowledge and skills of these expressions took place, and no new musicians learnt to perform them. By 2015, Musisi Mukalazi Livingstone was the only surviving royal musician who knew the repertoire and skills of *Entenga* in the entire Buganda kingdom. *Entenga* is a set of fifteen tuned drums played by six musicians. Song parts are played in octaves pairs in an interlocking manner, like the *Amadinda* (Baganda peoples' xylophone), with curved *Enga* (reed sticks).

To save the *Entenga* music tradition from extinction, I initiated a project to revive the performance of *Entenga* music. The project was funded by Singing Wells, a cultural organisation and recording label based in the United Kingdom. This project involved six Kyambogo University students and six non-university practising musician members of cultural groups. During the 6-month project, *Entenga* knowledge and skills were transmitted using pedagies that Musisi repeatedly described as 'that is how I learnt *Entenga* in the palace.' The *Entenga* music pedagogy involved holistic acts, storytelling, demonstration, collaborative problem solving, active learner participation, and real-life goal setting. The youths engaged intensely with joy and became proficient in 12 *Entenga* songs. After 6 months of engagement, they were invited to perform at public events including the king's coronation anniversary in 2016, and they have been invited annually to play at those anniversaries. This chapter thus focuses on the pedagies that this master musician used to transfer knowledge and skills of *Entenga* to university students and practising musicians.

Education, Research, and Music

Through my work as a music educator, Indigenous music revivalist, and researcher, I have come to understand the extraordinary value of creating opportunities for formerly colonised people to (re)learn and reclaim their Indigenous cultural practices. My previous work in this vein includes a study of the teaching and learning that took place during projects to revive various nearly extinct Indigenous music traditions (Isabirye, 2019, 2021a). The studies showed that 'nurturing identity, agency, and joy-filled passion among the learners were the main contributing factors that facilitated a successful transfer of knowledge and skills from the elderly master musicians to multitudes of youths' (Isabirye, 2021b, p. 239). An autoethnographic study (Isabirye, 2021a) of my experiences learning Indigenous music and applying Indigenous pedagogy in my classroom offered additional insights about how Indigenous learning and teaching processes support the development of learner leadership, ownership, agency, and identity.

I grew up in a musical village community, where we learnt to play *Embaire* (xylophone), *Endingigdi* (tube fiddle), *Enkwanzi* (pan pipes), and *okukuba Engoma* (playing drums) in contexts that could qualify as a *musical playground* (Marsh, 2008). My Indigenous community was a place for learning meaningful musicianship and constructive being, which is why I remain so deeply connected. I attended primary through graduate school in Uganda and became a high school music and drama teacher. Later, I became a music and drama teaching assistant at Kyambogo University. As a high school teacher, I always went back to the villages to learn music and teach it to my learners. Students were always enthused to learn musical expressions that emerged from their Indigenous communities, which were no longer performed—a discovery of their own selves. From those experiences, I realised that it is important for me to demonstrate for my teacher trainees how to connect with Indigenous communities, to enable them to recognise the potential and educational value that Indigenous communities offer. This could possibly transform the theory and practice of music and general teaching and learning in schools. Therefore, connecting learners with their cultural identities through rediscovering their musical expressions became my preoccupation.

I had discovered that some of the finest musical expressions of Uganda's communities were outlawed royal traditions that were no longer performed. It became a necessity for me to research, engage with the communities, and where possible, revitalise and revive some of their music. I worked with Basoga communities to revive the *Bigwala* (royal side-blown gourd trumpets), *Ekimasa* (royal harp) and the *Naizungwe* (royal drums), and *Entongooli* (bowl lyre); then with Buganda communities to revive the *Amakondere* (royal side-blown trumpets) and the *Entenga* (royal tuned drums). Revivals involved creating new musicians through the transfer of knowledge and skills of those kinds of music from surviving culture bearers—master musicians—to youth. I solicited funds from UNESCO and Singing Wells and transformed communities into places for my students to learn Indigenous musical expressions and research.

Historical Background

Uganda was created through the colonial overlay of a national political structure on diverse, culturally different, well-organised Indigenous kingdoms, chiefdoms, and clans. The people were culturally and linguistically different, but also interrelated; for example, Bantu dialects such as Basoga—my own dialect—and Baganda have similar cultures and histories (Nketia, 1974; Isabirye, 2020, 2021a). The creation of Uganda by the British was done without building consensus among communities. As Kasozi (2013) explains, the colonists created unbalanced social strata among the different ethnic societies within colonial Uganda, elevating collaborators and weakening resistors. Buganda had collaborated with colonisers and was, in turn, rewarded with a higher status in the colonial state, which ruled for 66 years. In 1962, Uganda gained independence, and the *Kabaka* (king) of Buganda became president of a highly plural and divided nation. The unification of Uganda necessitated negotiating the status of all ethnic societies and healing from the pains of colonial violence. Equal status for all ethnic societies became a problem that was compounded by the *Kabaka's* bias towards Buganda. Conflicts of interests were suspect, and the president/king appeared to pursue interests of Buganda at the expense of the state. Buganda preferred to retain their sovereignty and a higher status within the national frame, which disadvantaged nation building. Within Buganda were also disgruntled people who felt that the British privileges were given to a small elite Baganda group—*Mengo Establishment*—who controlled politics and all resources in the kingdom.

After attaining independence, the leaders of young Uganda focused on unification of the country, not the divisive interests of one ethnic society (Kasozi, 2013). Unfortunately, unification of these culturally and politically different peoples of unequal status turned out to be conflictual and required political consensus building among the ethnic societies. This conflict reached a climax when the central government opted for a military solution, attacking the Buganda kingdom in 1964 and exiling the king. The conflict ended with promulgation of a new 1967 constitution that illegalised all kingdoms and chiefdoms (Kirindi, 2008; Kasozi, 2013; Kafumbe, 2018) and by default all royal music traditions associated with them. This transformed Uganda into a republic. Some of the Baganda royal musicians were killed during the military attack on the palace; others were forced into hiding. As a result, the *eŋŋoma Entenga* music ceased to be practised—consequently, no new drummers learnt this tradition. This national false-start and turbulent political history affected all spheres of being in society, including education at all levels, additionally silencing all Indigenous music forms.

The problem of music education in Ugandan institutions of higher learning—particularly universities—comes out of this historic national context. In addition, there are very few lower secondary and high schools that engage in internal and national musical arts activities such as festivals, and very few students opt for music-related academic fields. As a result, very few teacher-training college students choose to be music teachers, and the very few that do opt for musical arts in universities. Worse still is that education in Ugandan institutions of higher learning remains rooted in Western epistemes that continue to frustrate meaningful learning and societal development. Institutions of higher learning mainly hire graduates with first or upper second-class degrees in their fields who become lecturers and professors in those academic areas. Many of those focus on research in their fields but lack orientation to music or even general education pedagogy. Because of the absence of literature on pedagogy within their programmes, many instructors maintain methods used by their teachers before them, sustaining distanced contemporary education pedagogy. This chapter thus offers a reflection on Indigenous pedagogies that yielded meaningful results in a university setting in an effort to improve pedagogy and learning in institutions of higher learning in Uganda and other similar contexts.

Indigenous Pedagogy

In Uganda, some educators take pride in following a British system, demonstrating the lingering impacts of colonial education systems. On the contrary, I take pride in an education that is rooted in the Indigenous systems of a community, a culture, and a place. Gruenewald (2003) advocates for such place-conscious pedagogies, arguing that the educational needs of different societies differ. Indigenous pedagogies have been discussed through various lenses by scholars such as Isabirye (2021a, 2021b), Kenyatta (1965), Marsh (2008), Nketia (1974), and Ssekamwa (1997). In short, Indigenous learning pedagogies entail learner participation (Wenger, 1998) in cultural experiences and engaging in meaningful, real-life experiences (Dewey, 1938/1998; Darron & Sharon, 2019), while facilitators of the learning offer support and scaffold student learning processes (Bruner, 1966).

Indigenous pedagogies embed 'humanistic interactive sociality' (Oviawe, 2016) and are transmitted through social interaction, cultural knowledge, and 'desirable social behaviours or manners, technical skills, customs, beliefs, values, laws, and institutions' (Ssekamwa, 1997, p. 1). Indigenous learning happens 'through playing and working, oral literature, and ritual ceremonies, as well as hunting... [that] prepares the child' (Okumu, 2000, p. 154). Deep learning happens when the young observe, listen, and imitate the more knowledgeable and skilled members (Kidula, 2019). Students acquire skills of 'imagination, thinking, shrewdness, literature, composition and art of public speaking' (Ssekamwa, 1997, p. 5). Teachers help learning to happen in a playful manner using 'games, songs, rhymes, storytelling... proverbs, riddles' (Ssekamwa, 1997, p. 5). In the case of Indigenous music education, learning enhances thinking, listening, memorisation, and music performance skills, and an Indigenous music educator 'remains in focus, serving as a guide to a child' (p. 250). Such Indigenous learning happens through performance experiences that embed the depth of knowledge, values, and beliefs of being within specific cultural communities (Idamoyibo & Akuno, 2019).

My Experiences as a Music and Dance Teacher

My experiences as a music and dance teacher in primary and secondary schools led me to wonder why teachers in Uganda revere Western epistemes exclusively and pursue pedagogies that are so controlling and typical of a banking education (Freire, 1970). Schools in Uganda are still entrenched in a colonial system that depends on high marks for the validation of learning, where learners grasp facts to regurgitate during tests and examinations. Teachers neglect learners' creative capabilities and focus on completion of bookish syllabus content so that students get high marks in examinations and secure their economic future. Then, learners cram those teacher-given truths without conceptualising content, retelling bookish knowledge at the expense of their own identity, agency, and intellectual growth and development. This education sustains oppressive practices, as Freire (1970) characterises:

> the teacher teaches and the students are taught; the teacher knows everything and students know nothing; the teacher thinks and the students are thought about; the teacher talks and students listen-meekly; the teacher disciplines and students are disciplined; the teacher chooses and enforces his choice, and the students comply; the teacher acts and the students have the illusion of acting through the action of the teacher; the teacher chooses the program content and students (who were not consulted) adapt to it;... the teacher is the Subject of the learning process and the students are mere objects.
>
> *(p. 73)*

To contrast Ugandan school reliance upon this oppressive way of teaching and learning, my teaching incorporated our childhood Indigenous learning that allowed us to participate in meaning-making. My goal was to support learners to take charge of their learning, pursue their own music learning paths, and practise what their passions engendered, as individuals, in groups, and beyond class.

Also, I knew that humans learn only when they decide to do so—to learn is a personal choice—and by engaging in experiences that are meaningful to them. I needed to create learning contexts that met those basic values of being. As a result, learners enjoyed the music and dance lessons I offered. I taught how to play *Embaire* (Busoga xylophone), *Enkwanzi* (Busoga pan pipes), *Endongo*[1] (lamellaphone of Busoga), and *Engoma* (drums) and the performance of Indigenous dances of Ugandan communities. I encouraged learners to participate in making strategies for us to all achieve class objectives, and they co-led the processes we pursued to achieve them. Learners brought their knowledge and skills into those contexts, negotiating best practices as I guided consensus building among them. I participated in all activities alongside and together with the learners—this always excited them, empowered them musically, and created communities of active participants. Each learner chose role models to learn from during the engagements, and my pedagogies were *socialising* the learners. Through my experiences teaching in schools for 16 years, I came to realise that meaning-making and meaningful active participation in a practice can support people to learn anything (Nketia, 1974; Wenger, 1998; Isabirye, 2019).

The Buganda Society

The Buganda society is organised according to clans, and each clan performs a specific *hereditary duty* in the service of the king (Kafumbe, 2018). Therefore, clan leaders/elders identify and train some of their members from childhood as successors. Those young servants dedicated to royal service undergo training as *Abasiige* (*Omusiige* for singular) and are trained by members of their clan in the palace—the context in which they would work. The *Omusiige* (a child dedicated to the king's service) is handed over by the parents to live in the palace and learn the responsibilities of their clan. A person was not welcome to learn the duties of other clans; a clan did not allow outsiders to interfere with their noble duties since it was a great honour to serve the king. Also, this could weaken the connection of the clan to the kingdom (Kafumbe, 2018). For example, the *Entenga* drums was a reserve of the *Lugave* clan; *endere* flutes was a reserve for *Mmamba* (lungfish) clan; and *Akadinda* (xylophones) was a reserve of the *Njovu* (elephant) clan.

Sometimes exceptions were made, however, and a non-member joined a clan to serve the king. For example, Musisi Mukalazi was an *Omusiige* of the *Mmamba*—his father was the *magumba* (title for head of the royal flutists, *Endere*-players)—not the *Lugave* clan. But Musisi was not interested in *Endere*. Musisi spent the entire time listening to and learning *Entenga* although the *Abatenga* (*Entenga* drummers) did not welcome him—he participated illegitimately on the periphery (Wenger, 1998). The young prince was equally interested in *Entenga*, which made Musisi a close associate of the heir to the throne. Due to that connection, Queen Sarah Kisosoonkole recommended to then leader of the *Entenga* ensemble in *SseKabaka* Edward Mutesa II's palace to accept Musisi into a practice of the *Lugave* clan, since he was highly talented and interested in the drums. The queen's recommendation transformed Musisi into a legitimate participant in the *Entenga* practice (Wenger, 1998), and this facilitated his learning. *Entenga* were a special ensemble that played for *Kabaka* Muteesa II during his leisure time and were not exposed to the public.

The palace had partitioned sections allocated to the different music ensembles. The ensembles included: *Abatenga* (*Entenga* drum players), *Abalere* (notched flutists), *Omulanga* (harpist), ab'*Akadinda* (*Akadinda* xylophone players), *Abatamivu* (*Entamivu* players), and *Abakondere* (*Amakondere* trumpet players). Musisi was allowed to move from the section of the *Abalere* into the *Abatenga*. Indeed, Musisi is not the only person to have been accepted into a practice when he was not a primary member of the clan. Kafumbe (2018) explains how the *Butiko* (mushroom) clan leaders allow non-primary members to join them in the performance of the *clan-royal Kawuugulu* music and dance. Therefore, the practice of modifying norms to address a need is part and parcel of the Buganda and indeed other cultural institutions in Uganda.

The *Entenga* Royal Drums

The *Entenga* drums comprise two sections: The melodic drum section and the rhythmic drum section. The melodic section comprises 12 hierarchically arranged drums according to size, with the smallest being the highest pitch. These twelve are played by four people. The highest drums are played by *Omukonezi* who plays the highest parts, which are added as embellishments. *Omukonezi* starts the songs, which is not the case with *Amadinda* (12-slab xylophone of the Baganda that is played by three musicians) where *Omunazi* starts the songs. The next person plays the *Omuwawuzi* (mixer) part. Some drums are shared between *Omukonezi* and *Omuwawuzi*, and the number of shared drums depends on the song. The third player is the *Omunazi* (starter), who plays the same notes as the *Omukonezi* at a lower pitch, except the additions that are possible only for the latter. The fourth player is the *Omuwawuzi ow'Amatengezi*, who plays the same notes an octave lower as the *Omuwawuzi*. *Entengezi* are the big drums among the tuned section of *Entenga* drums—and the *Omuwawuzi* who plays those drums are distinguished by alluding to the deep pitch of the drums he plays. Therefore, the *Entenga* melodic drums are played in octave pairs by four musicians, using long curved sticks made from *Enga*—a type of reed. The curved end is used to hit the skin surface of the drum and produces a refined sound.

There is a challenge with the curved sticks particularly because players hit the same drum at some points in the progression of the song. However, musicians are trained *okuyita waggulu* (to pass up when hitting a drum) and *okuyita wansi* (to pass down after hitting) particularly for songs that are longer melodies. For songs with short melodies, the players can hit drums without passing down or up because they might share only one drum, and in that case, each player cares to hit a side of the drum that does not cause the entangling of sticks.

The rhythmic section comprises the three big drums that provide the beat and add rhythmic texture. The largest and lowest pitch drum is called *Nakawombe*, and according to Musisi, that name was derived from the sister of Katende, the man who is believed to have brought the *Entenga* from Sese Island. According to Musisi, the *Abatenga* in *SseKabaka* Muteesa II's palace repeatedly said that these drums were brought from Sese island into the palace by a man called Katende of the *Lugave* clan, who had learnt this music from Busoga. Musisi says the *Entenga* surely originated in Busoga. This drum is placed at the extreme end. The next drum to the *Nakawombe* is called *Kyawakati*—one for the middle—a name that is derived from its middle location among the three rhythmic drums of the *Entenga* set. The *Nakawombe* and *Kyawakati* are played by one person. *Entemyo*, the third drum among the non-melodic, which is also the smallest and loudest, gives the central beat and is played by one person.

The *Entenga* Revival Processes

As a high school student at Kiira College Butiki, I read about *Entenga* music in Mukasa's (1977) Anthology on Uganda musical instruments and was fascinated because I had never seen or listened to tuned drums. I therefore wanted to see and listen to that music. Although I am neither a member of the *Lugave* (pangolin) clan, and not even a Muganda—of Baganda people—I was interested to know more about a drum tradition whose name—*Entenga*, is so connected to my dialect. I speak the Lusoga *Lutenga* dialect, one of the most spoken among the Basoga people. The Baganda and Basoga belong to the Bantu group of people, which offers another lens to frame my identities in *Entenga* culture. Therefore, my engagement in *Entenga* project could be framed through various lenses as a researcher, music educator, cultural revivalist, member of Bantu group, and one of the Lusoga Lutenga speakers. I spent my entire high school and undergraduate training researching and searching for any *Entenga* musicians to find out more about this unique music. My search and research revealed to me the sad political history of Uganda that nearly caused this and other royal music traditions to die altogether.

In 2015, I requested Singing Wells to finance the revival of *Entenga* music, a project that was carried out from Kyambogo University, since some of my students were Baganda (people of the Buganda kingdom). I needed to find a master musician to share the knowledge and skills of *Entenga* with the Kyambogo University students. I asked many Buganda kingdom officials, music teachers and lecturers, and all other musician friends whether they knew any such musicians who were still alive. The 2-month search enabled me to find Musisi Mukalazi Livingstone—the only surviving *Entenga* musician who had learnt the music in the palace during King Edward Muteesa II's reign as a boy in the 1960s.

The teacher-trainee students of Kyambogo were the primary target/participants in the *Entenga* revival project. I invited Musisi Mukalazi (Figure 6.1) to Kyambogo University to teach the knowledge and skills of *Entenga* to the students. The first week of teaching revealed slow progress by the students. They had an intense academic programme to attend and were left with limited time to learn with Musisi. He used to wait for the students for long hours, and at times not all students were free to learn *Entenga*. This was a major concern because Musisi's travel and living costs were funded by the project.

Concerned about the slow speed, I invited six practising musicians who have skills of xylophone playing. I had discovered that a skilled xylophone player could learn *Entenga* playing much faster. Therefore, the project funded the daily travel and living costs for the musicians and students. The students were offered only meals because they had accommodation in the university and did not need transport facilitation. Musisi and his *Entenga* learners enjoyed having meals together. In some cases when the students attended lectures, Musisi taught the other

FIGURE 6.1 Musisi Mukalazi Livingstone, the Entenga master musician.

musicians. This was advantageous because the musicians learnt the songs in a few days and supported Musisi to teach the Kyambogo students.

The first song Musisi taught was *Mubandusa*. He argued that this was always the first song on their repertoire and therefore they should learn it first. Musisi taught the student a repertoire bearing in mind a performance programme. To Musisi, *Mubandusa* song is the anthem of the *Entenga* music. The purpose of the song is *okubandula*—to open up a new thing. This song was always first on the *Entenga* programme in the palace and elsewhere because of its simple and repetitive melody notes, tunefulness, and textural meaning.

During the project period, the students and I interviewed Musisi about his palace life, the royal music ensembles, and the history of Buganda kingdom. The first *Entenga* lessons were conducted on the *Akadinda* (22-slab giant Baganda royal xylophone), which revealed the connection between xylophone playing style and *Entenga*. The drums were tuned by a drum maker—a craftsman called Gaira from Mpambire village (about 40 kilometres west of Kampala)—while the students and musicians observed. They learnt how to tune already-made drums because making drums would delay the learning of the music and require additional resources. Therefore, beyond the music, students learnt how *Entenga* are tuned, and the deeper Baganda culture that Musisi shared during the prolonged engagements.

Tenets of Musisi's Indigenous Pedagogy

The Indigenous ways of music learning that were used to transmit *Entenga* music to the youth and inspire agency among them to perform before huge crowds, as well as combining students and community musicians to jointly solve musical problems, was a new approach at Kyambogo. Musisi engaged in *Entenga* playing collaboratively with learners, but also allowed them to figure out musical concepts on their own, scaffolding them as individuals (Figure 6.2) and as a group (Bruner, 1966). Musisi encouraged fast ones to guide their peers, filling the experience with fun and laughter during the interactive learning engagements and avoiding stressful feedback to learners. He spent much time teaching individual learners, and this created intimate settings for addressing personal needs of each learner. The learners reached out for scaffolding countless times without fear.

Musisi spent time with learners talking about his great experiences in the palace, including how he played with the prince, who is the current king, and the origins and meanings of the songs he taught. Musisi used every opportunity to provoke learners to interact and tell their stories. He believed that learning arises from the interest of a learner, and that one cannot learn if they do not have interest in something. He narrated an experience to me that the Director of Ndere Troupe/Centre brought drummers from Burundi for him to teach them *Entenga* drumming. He promised them a higher salary if they learnt. They tried but gave up after one lesson—saying that *Entenga* drums were hard. Musisi argued that those Burundians did not have interest in *Entenga*.

FIGURE 6.2 Musisi scaffolding Entenga student.

Musisi believed that to teach well, one must behave like a parent to the learners. He often cracked jokes, which enabled the learners to not fear him and to better learn the music. Musisi also challenged the students to improvise their own ways of playing the songs. He used nicknames to refer to them whenever they performed very well. A famous nickname was *Embwa* (dog) for anyone who performed well. He used to say: *embwa eno ekuba ekintu* (this dog plays the thing [song] extremely well).

To teach a new song, Musisi started by humming it. Then, he played the parts of a song on the *Entenga* as it is supposed to be. Then, he slowed the speed of the song and provoked the learner to join him. He observed the learners to see the level of difficulty they were facing. As the learners observed, he then broke up the song into parts and showed them how the parts connect to make up the song. He made sure that the parts match the learners' abilities. Then, he stepped aside but paid attention as the learner worked without his interruption. He treated every moment of the teaching with love and respect for the learners.

Musisi's example aligns with the literature on an effective music teacher. As Erwin, Edwards, Kerchner, and Knight (2004) suggest, a good teacher does work with love and inspires learners to desire to learn more so that they do not fear the hardship of learning. As the more knowledgeable person interacts freely with the learner, the welcoming atmosphere increases learning by allowing the student to seek support or scaffold (Bruner, 1966). This opens many paths for joy-filled learning to take place (Isabirye, 2019). Music is a social activity that requires teachers to engage together and deeply with learners in a musical context that they have created (Campbell, 2008). Learners engage in intense listening and observation, which enables them to initiate and participate with others collaboratively in learning problem-solving agendas. At the beginning of the project, the university students were slower than the musicians, but since they were working as a group, everyone supported each other to learn *Entenga* songs very fast. The songs to learn were a group problem, and learners mediated the learning of their peers so that the group could be proficient and have a broad repertoire.

Musisi used pedagogies that allowed the youths to ask questions among themselves, suggest answers and seek his support only when necessary. This learning was guided by the questions that learners asked. Learning is an endless 'process of inquiry' (Kramer & Arnold, 2004, p. 44), and seeking answers to musical learning problems involves understanding the sound, the setting, the significance, and the meaning. In this project, learning problems to be solved included learning the interlocking nature of *Entenga* sound, the Buganda context, the meaning of the *Entenga*, and how all these aspects come together. The learning-problem-solving approach nurtured confidence in the students to come up with their own ways of understanding *Entenga*, which motivated them to work harder and to grow—this was not just about learning *Entenga*. This learning was about negotiating and renegotiating their identities and growth as individuals and as a group (Isabirye, 2019).

Entenga Public Performances

When the learners gained proficiency, they needed to share their newly acquired music culture with the kingdom since it was royal music. However, it was not possible for anyone to reach the officials and inform them about the new generation of *Entenga* musicians at Kyambogo University. Then a friend and organiser of the DoaDoa festival contacted me about making a paper presentation at the festival. I informed him about a new generation of *Entenga*—he had never heard of this music genre even though he was a Muganda (from Buganda) himself. This was the first public performance of *Entenga* in Uganda since the attack on Buganda kingdom palace and the exile of the *Kabaka* in 1966. On that day, the students decided to include *Akadinda*—a 22-slab xylophone—of the Baganda people in their performance. This performance enabled the students to gain confidence and provided exposure. A kingdom official came to know that *Entenga* had been played at DoaDoa, and organisers of the coronation anniversary decided that those *Entenga* players should be invited for the *Kabaka*'s coronation anniversary.

The students' involvement in kingdom rituals lasted for 4 years and was interrupted by the COVID-19 pandemic in 2020. The first event where they played was at the 23rd coronation anniversary of Kabaka Muwenda Mutebi II, at Kabasanda in Butambala (2016). The *Entenga* drums fascinated the event organisers, who were also new to them. The *Entenga* were located directly facing the king (Figure 6.3) to enable him to enjoy this music. This event was followed by performances at the subsequent coronation anniversaries: The 24th anniversary at Kasanda in Mubende district (2017), the 25th anniversary in the palace at Mengo (2018), and the 26th anniversary at Nkumba University in Entebbe (2019).

FIGURE 6.3 New generation of Entenga players at coronation 2016 anniversary of the Kabaka.

Kyambogo students were amazed to see the rehearsals in preparation for the coronation anniversaries and to participate in them even if some of them were not Baganda (people of Buganda kingdom). The *Lugave* clan members realised that they lacked musical skills to play *Entenga*, and so we came to fill their gap in the service of the kingdom. Buganda culture officials donated bark cloth to the students and asked us *okusumika* (to wrap backcloth over the kanzu dress and knot it atop the shoulder), which made us become part of the entire Buganda cultural setup. Before the performances, the *Kawuula* (head of *Mujaguzo* drums) always knelt in front of the drums, owned *Entenga*, and introduced the performance as part of the *Lugave* clan.

I raised a question to the minister in charge of *eby'obuwangwa n'enono* (culture), Ow Walusimbi, and he confirmed that it was okay for a non-Muganda to perform for the *Kabaka*. He added that the *Kabaka* is the overall head of cultural matters, and he has the powers to alter any norms if the alteration does not cause conflict in the kingdom. The minister concluded by saying that Buganda kingdom has always been an open society that welcomes people from other lands into the service of the kingdom. For example, King Kyabaggu invited musicians from Busoga and even allocated them land in the kingdom. Indeed, two places in the Buganda area are named after places in Busoga and have been allocated to Basoga musicians: Kyebando (on Kampala-Gayaza Road) and Kisoga (on Mukono-Katosi road).

During the second coronation anniversary at Kasanda, the *Kabaka* was so impressed when the youths played (Figure 6.4), he specifically acknowledged the *Entenga* youths for playing in exactly the same manner as the ones he had seen when he was a prince. These players had later taught Musisi. After the speech, he invited the *Entenga* players for a public handshake and promised to invite them to his palace. The appreciation by the king increased the agency of the *Entenga* youths, and they vowed to work even harder. They resolved to learn the *Akadinda* so that during the

FIGURE 6.4 Entenga performance at Kasanda on July 31, 2017.

next invitation they could present it as well. The increased agency empowered them, and since the styles of *Entenga* and *Akadinda* are slightly similar, they learnt much faster. Indeed, during the 25th coronation anniversary in Mengo palace, the *Entenga* youths were invited to play the *Akadinda* as well. The youths were not only inspired by the *Kabaka*'s attitude but also the uniqueness of the music.

The anniversaries attracted huge crowds, and their music stood out as the real culture that had been lacking. They became a true community of practice, which exist in all human societies and are part and parcel of our being (Wenger, 1998). They enable members to participate as individuals and in groups, and using this approach enables learners to support one another to engage in the learning process, each contributing a segment to the whole. This is similar to the ways of being at home and outside the formal institutional setting. Students develop—through intersubjective interchange (Bruner, 1996)—more applicable approaches to problem-solving, and find pathways to solve learning problems that would be impossible for them as individuals. Wenger (1998) adds that individuals endeavour to learn in order to contribute to the practice of their communities to which they aspire to belong in meaningful ways, which translates into an improvement in their trade.

Benefits to the Students

The students shared information that they gained from interacting with Musisi and the Buganda cultural leaders. For example, there is a palace at Kabowa near Kampala for the *mujaguzo*, or royal drums. In that palace, the drums are kept in a house called *Ndoga obukaba* (heal my ungovernable sex drive). Anyone or the *Kawuula* (title for the head of the *mujaguzo*) who takes care of the royal drums is supposed to avoid any sexual relations for the week before the *mujaguzo* are played before the Kabaka. It is believed that if the *Kawuula* engages in a sexual relationship in that period, the drums will not sound, and everyone will know the cause. In such a case, the king might sentence the *Kawuula* to death for the abomination. Royal regalia are very powerful even in other kingdoms. For example, Kirindi (2008) explains the *Bagyendanwa* royal drum of Ankole kingdom has its own palace at Kamukuzi, in addition to wives, property, and an entourage during its tours, and is accorded royal respect like a human being.

The Buganda court and indeed others such as Ankole are places to learn cultural practices and their meaning. The teacher trainees experienced the Buganda court manners that differ tremendously from common place behaviour, and this was transformative. The students repeatedly asked Musisi why he was so humble, and he kept on referring to the days when he lived in the palace as a youth. Kirindi (2008) explains that the court was a formal context where children were trained in culture, etiquette, and leadership to prepare them for a life of service to the kingdom.

These processes elevated students' self-esteem, and they were further inspired to work with their own pupils when they finally joined the world of work as teachers. Students also discussed directions they would pursue to revive music traditions in their own communities. These initiatives are highly important since Indigenous music of the culturally plural Uganda remains under threat and is in need of revival. As Kirindi (2008) explains the 'culture of our society is now passing on without being recorded for the benefit of future generations and posterity' (iv). The participation of teachers to lead initiatives to revitalise Indigenous cultures is critical. Thus, engagements in *Entenga* offered teacher trainees necessary skills that they would use to work beyond the classrooms and connect in relevant ways with the communities. As Kirindi suggests, it is possible to safeguard still-surviving music and folklore heritage of African societies.

Through this project, students were exposed to the wealth of knowledge that the older generations offered. While the focus of the project was to safeguard the music from extinction, kingdom officials invited the students to join others in royal service. The Kyambogo students developed interest in *Entenga* music due to various factors. *Entenga* are a unique type of drum, both in make—together with the curved sticks that are used to play them—and the music that they produce. The uniqueness of a culture makes it new, which attracts attention and interest. Pond (2004) suggests that a teacher's calling is to guide learners 'to move into the learning zone' (p. 33) and gain a new understanding of a learning problem based on engaging in a new experience. One of the students, Shaban, explained why participating in the *Entenga* revival was important:

> I am really very happy to be part of this initiative because it is my culture, my identity. When this music was not there, we had no identity. We could find ourselves anywhere. Now we have what we can be identified with. That this is Buganda. Without a culture you cannot belong anywhere. In this band we are trying to keep the culture alive. It is the best any parent would wish except those who adopt the Western lifestyle. The African way is that you pass on the heritage from one generation to another, that is the education. Knowledge and skills are passed on from one generation through practicing the culture.
>
> *(Shaban, personal communication, February 10, 2021)*

The students did everything possible to learn *Entenga*, and to perform at Doadoa and the royal ceremonies, with pride. Their identities kept on changing from interested music education students, to drum players of *Entenga* music, and finally royal musicians whose performance was central to the coronation anniversary—the main event where the *Kabaka* appears in public annually. The *Entenga* experience offered students the opportunity to assess their proficiency as individuals and as a group that was transforming into a community of practice (Wenger, 1998). The *Entenga* musicians realised that they had gained proficiency and were starting to own the practice. This increased my own agency and strengthened my belief in Indigenous education processes (Isabirye, 2021a) that Musisi used to teach my students. Also, those processes had not only enabled students to learn the music but contributed to the revival of *Entenga* as meaningful to the culture bearer and indeed the king.

As a music expression, *Entenga* was giving the students an opportunity to negotiate their identities as revivalists and discoverers. Their classmates were amazed to see and listen to the music that had been a focus of their 2-months learning engagement, a sacrifice in terms of many things including time, energy, and patience with new and shifting identities. The newness of *Entenga* music gave them the feeling of—*look what we have found that you did not know exists*—being powerful revivalists. What stood out as key motivations for their participation in the revival are that the *Entenga* embedded cultural identity (Isabirye, 2020), embodied their sense of belonging, and represented intergenerational transmission (Brannen, 2006).

Implications

Music and indeed general education in universities might be meaningful if the knowledge and skills are created and recreated in ways that allow students to bring their community's cultural resources into learning contexts. Students can contribute to the growth and development of society as part of their learning; therefore, isolating them from the community is a huge loss for the students and the community. Such isolation denies students opportunities to research and learn ways of being and working in community. The communities miss the benefit of growing from the knowledge and skill that students contribute. Furthermore, university education might thrive when faculty create meaningful learning communities and desist from promoting individualistic Westernised approaches that nurture graduates who cannot work well in groups or in communities. Also, culture bearers—experienced professionals of a field—can be invited into universities to facilitate the construction and reconstruction of applied knowledge and skills beyond what faculty can offer.

Note

1 This instrument should not be confused with *Endongo* (eight-string bowl lyre) of Buganda.

References

Brannen, J. (2006). Cultures of intergenerational transmission in four-generation families. *The Sociological Review*, 54(1), 133–154. doi:10.1111/j.1467-954X.2006.00605.x
Bruner, J. (1966). *Toward a theory of instruction*. W. W. Norton & Company, Inc.
Bruner, J. (1996). *The culture of education*. Harvard University Press.
Campbell, S.P. (2008). *Musician & teacher: An orientation to music education*. W. W. Norton & Company, Inc.
Darron, K., & Sharon, P. (2019). A critical conceptualization of place-conscious pedagogy. *European Journal of Curriculum Studies*, 5(1), 732–741.
Dewey, J. (1938/1998). *Experience and education*. Kappa Delta Pi.

Erwin, J., Edwards, K., Kerchner, J., & Knight, J. (2004). *Prelude to music education*. Pearson Education, Inc.

Freire, P. (1970). *Pedagogy of the oppressed*. Continuum.

Gruenewald, D.A. (2003). Foundations of place: A multidisciplinary framework for place-conscious education. *American Educational Research Journal, 40*(3), 619–654. doi:10.3102/00028312040003619

Idamoyibo, A.A., & Akuno, E.A. (2019). Systematic instruction for music education: Towards skill development and cultural growth. In E.A. Akuno (Ed.), *Music education in Africa: Concept, process, and practice* (pp. 249–261). Routledge.

Isabirye, J. (2019). *Nurturing identity, agency, and joy-filled passion through revitalizing Indigenous music education practices: Learning in and from a cultural revival project in Busoga, Uganda* [Unpublished doctoral dissertation]. Oakland University, Rochester, Michigan.

Isabirye, J. (2020). Namadu drum music and dance as mediation of healing rituals among the Bagwere people of Uganda. *Muziki, Journal of the Musical Arts in Africa, 17*(1), 46–71. doi:10.1080/18125980.2021.1885304

Isabirye, J. (2021a). Can Indigenous music learning processes inform contemporary schooling? *International Journal of Music Education, 39*(2), 151–166. doi:10.1177/0255761421996373

Isabirye, J. (2021b). Indigenous music learning in contemporary contexts: Nurturing learner identity, agency, and passion. *Research Studies in Music Education, 43*(2), 239–258. doi:10.1177/1321103X20954548

Kafumbe, D. (2018). *Tuning the kingdom: Kawuugulu musical performance, politics, and storytelling in Buganda*. University of Rochester Press.

Kasozi, A.B. (2013). *The bitter bread of exile: The financial problems of Sir Edward Muteesa II during his final exile, 1966–1969*. Progressive Publishing House.

Kenyatta, J. (1965). *Facing Mount Kenya: The tribal life of the Gikuyu*. Random House.

Kidula, J.N. (2019). Music and musicking: Continental Africa's junctures in learning, teaching and research. In E.A. Akuno (Ed.), *Music education in Africa: Concept, process, and practice* (pp. 14–30). Routledge.

Kirindi, P.G.N. (2008). *History and culture of the kingdom of Ankole*. Fountain Publishers.

Kramer, J., & Arnold, A. (2004). Music 200 Understanding music: An inquiry-guided approach to music appreciation. In V.S. Lee (Ed.), *Teaching & learning through inquiry: A guide for institutions & instructors* (pp. 41–50). Stylus Publishing, LLC.

Marsh, K. (2008). *The musical playground: Global tradition and change in children's songs and games*. Oxford University Press.

Mukasa, D.G. (1977). A brief anthology on Uganda musical instruments. Comb Books. https://etheses.whiterose.ac.uk/315/1/uk_bl_ethos_487748.pdf

Nketia, J.H.K. (1974). *The music of Africa*. W.W. Norton.

Okumu, C. (2000). Towards an appraisal of criticism on Okot p'Bitek's poetry. In E. Breitinger (Ed.), *Uganda: The cultural landscape* (pp. 133–158). Fountain Publishers.

Oviawe, J.O. (2016). How to rediscover the ubuntu paradigm in education. *International Review of Education, 62*(1), 1–10. doi:10.1007/s11159-016-9545-x

Pond, S.B. (2004). All in the balance: Psychology 201 Controversial issues in psychology. In V.S. Lee (Ed.), *Teaching & learning through Inquiry: A guide for institutions & instructors* (pp. 31–40). Stylus Publishing, LLC.

Ssekamwa, J.C. (1997). *History and development of education in Uganda*. Fountain Publishers.

Wenger, E. (1998). *Communities of practice: Learning, meaning, and identity*. Cambridge University Press.

7

ON LANGUAGE, COLONIALITY, AND RESISTANCE

A Conversation between Abdirachid Ismail and Christopher B. Knaus

Abdirachid Ismail and Christopher B. Knaus

Abdirachid M. Ismail holds a Ph.D. in Somali dialectology. He is a teacher at the University of Djibouti and Vice President of the Independent Research Institute of the Horn of Africa (IRICA). His parents were born in Somalia and migrated to Djibouti, where young Abdirachid was born and raised. Abdirachid's first language is Somali, and he also speaks French, English, and understands local Arabic. Our conversation was held via remote technology, transcribed, and edited for clarity.

ABDIRACHID: I became a professor in 2003, and before then I worked in France where I did all my university studies. I went to France because Djibouti was colonised by the French and back then, there was no university after secondary school. So after secondary schools, we were automatically sent to France, with a national or French scholarship. After my studies, I worked in different professional positions in France, one of them being a position as a purchaser for some big companies…It was destiny that I had to come back to Djibouti, not to stay there indefinitely, and then to become a professor at the University of Djibouti, to shift my purpose…and then to meet you!

CHRIS: Definitely destiny, my brother. In your writings, you talk about English as the most recent colonising language, on top of French and Arabic before that, which are all on top of Afar and Somali. How did we get to the place where we just continually push down local languages? And elevate outside languages?

ABDIRACHID: Well, the sociolinguists say this is linked to a very simple factor. In the marketplace of languages, each one has an economical weight. If a language gives economic opportunities, enables access to a higher standard of life, then people tend to learn that one language. They appreciate that one language. That's the predominant factor...In Djibouti, this factor was not determinant for the French, instead that is a sociopolitical factor which has established its domination, as well as for Arabic. For example, children learn mainly French in the beginning, and then Arabic, and finally English in school. Arabic is taught nowadays from almost the first year of school, it is more present than in my time, whereas it does not offer more economic opportunities yet. It is the second official language of the country. But we do not have the opportunity to learn Somali or Afar in schools.

CHRIS: Wait—the Somali-speaking population in Djibouti is large.

ABDIRACHID: The population of Djibouti is around one million, and proportionally many of them speak Somali. But we have three Communities in Djibouti, and it has not been easy to choose only one language for all these Communities. They have gone through conflict and power disputes all along the colonisation period, and even after. That was the reason why Djiboutian authorities decided not to change the colonial educational system based on French language, to maintain peace, and to give equal rights to all these communities, especially between Afar and Somalis. So, if one language is taught, then the other has to be taught, too. That means that Somali children, as well as the other communities' children, learn their respective mother tongue among their family, their neighbours, and, in one word, outside the schools.

CHRIS: So, we use the term equality to make it so that nobody learns Indigenous language. I don't think that's what equality means.

ABDIRACHID: Yes, since we cannot do for one, we will not do for both. Equality for all is inequality for all.

CHRIS: I mean we're laughing but obviously this is a colonial decision. I'm imagining in Djibouti, like most countries on the continent, people don't speak French or English when they're with their families or when they're out shopping or just hanging out. They mostly speak Somali, right?

ABDIRACHID: Right. Or Afar or Arabic. And when they are in official or more formal places, they switch to French, sometimes to Arabic.

CHRIS: This is how colonisation works. I mean you said it—it's an economic language, to speak in a colonial term, and if you want to speak your own language, we withdraw the money from it.

ABDIRACHID: Yes, to some extent, that's it. In the formal situation, we use foreign language. And informal situation, we use our own national languages. In media or at work, during meetings, we sometimes use mixed languages. We call that code switching, when we go from one language to another. That is something very common among educated people in Djibouti, as in any diglossic or multilingual context.

CHRIS: I notice that you use the term 'foreign language' for French or English and then national language for Somali and Afar.

ABDIRACHID: Yes, French is historically related to colonisation, and English is socially implemented in these last 20 years…almost as a heritage of September 11, 2001. That's why we speak about 'foreign languages'…Arabic is an official language, and the Djiboutians use certain dialects of Arabic, more precisely South-Arabian dialects. It is difficult not to count these dialects among national languages. So official languages are Arabic and French, and the national languages are Somali and Afar and dialects in Arabic, but the latter are not given official status. These terminologies hide the fact that the majority of people speak national languages but cannot use them in official national conversations.

CHRIS: That is so problematic, especially because, as may have written about, people prefer the language they grew up with, especially if that has a cultural connection to family history.

ABDIRACHID: Yes, people love their languages…at least, I know that Somali people love their own. Somali is seen as a language embedded with so much poetry and oral literature, stories, proverbs, sayings, that are very rich. An old Somali intellectual has written that

> Somali is a copious language, with a great number of words; in every respect it is a rich language, its words and expressions, its poetry and proverbs, its odes and elegies, its poems and plays, its songs and ballads, its stories and tales, its written and oral genres, whatever aspect we consider, it is a great language, full of wisdom and sayings that convey profound ideas.
>
> *(Ciise, 2005, p. 13)*

I don't know if you have ever read or heard about Richard Burton and Waterfield's (1856/1966) *First Footsteps in East Africa*. He depicted Somali people as a nation of poets and storytellers. Somalis are fond of poetry and storytelling, but not that much in French. In Djibouti, young people who attend to schools in French are not so fond of their own culture and language. That is somehow the result of the type of colonisation which has prevailed in Djibouti, based on assimilation to French culture and promoted through the educational system which excluded local languages and cultures. In the other parts of East Africa, in other Somali territories, Somalis use their language in official and formal situations, in media, business, university, everywhere. And of course those Somalis mastered the language and use it in all its potentiality. The language there reflects their cultural backgrounds and is very rich. Djiboutians and Somalis love Somali. When we are a certain age, we tend to try to sing in Somali and to learn poetry, but we do not have the opportunity to learn it in school.

CHRIS: So where do you learn Somali?

ABDIRACHID: At home, on the street, in informal places. It's why when we gather with Somalis from other parts of East Africa, sometimes they mock us, saying 'Oh, you don't speak very well,' [laughter] 'Your Somali is not that strong,' etc. They mock us if we speak 'Djiboutian Somali.'

CHRIS: So other Somali speakers who may have been able to study it more look down on those who live somewhere where they cannot study it.

ABDIRACHID: Exactly…There is a special form of Somali language emerging in Djibouti, with many, many words in French. One of my students and colleague, Hawa Abdillahi, recently defended her thesis on Djiboutian Somali, used specially by young generation of Djiboutians. This variety is becoming a mixed language in the proper sense. Hawa Abdillahi's thesis clarifies sociolinguistic dimensions and how this variety works.

CHRIS: Beautiful. Young people doing this on their own, making language because they're not learning this in school.

ABDIRACHID: Yes. And the French is so present, it almost becomes their first language. So they use the two, they mix it with Arabic dialects, too.

CHRIS: That's beautiful, isn't it? Young people essentially saying, 'You're not going to teach us Somali but I'm still going to use this language and I'm going to bring in other words from other languages that I have to speak in.'

ABDIRACHID: In a certain way, maybe, but it is a natural outcome in a languages contact situation…now we are in a kind of linguistic transition, with different languages in competition. In this unstable linguistical context, youth are expected to have sound and stable linguistic competences…Whereas the infant, 3 or 4 years, is put in the school where he or she only hears French or Arabic, although her or his own language system is not yet stable and they get another system on top of it, and this is problematic.

CHRIS: Right! That's why you start using the language that you know, so you incorporate French words into Somali, you still make language but you're making language with a foundation that isn't fully developed. I mean it's beautiful, in the sense of how young people make language work for them. But also to your point in your writings, we could be providing that foundation for both languages.

ABDIRACHID: Exactly. That is what I am advocating for. But we see the youth mixing languages, inventing a new form of expressing themselves, we won't say 'Beautiful! That's great.' No, no! Because of our prescriptive set of mind, we judge them negatively, saying that they are incapable of speaking rightly their language. In one hand, we do not permit them to learn their mother tongue, and we put them in a situation where their first language is undervalued, and in the other hand, when they use their own skills to adapt their language, invent new forms of expression, we disqualify them.

CHRIS: You say that you are advocating for teaching local languages, how do you make that happen when the school system in Djibouti won't do it? Look, I'm in the United States, we teach English as if it is the only language that exists, so I recognise that teaching children to be multilingual is a political problem. But how do we get school systems to say we're going to teach all five languages?

ABDIRACHID: That's it! You are right, the answer is not so simple…that question has been discussed for a long time in Africa, since independences at least. My personal view, after some assumptions, is that we should not begin to introduce national languages in the elementary school in Djibouti, but first in nursery schools (see Ismail, 2015). You have to learn your national language, your home language, in nursery school. To first learn a foreign language in nursery school is cognitively nonsense. Someone has said that if we do not teach a language, we condemn it to death, but we need to put in place a strategy which is sustainable. To really teach a national language, we have to adopt a systemic strategy. The first is to teach it in nursery school until 3 or 4 years, if we have to begin the formal education from nursery. In elementary classrooms, that is more complex, because we have this pyramidal system where elementary schools are so numerous…So introducing the national languages at that level means a great amount of money. Financially it is very expensive. Also, it is far more complex than in the other levels of education because we have certain schools with more Afar, and others with more Somalis, so how do we teach both without separating children? Without implementing some separation in their minds that they are different? Because of these difficult questions and other reasons, Djibouti decided not to introduce national languages in the educative system, neither in the nursery, which still belongs mainly to the private sector, nor anywhere. The education professionals think home language development is pertinent to youth at the elementary stage, indeed it's ideal. But practically it is very difficult.

So I think that it is more efficient to introduce Somali and Afar in secondary school, when youth have more interest in learning their own language. And they can put themselves into the language class they prefer. As there are less schools, less classes in the secondary, so we would need less teachers, compared to elementary schools. So in the secondary schools, you would have both Afar and Somalis in the same classes. This means we would not separate at elementary levels, but in secondary, where we can create more specialisations, we can deepen national languages and culture classes, and children can choose the language they want to follow.

And at university, we should also have mandatory courses. I think that we can introduce Somali and Afar most smoothly at the end first, and then we begin, 1 year before each year. And year by year, until we integrate through elementary schools. So you build it from the end first, and move towards the beginning. But, people think usually to begin at primary school, but that has not worked, even in other parts of Africa. If we begin in secondary school, at least it will be easier. I published this in 2015, and yet there is no reaction so, here we are.

CHRIS: Ha! Part of the problem is when we write things, who is reading? Who has access?

ABDIRACHID: That is right. In most African countries, there are not scientific medias. So researchers have to share they writings with those they may interest, especially with decision-makers. It is what I have tried to do with this article by sending it to the Ministry of Education. But, you see usually the politicians prefer not to tackle the difficult problems, especially if these issues seem not urgent or vital.

I think that the problem is not that the official languages are foreign languages. In some developed countries, the official is a foreign language like in Singapore, where the first and official language is English. But we cannot simply think of language in terms of economical profit. We have to think of language teaching as helping to implement a certain mindset, linked to a certain cultural ecosystem. And if you just download some others from outside that are different from your own ecosystems, sometimes, it can be problematic. Very problematic. Languages are so closely related to culture, and sometimes we may cut off the link if we only teach the languages valued only in the market.

CHRIS: I think about the idea of singing in somebody else's language. South Africa has 11 official languages, but in practice, the official language is English. But there are ten other official languages. I guess it's nice to be called 'official' but the all the exams are in English, with the exception of language exams, which are obviously in Zulu or isiXhosa or Setswana or one of the other official languages. But all of the other required subjects are in English. So while it is nice that everybody can speak one language…

ABDIRACHID: …Every generation speaks less and less the national languages. It is why we speak about endangered languages. We are erasing systems, both locally within the country and across Africa. What about in their families? Do they speak English and their own national languages in South Africa?

CHRIS: Yes! Most families will prefer to speak their own language. And apartheid intentionally segregated by race, culture, and language to where most of an entire township speaks one language. So almost everyone in a specific township, or at least a neighbourhood within a township, shares one language. For example, this is an Xhosa township, this other is more Tswana, and this could be more of a Zulu-speaking township.

ABDIRACHID: There is a kind of nationalistic behaviour there. So, is Zulu the predominant language?

CHRIS: Zulu is the most common of the nine African languages. There are two languages that I'd consider foreign for this conversation, English and Afrikaans, though that is much more complicated as Afrikaans is a localised adaptation between Dutch and so-called Coloured linguistic communities. But yes, there are nine compared to the two in Djibouti, but even then, there are others, including more recent immigrant communities, and Khoi and San, which are historic Indigenous languages. And everybody speaks a little bit of English. If you grew up in South Africa, if your family language is Zulu, you tend to speak Zulu first. Especially if you are raised in a township, where your local crèche [preschool] is likely to still be in Zulu. English might not come until formal school starts. So there is a strong foundation, but not the model you propose and there are huge issues with validating capitalistic languages.

ABDIRACHID: I think, to your point, it is still not enough and it seems that globally, instead of increasing the amount that we teach language, we're decreasing.

CHRIS: Totally. So why do you keep fighting when you know we just keep losing?

ABDIRACHID: [Laughter] You know—I'm not fighting any longer!

CHRIS: [Laughter] Did you stop?

ABDIRACHID: [Laughter] In languages, I think so. Because I feel that we have done what we can do as a scholar or researcher. Our role is to think, to study, to write, sometimes to teach. And then the job is over. Instead, we need the politicians for this. I think that today, we have ideas of how to tackle this problem. But for political reasons, we don't want to. So maybe we need to wait for another generation of politicians, a younger generation. I hope that it will be not too late for Indigenous languages.

CHRIS: Yeah, I don't think young people want to wait very long.

ABDIRACHID: I hope so! But you're right, we know what we need to do. You see, we are thinking about this concept of decolonisation, and even if we may have some reserves to use this term, in higher education, in research, in knowledge production, and many other aspects, this is a central issue. Even if you speak a foreign language as a first language and you try to adapt it to your needs, it will take more time to adapt this language to your current local ecosystem. But if we can create our own representations, imaginations, our own realities with our own concepts, ways of thinking with a foreign language, why not after all—at least we have this possibility. Knowledge, understanding, creativity, that is what matter after all. Language is a means, above all. Indeed, every language has born and grown up in a specific cultural, civilisational field, and is most adapted to that. But if you want to grow apples in a semi-arid land, don't be surprised if you don't get granny or golden apples, expect to get other kinds of apples, if you can still call them 'apples.'

The trouble is that we honour just one way of thinking. And even in science, this is a huge issue for us, because there are certain postulates and assumptions that we do not really agree on. And this is one of the big reasons that Africa is not going down the path of what you call development, because the assumptions behind modern science are not the same as those on which the cosmovisions of Africa are based. And language is part of those assumptions and that vision. For example, in the modern world, the writing is much more valued than orality, whereas in Africa, the spoken has word much more power that the written one. You may have heard this famous Sufi story of the man who has lost the key to his house and was looking for it under a street-lamp, but without finding it. When he was asked if he was sure he lost it there, he replied 'No!,' and pointed his finger towards a remote dark place. So, why was he looking for it at that place? 'Because,' he said, 'there is no light over there.'

CHRIS: What you're saying challenges 'development' as a colonial tool, raising questions as to what we mean by decolonisation. So if you're on a pathway to being colonised, then you may be able to be more developed but that means you have to embrace some assumptions that are very singular.

ABDIRACHID: Singular, and historically dated, that is one point. The other point is that colonisation never leads to development of any kind, but to impoverishment of every kind…

CHRIS: One aspect of decolonising is recognising and honouring and strengthening language. National languages, Indigenous languages, whatever the term. But even if you do that without also helping people recognise that this is just one way…

ABDIRACHID: Exactly. There has to be recognition of more than one way. Even if people in Somalia, in Ethiopia, if they can speak their own language everywhere, it doesn't mean that the knowledge they use are from themselves…the knowledge production, the academic books, etc. they still come mainly from outside. So even if you can speak in your language, everything is from outside, science, education, medicine, technology, industry, etc., all this conveying a certain model of thinking and a particular relation to life and to the outer world… an interiority and an exteriority that implies a particular ontology. They are just downloading and trying to adapt themselves to this one way. This is what we are doing, across Africa, and maybe across the world today.

CHRIS: I like how you say that they're just downloading, versus creating knowledge. Earlier, you said that the Somali language is a language of poets and storytelling, but if we're just downloading, we are not creating a story, or creating poetry. You may be downloading poetry, but you're not creating it.

ABDIRACHID: Yes! Until now we see Somali poets who are conscious about this. Who are struggling against the invasion of cultural by-products of invading civilisations, who discuss the trap of what is given, made available, offered turnkey, versus what is created, thought, imagined by oneself…in a sense the conflict between traditionalism and modernism, and we have lenses, across time, from poets to this kind of confrontation. And they are seeing what is happening, how things are changing. We have really big poets, who are very deep thinking. And today some of them have travelled outside, they've been in the U.K., in Europe, in the States. And they have got the opportunity to see other realities to compare to their own reality and then to produce some knowledge, some powerful thinking, a very rich poetry.

CHRISTOPHER: This sounds like they are talking about survival. Intellectual survival.

ABDIRACHID: Sure, in a certain way. Intellectual survival. That's it....
I'm now writing an article on African scientific research, trying to understand why it is still down and not going up... So we see the gap between these two kinds of visions. One vision based on European ethno-science developed in the sixteenth to nineteenth centuries—so this is all very recent. And another vision based on traditional African science, deep rooted in the African cosmovision. So it is difficult to change it. We already have a hardware in mind and we like to replace it with a software coming from outside, and we are all surprised because the applications of that software are not working...we keep forcing these applications to work, that is fundamentally of colonisation is about.

CHRIS: That's right—because they're designed to be singular. Like we have trained people to be singular, to cancel out multiple perspectives. So the program or research or educational approach is literally not designed to acknowledge multiple conflicting things happening at the same time. But that's the world, multiple conflicting things happening at the same time.

ABDIRACHID: Exactly! We do not accept multiple possibilities. For example, we have the assumption that unity is wonderful, that unity is peaceful. And we try unity like it's an algorithm, like we can just program it, or we can just produce, unity. But we cannot, because we are not singular. Humanity is a wonderful machine that can cope with diversity, complexity. And this is what makes the difference between humans and machines.

This rationality on which everything is based now today is good for machines. It works. Yes, a computer can beat Gary Kasparov at a game. But, it can't have what human beings have. It cannot have intuition and many other human competencies. Thinking and rationality, yes, we can ingrain it. But happiness and love? It can imitate, but human energy, and what we are? No. That complexity that makes us human—only human beings can cope with something as complex as us.

CHRIS: What you are talking about is decolonising the entire system. Not just education, but the entire way that we think about and structure society.

ABDIRACHID: Exactly. Education is just one piece. Language is just one piece. Economy. Competition. Profits. We can live differently. Why always competition? Yes, for profits. But what kind of profit? How?

When I came back to Djibouti, and as I have been in a business school in France, I said to my family, I will create for you a business. So, what kind of business? I thought about it, I saw what is happening in Djibouti and in our small neighbourhood square, and said, 'Okay, a company which provides goods to little shops in a certain area.' So the big one who provides for the little shops, because these big shops do not exist in every quarter, in every part of town. So I said I will build this for you and then you will have revenue. And Mom says, 'No, I don't want this great thing. Just a little shop. It's enough for us.' I said, 'Mom, there are so many little shops. We can see five shops in just 100-meter square, we cannot compete here.' She says, 'Competition? No? God provides to everyone. We do not take something else. We do just our own business.'

She, and my family and everybody here are convinced that you will not take the revenue of another person. Life is already predestined. But at the same time, they will not do an action to try to get other customers and to make any others fail. They would not try to make another business fail. So no marketing. Just living at the same place and in the same way. So we have done that, and the little shop is still there. It's just a different way of doing the economy. Of doing the economy in harmony.

CHRIS: I appreciate that example because I'm thinking of the term you used earlier: That's unity!

ABDIRACHID: Yes, exactly. It is unity, a living unity, not an ideologised unity. The basic assumptions are equality, respect, etc… It is what is in the culture. Everyone has the same right.

CHRIS: Right. That's a beautiful cultural foundation that recognises that taking from someone so that you can have more is actually not unity; it disrupts unity. Good people do not do that.

ABDIRACHID: Yes, it's actually not fair. Normally, good people do not do this. But today, it is normal. And this is what we teach in the schools: Teach how to get the revenue from others, to kill other businesses, to grow at the expense of the others, to attract all the money, all the energy, because money is energy, to extract all the energy around, to keep it for oneself in a bank. This way of acting is the norm, the one that must be followed, the one that allows the development they say! What development?

CHRIS: That's right. We teach this. Do we not begin this system, when we give a grade to a student? When we say, 'You, you have high marks, but you here, you don't have high marks.' Not everybody can pass, we must have failures. But why not? Why can everyone not pass?

ABDIRACHID: You are right, every aspect of this worldwide system has to be questioned, because the old assumptions on which this system is based are no longer workable. And you are right, everyone has special competencies, but because we have neither the tools nor time to know that, and because our system is built on a certain vision of excellency, we judge kids according to that binary good or bad assessment.

CHRIS: You just broke down capitalism in 1 hour!

ABDIRACHID: [Laughter] Capitalism is so strong. We need some kind of David [to battle Goliath].

CHRIS: [Laughter] We need a lot of David! But he's probably not going to be named David, he's probably going to be Mohammed or something.

ABDIRACHID: [Laughter] I don't know because you see, Muslim countries are not less capitalistic. Some days I am feeling that they are more capitalistic, in some ways like the old Europe.

CHRIS: Listen, we can't go anywhere in this world that isn't colonised by the West. And at some point, capitalistic infused. I don't think there's anywhere left.

ABDIRACHID: Yes, but you see Chris, the feeling that today we are all colonised is widespread, maybe everywhere in the world. Because I've been living in France for a long time and been to many countries in Europe, and the people in Europe are also feeling that something is not going right, the idea that we are colonised by a certain mindset, felt by many Europeans, not the big companies, not the temples of science, is something tangible, I call it the narrow-minded rationalistic science, and its offspring, this ridiculous capitalism which poisons the earth on which it has emerged, deprives the world of the energy from which it has sucked, saws off the branch on which it sits. This way of thinking has uprooted the spiritual, non-rational ways of thinking. If we stay at this level of rationality, we become machines. If we stay here, we will remain very rational. So we need to become non-rational again…

CHRIS: Or we fail at love.

ABDIRACHID: [Laughter] Exactly. The bearer of this mindset is Westerners, scientific organisations, capitalistic institutions, etc. These big organisations promote this mindset, and we see what has happened with COVID-19. And the discrepancy between common sense and the scientists with their trials and tribulations. In France, we have followed this. Totally mad. We have seen how science can be made to lie…how it can be easily distorted, because of capitalist interests, and power control issues…

CHRIS: You are right. This disjoint between reality and imagination, in part because science has been so singular in its approach.

ABDIRACHID: Exactly. We have gone through all of this kind of situation before. And they were rougher then. When a certain cosmogony dominates and structures our way of seeing the world, it leaves no chance for another truth to emerge, simply because this way of seeing the world has become the stock-in-trade of a certain social class…this is something classic in history. So we are in the same kind of transitional period, and we have to face it, so that the next generations can have less rough of a situation. Our positivity is very important! If more people are positive, I think something can happen. So not to lose heart, because losing heart means that life is just finished in this world. As most of Africans, I think that life is not only limited to this world. There is a continuity. We are living for just a short time and we must try to live as best as we can, and to do what we can do in the best manner. And then go onto another experience.

CHRIS: That's the Somali poet coming out of you.

ABDIRACHID: [Laughter] No, no, Somali indeed, but not a poet…I never fully learned Somali in the right ways. But Somalis are still great poets, they seem free in their mind, they have not yet mentally been colonised, at least they think so, maybe wrongly. But even that leads to problems. Sometimes we think we are the best thinkers, the best poets, the best everything. We maybe think that all other people have faults. Either they are Christian—that's not good. Or Jewish—that's not good. They are African, they are Arab—all not good!

CHRIS: [Laughter] That's not unity!

ABDIRACHID: [Laughter] No, but that's a big problem we still have.

CHRIS: That's universal, isn't it?

ABDIRACHID: Yes, probably.

CHRIS: Thank you so much, brother, for your time, energy, and insight! I appreciate that we moved from language to coloniality to looking at a new vision for the world, where we challenge capitalism, knowledge, and singularity of a taking vision towards one that is more aligned with your mom's notion of a business.

ABDIRACHID: Thank you for this informal conversation, without much filter, and for having given me the opportunity to share with you on these important topics.

References

Burton, R., & Waterfield, G. (1856/1966). *First footsteps in East Africa: An exploration of Harar*. Praeger.

Ciise, J.C. (2005). *Himilada Maansaddii hore: Geela, Fardaha iyo Haweenka*. Xarunta Cilmi Baadhista ee Jabuuti.

Ismail, A.M. (2015). Enseigner les langues nationales à Djibouti, une autre approche. In C.M. Ismaaciil, C.C. Mansuur, & S.A. Sharci (Eds.), *Afmaal: Proceedings of the conference on the 40th anniversary of Somali orthography*. Akadeemiye-Goboleedka Afsoomaaliga (AGA).

8
(DE)COLONISING PHYSICAL EDUCATION IN GHANA

Bella Bello Bitugu and Austin Wontepaga Luguterah

Education and training for the acquisition of skills and knowledge are critical components of human development worldwide (Wilson, 2014), and Ghana and the African continent are no exceptions. Formal education provides not only high-level skills necessary for labour markets but also the training essential for the human resources needed to run and operate within systems (Johansson, Fogelberg-Dahm, & Wadensten, 2010). It is these human resources that drive and direct organisations to make important decisions which affect society. The process, however, is not nearly as straightforward and smooth as it sounds, especially for countries of the Global South who had Western systems of teaching, learning, and training imposed through colonisation.

In Ghana, one key area of national development that has been greatly influenced by colonial mindsets and perspectives is physical education. Most often through sport and games, physical education aims to develop students' physical competence, knowledge of movement and safety, and their ability to perform in a wide range of activities. It permeates all aspects of life from infancy. The realm of physical education, which includes competitive physical activity through casual or organised participation, is a platform that is often overlooked in its need to decolonise. Yet physical education has played an important role in the development and decolonisation of Ghana because children and youth, spanning all levels from nursery to university, have opportunities to engage in it (Asare, 1982). The strength of Physical Education in developing the cognitive, psychomotor, and affective skills of the individual invariably contribute to the development of self, community, and country; this means that physical education curriculum and teaching must be purposeful and localised to intentionally benefit Ghanaian society (Amusa & Toriola, 2010).

DOI: 10.4324/9781003158271-8

In traditional educational settings, physical activities teach diverse lessons and serve many purposes. The reality of physical education in Ghana after the adoption of Western systems, however, misses the localisation and contextualisation of movement, sport, and related skill sets. The adoption of such Western systems, then, minimises the results of a physical education curriculum, and instead limits the development of students, teachers, and the education system (Chepyator-Thomson, 2014). This coloniality can be traced to how physical education was introduced and integrated into the education system and its impact on education and Ghana (Aissat & Djafri, 2011). This chapter thus identifies the process of colonisation and decolonisation of physical education in Ghana, providing examples from other countries with similar backgrounds and history.

This chapter introduces the purpose and nature of the various systems of education in Ghana, by tracing and identifying the traditional systems of education, values, philosophies, and societal purpose. This is followed by analyses of the colonial system of education first introduced by missionaries and merchants. Physical education during independence and post independent Ghana is then discussed, highlighting strategies towards decolonising physical education. This chapter clarifies that even though there have been intentions, practical steps, and measures to decolonise physical education in Ghana, decoloniality has not been realised. This is mainly due to the deep-seated colonial infrastructure that shapes physical education. In addition, the strategies adopted by independent Ghana to address and tackle the colonial system of physical education ultimately continue what was inherited before political independence. Finally, we suggest strategies to decolonise, including prioritising and standardising the training of traditional sports and recreation activities into the foundation of physical education.

Physical Education in Ghana

The first and still existing system of physical education in Ghana is the Indigenous system of education, which started in pre-colonial society. While colonial school systems have limited the transmission of Indigenous education, many Indigenous forms have persisted and have evolved to the present day. Physical activities play a vital role across traditional Indigenous curriculum and permeate almost all aspects of life (Abdou, 1968). Traditional games have been recognised as significant parts of the cultural heritage and the system of traditional education in Ghana (Amusa & Toriola, 2010). Rather than foster competition, traditional games and sports provide unique opportunities based on fun and participation, providing more benefits than contemporary games and sports (Pic, Lavega-Burgués, & March-Llanes, 2019). Traditional games and sports are expressions of Indigenous cultures and ways of life, which contribute to the common identity of both colonial and post-colonial Ghana.

In traditional society, recreational subjects include wrestling, dancing, drumming, acrobatic display, and racing, while intellectual training include the study of oral history, legends, the environment, local geography, plants, animals, poetry, reasoning, riddles, proverbs, and storytelling. Traditional games have proven to be the most important and attractive ways to improve physical, mental, affective, and social health of members of a society. Such activities promote physical health, improve one's spiritual and mental state, and institutionalise cultural values (Edwards, 2009, p. 32). Such physical activity is therefore an integral part of the life of old and modern Ghana, both as recreation and as a profession (Biritwum, Gyapong, & Mensah, 2005).

Historical background of traditional games in Ghana shows that they have always formed an integral part of the social life of the people (Asare, 1982). Games and sports in the traditional setting have two main functions, namely improving physical stamina and practising rituals. In the traditional system, physical strength was seen as a community asset and not for personal purposes. Traditional games involve actions infused with religious and mythical touches for observing rituals. Indeed, in addition to the functions mentioned above, traditional games are used in performances during festivals and special occasions (Greene, 2002). During festivals, traditional games combine aesthetic features with tenacity to bring about cultural values, as well as foster cooperation and unity, entertainment, and valuable social impacts (Newell, 2002).

Among the Mole-Dagbani, the Bulsa, the Kassena, and Sissala ethnic groups of northern parts of Ghana, traditional games and sports were seen as the avenue to display manliness and physical prowess. It was also seen as a way to maintain physical health and improve one's spiritual and mental state. Generally, traditional games and sports, as practised in the northern parts of Ghana, were designed after war victories and as such involved vigorous physical activities. Games and sports were therefore considered to be valuable tools to shape an individual's ethnic and community identity and to organise specific cultural values and beliefs (Thomas, 1974).

The practice of physical education is thus inherently deep in the various ethnic communities in Ghana, which developed physical prowess as an integral part of the traditional process associated with games, dance, food gathering, hunting, pastoral activities, and farming (Nabie, 2008). Apart from inculcating in the individual psychomotor, cognitive, and affective skills, these cultural activities also expose the individual to the cultural values of the community (Asare, 1982). And all these mean they are purposeful and serve the community and nation, for such activities are made by the people and for the people. Traditional games and sports in Ghana were designed to develop a holistic child who would be useful to themselves and the society. The games involved feats of strength, endurance, balance, focus, reflexes, flexibility, agility, and patience. Even under the moonlight, traditional games kept children busy physically and mentally. Some traditional games and sports in Ghana include wrestling, *Ampe, Ole, Oware, Pilolo, Chaskele*, and *Tia Mu Na Tow*, among many others.

Ampe

Ampe is a rhythmic girls game from Ghana, which involves clapping, jumping, dancing, and singing activities for several minutes. The game helps in bonding communities, enhances physical fitness, coordination, and encourages teamwork (Agbenyega, 2009). The game also helps to build skills in all the domains of physical education (physical, cognitive, social, affective).

FIGURE 8.1 Ampe.

Tumatu

This is a Ghanaian version of hopscotch. This game uses the strategic acquisition of more 'rooms' in the forms of boxes. The participant jumps into box after box until the end of the last box, and then returns to the starting point in the same manner. After successful completion of the jumps, the participant can 'acquire' a box that no one can step into. The more boxes you have, the more power you have. Other participants have to jump over your box house into an empty box to continue. The point of the game is to put your opponent in a position that forces them to make and hopefully fail at near impossible jumps. This game develops balance, socialisation, teamwork, and coordination in the participants (Dennis, 2018).

FIGURE 8.2 Tumatu.

Pilolo

The game is played among five or more children with one child chosen to be the leader of the game. An object—usually a stick—is used and the number of sticks to be used is dependent on the number of children. The leader hides the sticks away from the participants and later signals them to search for the sticks. Any person who sees the stick, picks it, and runs to a finish line. Apart from enhancing social interaction, the game builds participant agility and alertness and helps develop observation and reaction time (Komabu-Pomeyie, 2020).

Oware

The game of *Oware* requires a board with two straight rows of six pits each. Each pit is called a house, and the game is played with 48 seeds. Each player controls the six houses on their side of the board where seeds can be captured by the opponent. The game begins with four seeds in each of the twelve smaller houses. The objective of the game is to capture more seeds than one's opponent. Since the game has only 48 seeds, capturing 25 is sufficient to win. *Oware* has many variations and is considered a therapeutic tool to build self-esteem and improve critical thinking (Stoffle & Baro, 2016).

FIGURE 8.3 Pilolo.

Chaskele

This is a local bat-and-ball game, similar to cricket, played between two teams of two players or more. The game is played with a stick, a bucket, and a crushed can. Each player holds a crushed can and stands behind a line that is 5 to 7 metres away from a hole; by taking turns, they then attempt to throw the crushed can into a hole. After a round of throws, the players who get their crushed can in the hole will stand by the hole and prevent the others from getting their cans into the hole by hitting the cans as far as possible with a stick. The game of *Chaskele* improves endurance, stamina, balance, coordination, physical fitness, and hand-eye coordination (Gyadu, 2014).

Ole

The game is played with a basket placed 10 metres away in front of a demarcated line for each group. Players stand behind the lines and hold one orange each. When their number is mentioned, a player steps forward to throw the orange in the basket. The group with the highest number of oranges inside the basket wins the game. This activity can be repeated any number of times, but mostly in an odd repetition (e.g., 3, 5, 7, etc. times). This game aims at developing balance, socialisation, team work, and coordination in the participants (Dennis, 2018).

FIGURE 8.4 Oware.

These Indigenous games incorporate the four domains of learning: Psychomotor, cognitive, social, and affective. These domains are important in the development of young people. The psychomotor domain is concerned with the physical component of learning, including aspects of movement, coordination, and motor or physical skill. The cognitive domain is centred on intelligence and developing new knowledge and mental skills. The social domain is concerned with the interaction among people involved in the activities. The way they speak to each other, listen to each other, and physically respond to each other can affect their motivation and willingness to move. The affective domain is focused on emotional development. They are games that have helped develop the minds and bodies of young people while instilling in them Ghanaian values of collaboration, community, and creativity.

These are examples of historically rooted pre-colonial games that are still widely played today despite missionary and colonial attempts to centre manual labour or European sports as part of the colonising effort. In the following sections, we explore missionary and colonial forms of physical education and how these excluded Indigenous forms of physical education from the official curriculum.

FIGURE 8.5 Chaskele.

Missionary Education

The external system of education that exerted the most influence on physical education in Ghana were the missionary system, and later, the colonial system of education. The system of education that we know today and regard as the formal Western system of education was first introduced by Christian missionaries. The pioneers of the missionary system of education were the Portuguese who arrived on the West Coast of Ghana in the fifteenth century (Graham, 1976). In 1529, King George the Third of Portugal ordered the Portuguese governor at Elmina to teach the Ghanaians reading and writing of the holy scriptures. The Portuguese language was to be used in the schools, and every teacher was to be paid 240 grains of gold a year for each pupil he taught (Graham, 1976).

The scriptures and the languages of the missionaries were the media used to achieve the stated objectives of the system, which were mainly focused on spreading Christianity. Fafunwa (1967) observes that commerce, Christianity, and colonialism combined to exploit African souls. Lord Lugard (1965) asserted that, from a Western colonial orientation, African culture and religion had no system of ethics and no principle of conduct. The primary objectives of the early Christian schools were to convert the 'heathen' or the 'benighted African'

FIGURE 8.6 Ole.

to Christianity through 'western education' (Graham, 1976). The ability to sing hymns and recite catechism as well as the ability to communicate in colonial languages both orally and in writing were considered essential for a good Christian (Bitugu, 1997). This was the mindset of both the missionaries and the colonialists who ran the schools. The stage was indeed set for the colonialists to execute the mission of 'educating' and 'civilising' the colonies.

Mumford (1929) states that 'after a continual contact with the white races, the early Africans almost invariably deteriorated in art, morale and physique, and became disconnected or idle' (p. 139). McElligot (1950) also maintains that Africans must extract from Western culture only that which can harmoniously be fused with African culture. However, under colonisation, such extraction was nearly impossible; Africans had no say and determination in what was taught and included in the syllabi and curriculum. Given the nature of traditional education before the arrival of the Europeans and missionaries, one would have imagined and hoped that physical activities occupied a central stage in the curriculum of the missionaries when running their schools. But this was not possible.

Instead, whatever happened to be described as physical education was doing physical work like carrying, pushing, and manual work to instill morals and disciplines and to enable the execution of the general day-to-day activities of the people (Asare, 1982). McWilliam and Kwamena-Poh (1975) noted that the missionaries attempted to replace the existing African beliefs with Christianity by banishing traditional forms of training for citizenship, which they regarded as bulwarks of Satan. It was further observed by Asare (1982) that the missionary physical education least resembled the ideal physical education for young Ghanaians and was fraught with masculine, Christian, and Victorian British values. With the newly introduced Western system, Ghana started seeing the missed opportunity of streamlining and developing physical activity that had been very central in its survival and existence. This is to the extent that physical education was only given official recognition and inclusion in schools well over 400 years after contact with the first Europeans. This translates to 400 years of denial and exclusion of such a vital sector of the lives of the people—this was 400 years of the colonisation of the mind, system, and process.

Colonisation, Sports, and Physical Education

The British Government officially took over the rule of Ghana, which was then the Gold Coast, after the Foreign Jurisdiction Act of 1890, when Ashanti was declared a colony and the northern territories a protectorate (Colonial Office, 1950). In 1900, orders in Council were also passed which annexed all territories in the Gold Coast south of the Ashanti as a British colony by settlement. Colonisation took control of every aspect of the society. The colonialist, irrespective of the power it wielded over the colonies, came to see the introduction of Western types of schooling and education as essential to the objectives set for their coming to the Gold Coast. They took full control of education by taking over its organisation and administration from the missionaries. However, the physical education that was part of the missionary education did not feature in the curriculum of the schools at the beginning of colonialism (Asare, 1982).

Governor John Rodger (1909) of colonial Kenya argued that the British colonialists ought to develop all the native races on the lines of their natural evolution and not to substitute Indigenous laws and customs with something that the colonists thought was better merely because it happens to be in force in Britain. But Governor Rodger's observation was neither heeded nor noted. Britain went ahead and imposed its own idea of physical education in the colonial education system. Asare (1982) indicates that gaining insight into the aspects of physical education in the Gold Coast could only be understood by juxtaposing what was happening in Britain itself.

Thus, the physical education that was introduced in the twentieth century in Ghana through the British was a replica of what was happening in Britain. Physical education in the early twentieth century was revised in the curriculum in Britain in 1905 and 1909 (Asare, 1982). The defining object of physical education in Britain was to promote health in body and mind (Board of Education,

1909). In order to improve physical education in Britain, colleges were established in 1903 in Manchester, Bournemouth, and Bedford (Asare, 1982). According to Asare (1982), when Governor Clifford assumed office in Ghana in 1904, there were no government-owned training colleges because most were educated in missionary schools. In 1900, a government training college was established to train local teachers. At the college, drills, and physical instructions were given twice a week.

This prompted Rodger (1909) to address the African Society, which was an association aimed at promoting relations between Britain and colonised African countries and producing scholarly works with programmes in education, politics, business, and arts and culture. Rodger (1909) outlined the progress being made in the field of sports and games to observe that the schoolboys were also devoted to cricket, with great natural aptitude for the game and hoping that within the next few years, the British colonialists may have the pleasure of seeing a team of West African cricketers come to play in Great Britain, and, if they do, he felt they will give a good account of themselves.

By far, however, the epoch that determined physical education in the Gold Coast was during the governorship of Governor Gordon Guggisberg. He is credited with laying the foundation for teaching physical education. The first physical education syllabus was introduced to schools during the Guggisberg era (Agbodeka, 1972). Guggisberg, under the Education Ordinance of 1925, formulated what was known as the 16 Principles of Education (Joyce, 1995). Among the formulated 16 principles was the requirement that games form a part of school life (McWilliam et al., 1975). It also emphasised the importance of character training and physical education training in the educational curriculum. The most important aspect of the policy was the compulsion for the construction of playing fields in all schools. Because of the physical education policy, physical education, sports, and organised games were made core subjects of the educational curriculum. Guggisberg also formed inter-schools sports competitions at the elementary and secondary school levels (Kirk-Greene, 1989). Achimota School (from Accra), Presbyterian Training College (from Akropong), Mfantsipim and Adisadel College (from Cape Coast) competed in 1926 for the Aggrey Shield sports competition, for instance. After 1933, a new curriculum replaced Guggisberg's educational reforms (Ocanse, Sofo & Baba, 2013). The new physical education syllabus emphasised rhythmic free movement, good posture, and agility without making provision for self-expression and individual skill learning. Nevertheless, the new syllabus allowed teachers to use local materials to create innovative teaching aids to teach physical education (Baba, Amui, Boateng, & Asiamoa, 1993).

It must be mentioned though that teachers of physical education had no expert guidance. In an attempt to salvage sports, according to Van Dalen and Bennett (1971), physical education became a school subject after the passage of the 1944 Education Act. The Act introduced three slots of 35-minute physical education lessons per week in elementary schools and two slots of 40-minute lessons per week in secondary schools. The new education act compelled each classroom teacher to be responsible for the teaching of physical education despite the fact that they were not specialist teachers, nor even trained, for physical education. In order to train teachers to have physical education knowledge, in 1950, a 1-year programme for physical education teachers was introduced at Achimota College and later transferred to the University College of Science and Technology, Kumasi (now Kwame Nkrumah University of Science and Technology) (Opoku-Fianko, 1985). In 1959, after evaluating the 8 years of training physical education specialists, the programme was upgraded to a 2-year programme of training and moved to the Government Training College in Winneba. Thus, the Gold Coast went through a similar process as Britain, paralleling a colonial development of physical education.

As physical education evolved over time, the needs and desires of Ghanaian society remained excluded, as colonising undertones remained the foundation. The new physical education syllabi emphasised the imposed physical activities, while continuing to ignore the values of Indigenous African sports and games (Ocansey et al., 2013). Contact with the European on Ghanaian soil thus marked the beginning of the erosion of the traditional games and sports in Ghana, and the beginning of the new chapter of European games and sports (Amusa & Toriola, 2010). The establishment of colonial and missionary models of education in Ghana created an environment where Indigenous physical activities were regarded as primitive, immoral, and anti-Christian (Joyce, 1995). According to Booth (1997), colonial education excluded several traditionally desired skills and behaviours from the curriculum.

To Asare (1982), the physical education department in Ghana was so chained to British ideals and methods that it never took into account any philosophy that privileged local perspectives or needs. Coward and Lane (1970) observed that physical education in Africa was too often regarded as a second-class subject—in part potentially because of Ghanaian apathy—and because it was often neglected, taught half-heartedly, or not at all. This observation may be attributed to limited teaching tools and trained teachers in the area. According to Whitehead and Hendry (1976), the curriculum allocated more time to practical lessons, while the theoretical aspects received less attention, thus further removing the historic connection between the intellectual and physical challenge of Indigenous sport and game. Adedeji (1980), for example, expressed the concern that the British should have devoted time towards the Indigenous cultures of Nigeria, but instead prepared Nigerians to participate within the allied forces in the First and Second World Wars. Likewise, in an attempt to identify the physical activities that are Indigenous in origin and sufficiently suitable enough for constructing a physical education syllabus for Nigerian elementary schools, Ajisafe (1976) criticised the British 1933 Physical Education syllabus that was transposed to Nigeria for failing to satisfy the developmental needs of the children in Nigerian culture.

From Independence to Institutionalising Sport

Despite educational reforms made after Guggisberg, physical education had not fundamentally transformed. The method of teaching physical education in the schools still mainly consisted of daily drills from ex-military men and war veterans, with the sole aim of instilling youth discipline (Opoku-Fianko, 1985). After becoming independent in 1957, the quest for national identity, African identity, and international recognition in all sectors became intense (Baba, 2000).

With the teaching, practice, and organisation of physical education in Ghana determined by European missionaries and colonialists, one would have expected that once independence was achieved, conscious policies and strategies would purge colonial structures. Indeed, this process of decolonising every aspect of life in Ghana, especially physical education, was to have started when Nkrumah took the lead in Ghana's independence struggle and then became the first president of Ghana with a Pan African ideology. In 1961, Nkrumah enacted his vision of a Ghana with national competitions to produce athletes for international contests. The entire educational system was intentionally aligned to provide continuous supplies of distinguished sports men and women (Charway & Houlihan, 2020). The introduction of the award for best sports men and women was introduced and named Osagyefo Meritorious Award for The Most Distinguished Sportsmen after the president of the republic. The president also appointed Ohene Djan, a trusted protege with little qualification in sports, to control everything related to sports (Adum-Kyeremeh, 2019). All these moves were clearly political interventions in sports rather than educational strategies to decolonise that are devoid of political, personal, and other interests.

Still, interest in sports grew among schools and the public, which led to long-term sports programming and competitions guided by a policy of compulsory intramural sports programmes for all school children in the newly independent nation to foster unity (Amusa & Toriola, 2010). Most of the schools and colleges in the country established departments of physical education with programmes for mass gymnastics and competitive sports such as football, track and field, boxing, table tennis, and cricket (Asare, 1982). Apart from competing in the Empire Day Games, sports programmes were taught and managed mostly by classroom teachers and military ex-servicemen (Opoku-Fianko, 1985).

Nkrumah's government responded to national expectations to promote physical education and sport by restructuring the course syllabus of the Teacher Training Colleges (TTCs) in Ghana to include physical education as one of the eight 'core' subjects of general education (Graham, 2013). To improve the quality of physical education in schools and to remove the colonial mindset, teacher education in the field of physical education was established to train teachers with intentional methodology (Sofo, Kpebu, & Belcher, 2007). In all these changes in the curriculum, however, traditional sports and games remained excluded. Even though all colleges of education in Ghana were producing teachers for basic and secondary schools, there were still some concerns that teacher college graduates did not develop the general and subject-specific competencies required by the basic schoolteacher, especially in physical education and sport (Mereku, 2019).

In the mind of the Ghanaian public, sports were synonymous with physical education and vice versa. The growth and popularity of physical education and interscholastic sports and the government's commitment to harnessing the sporting activities of schools and colleges resulted in the formation of the Schools and Colleges Sports Association in 1961 (Hardman, 2008). The growth of organised sports from 1961 to 1966—especially in football, athletics, boxing, field hockey, table tennis, and cricket—influenced professional preparation programmes in physical education in colleges and universities. To support the growth of physical education, the Central Organisation of Sports (COS) was established (Amusa & Toriola, 2010).

Between 1962 and 1966, the physical education training programme transformed into a 4-year diploma programme producing physical education teachers who were employed by the Ghana Education Service (Asare, 1982). Some students from the specialist training college in Winneba were offered scholarships to continue their studies in physical education in Britain and the Soviet Union (Amusa & Toriola, 2010). Adum-Kyeremeh (2019) observes how the newly independent Ghana started to establish new sports structures by sending coaches and athletes to the German Democratic Republic, Czechoslovakia, and Russia to train as physical educationists, who then returned to manage the system. That was certainly not a process that was supposed to seriously decolonise. One observes from the above political undertones the intent to move from the West to the East. Nkrumah simply moved towards the Eastern bloc for expertise, exchange, and capacity building (Adum-Kyeremeh, 2019). The continuation of this strategy after independence meant that decolonising physical education—as an area of study, curriculum, and sport organisation—was unrealistic.

Policies of Ghana's re-investment in sport thus promoted international competitions, which invariably did not promote Indigenous games and sports. The Real Republicans Sporting Club was established to help develop and promote boxing, football, athletics, and ping pong under Nkrumah. The Nkrumah government also saw sports as a means of creating African unity and created the Pan African Sports Magazine in solidarity with other African countries (Darby, 2013). Subsequent governments after Nkrumah developed sports in the same policy approach (Mensah, 2016). These were all practical actions that were framed to decolonise physical education in Ghana (Adum-Kyeremeh, 2019; Charway & Houlihan, 2020), but the content of the strategy reinforced the colonial structures. Football, for example, by far the country's most popular sport, was organised and played exactly in line with how Britain, the former colonial master, organised its football leagues. George Ainsley was brought in from England as Ghana's first professional football coach; then many others from England and other parts of Europe came, and Ghanaians were sent to Europe to be trained

(Adum-Kyeremeh, 2019). This was such that the education, training, curriculum, organisation of sports, and training of teachers were all either inherited from the colonialist or, ironically, new structures were introduced but with the same content of the past so as to attract international recognition.

While these strategies were stated to decolonise physical education, political interests were more strongly aligned with pan-Africanism, socialism, and the cult surrounding the first president's ideology along with recommitment to foreign sport infrastructures. This is not an effective recipe to decolonise, and Nkrumah's efforts created a path that future leaders continued. During the National Redemption Council/Supreme Military Council government from 1972 to 1976, sport was, for the first time, attached to the Ministry of Education, Culture and Sports (Herbst, 1993). This made it the first ever sports legislation in Ghana in the process of decolonising physical education. General Kutu Acheampong, Chairman of the Supreme Military Council, attempted to instrumentalise sports to improve the domestic image of the Ghanaian military to the extent that he made himself the minister of sports during this time (Agyekum, 2019). General Acheampong further established the SS74 Sports Club, the military sports and athletics club that organised participation in local, regional, national, and international sports tournaments and programmes. This is just like what Nkrumah did with the Republicans during the first republic (Agyekum, 2019).

The Government of Ghana continues to be the main financier of national teams and sports programmes and therefore influences the development of sports in the country. This has meant, however, that government programmes have not given space to traditional sports (Mensah, 2016). For example, the National Sports College in Winneba, created by the Provisional National Defense Council (PNDC) government in 1984 under SMC Decree 54 of 1976, was mandated by law to develop the technical and human resource needs for sports in the country by training coaches and sports administrators on modern skills in sports (Bitugu, Luguterah, & Ahiable, 2020), but this does not include traditional sports and games. The international sports politics of the International Olympic Committee (IOC) also influenced the development and promotion of sports in Ghana. The IOC continues to promulgate Western sports and games through their policies in Ghana, which invariably overshadow any attempt to promote local and traditional sports. All these certainly do not compliment any meaningful strategy to decolonise physical education in the country.

The fourth republic from 1992 to date spearheaded the design of the National Sports Policy in 1994 to provide guidelines and strategies for policy implementation in Ghana. This policy is historical because it led to the creation of Women's Sports Association of Ghana and Association of Sports for the Disabled as well as further inter-ministerial and multi-stakeholder strategy (Charway & Houlihan, 2020). However, Ocansey (2013) observed that the activities were not free from political influence with personal interest. The introduction of the 2016 sports policy was expected to give Ghana sports some local and Indigenous context.

However, the policy does not challenge the colonised perception of sports, does not transform funding mechanisms, and does not treat traditional games as vital in the process of decolonisation. Relatedly, there still is no physical education degree in Ghana that offers traditional games as a specialisation, and if traditional approaches are treated at all, they are brushed over as leisure and entertainment, rather than as a serious sport.

Integrating Decolonial Sport

The content, organisation, and running of physical education after independence did little to further the decolonisation of the Ghanaian system. This is despite a rich history of physical activity in the daily lives of pre-missionary communities in what would become Ghana. In analysing post-independence physical education in Ghana, there were clear and explicit attempts to decolonise physical education. Politically however, the first post-colonial government rather wanted to use physical education to rub shoulders with other countries, especially with the colonial masters. Even if the aim of decolonising physical education was serious, strategies drove towards international recognition and acceptance rather than a return to Indigenous-centric ways, despite the widespread use of such activities in informal spaces. Subsequent governments also tried but similarly ended up using sports for political, personal, and economic gain. These strategies, engagements, intentions are insufficient to decolonise physical education. We are not arguing that all Western games need to be removed from Ghana because they have become a part of modern Ghanaian culture. The incorporation of Indigenous sports and games is important in the decolonial process. Traditional games and Western games and sports can complement each other when properly organised, administered, and managed.

To decolonise physical education, we suggest three strategies. The first relates to core Ghanaian values. Colonial systems have bestowed and reinforced the narrow values of physical education to be militarisation, discipline, and professional participation in sports. Physical education entails much more than these limited framings. This calls for Ghanaian values to be promoted in teaching and organising physical education, with a focus on moving from competition towards collaboration and collegiality.

The second strategy to decolonise physical education relates to the standardisation across the field, across the school system, and across communities. Physical activities that are not standardised within a Western-oriented school system are not regarded as sports, relegating traditional sports into the background. Therefore, the curriculum of physical education must include Indigenous games as central to everyday recreational activities, related to student promotion, and integrated into teacher training.

The third strategy to decolonise physical education rests with engaging in the infrastructure of sport. All sporting activities in Ghana are organised based on colonial legacies and standards. This is especially true of school and amateur sports, which, due to efforts imposed during the transition towards independence, have become the bedrock of national sports teams. The criteria and content of sports organisations must therefore be redesigned to meet local contexts and circumstances. This requires not only valuing Indigenous physical activities and integrating such into the educational curriculum, but also transforming Ghanaian overreliance upon only Western sport. The journey towards decolonising physical education cannot be complete without a return to community values, and these, within Ghana, are based in part upon traditional physical education activities.

References

Abdou, M. (1968). *Education in Africa*. Deutsch.
Adedeji, J.A. (1980). The ascendency of Physical Education 1900–1960. A study of Physical Education as a teaching subject in Nigerian schools. *International Journal of P. E.*, 17(3), 24.
Adum-Kyeremeh, K. (2019). Political action in Sports development during the National Liberation Council Era in Ghana. In M.J. Gennaro & S. Aderinto (Eds.), *Sports in African history, politics, and identity formation* (pp. 59–72). Routledge.
Agbenyega, J. (2009). Enhancing anticipation, coordination and conflict resolution skills in children through 'ampe.' *Every Child*, 15(2), 22–23.
Agbodeka, F. (1972). *Ghana in the twentieth century*. Ghana Universities Press.
Agyekum, H.A. (2019). 'The best of the best': The politicization of Sports under Ghana's Supreme Military Council. In M.J. Gennaro & S. Aderinto (Eds.), *Sports in African history, politics, and identity formation* (pp. 73–88). Routledge.
Aissat, D., & Djafri, Y. (2011). *The role of colonial education in retrospect: The Gold Coast case in the era of imperialism*. University of Abdelhamid Ibn Badis, Algeria.
Ajisafe, M.O. (1976). An Indigenous syllabus of Physical Education for the Nigerian primary school. *International Journal of P. E.*, 13(4), 27–33.
Amusa, L.O., & Toriola, A.L. (2010). The changing phases of physical education and sport in Africa: Can a uniquely African model emerge? *African Journal for Physical, Health Education, Recreation & Dance*, 16(4), 666–680. doi:10.4314/ajpherd.v16i4.64095
Asare, E. (1982). *The impact of British Colonisation on the development of education and Physical Education in Ghana* [Unpublished doctoral dissertation]. University of Leicester.
Baba, J.A. (2000). *An appraisal of the implementation process of sport policy in Ghana*. Kinesiology, Sport Studies, and Physical Education Master's Theses. 45. https://digitalcommons.brockport.edu/pes_theses/45
Baba, J.A., Amui, J.C., Boateng, T.A., & Asiamoa, T. (1993). *Physical education for senior secondary schools*. H. Gangaram & Sons.
Biritwum, R.B., Gyapong, J., & Mensah, G. (2005). The epidemiology of obesity in Ghana. *Ghana Medical Journal*, 39(3), 82–85.
Bitugu, B.B. (1997). *Ghanaian systems of education with a case study on the formal education of Moslems* [Unpublished master's thesis]. University of Innsbruck.
Bitugu, B.B., Luguterah, A.W., & Ahiable, G. (2020). Managing community development through sports. In A. Goslin, D.A. Kluka, R.L. de D'Amico, & K. Danylchuk (Eds.), *In managing sport across borders* (pp. 169–184). Routledge.

Board of Education. (1909). *Syllabus of P. E. for Public Elementary Schools*. H. S. M. O.
Booth, M.Z. (1997). Western schooling and traditional society in Swaziland. *Comparative Education, 33*(3), 433–451. https://www.jstor.org/stable/3099500
Charway, D., & Houlihan, B. (2020). Country profile of Ghana: Sport, politics and nation-building. *International Journal of Sport Policy and Politics, 12*(3), 497–512.
Chepyator-Thomson, J.R. (2014). Public policy, Physical Education and sport in English-speaking Africa. *Physical Education and Sport Pedagogy, 19*(5), 512–521.
Colonial Office. (1950). *Gold Coast Report, 1949*. H. M. S. O.
Coward, V.R., & Lane, T.C. (1970). *Handbook of P. E. for primary schools (African)*. Evans.
Darby, P. (2013). 'Let us rally around the flag': Football, nation-building, and pan-Africanism in Kwame Nkrumah's Ghana. *The Journal of African History, 54*(2), 221–246.
Dennis, A. (2018). Promoting Ghana's traditional cultural aesthetics in Ghana's most beautiful reality television show. *Legon Journal of the Humanities, 29*(2), 176–196. doi:10.4314/ljh.v29i2.7
Edwards, K. (2009). Traditional games of a timeless land: Play cultures in Aboriginal and Torres Strait Islander communities. *Australian Aboriginal Studies, 2009*(2), 32–43.
Fafunwa, A.B. (1967). *New perspectives in African education*. Macmillan.
Ministry of Education (1971). *Education report 1968–71*. Accra: Ghana Publishing Corporation.
Ministry of Education (1986). *Report on basic education, 1986*. Accra: Ghana Publishing Corporation.
Graham, C.K. (1976). *The history of education in Ghana*. Ghana Publishing Corporation.
Graham, C.K. (2013). *The history of education in Ghana: From the earliest times to the declaration of independence*. Routledge.
Greene, S.E. (2002). *Sacred sites and the colonial encounter: A history of meaning and memory in Ghana*. Indiana University Press.
Gyadu, A. (2014). *Folk games and life skills development among children in public schools in the Central region of Ghana* [Unpublished doctoral dissertation]. University of Education, Winneba.
Hardman, K. (2008). Physical education in schools: A global perspective. *Kinesiology, 40*(1), 5–28.
Herbst, J.I. (1993). *The politics of reform in Ghana, 1982–1991*. University of California Press.
Johansson, B., Fogelberg-Dahm, M., & Wadensten, B. (2010). Evidence-based practice: The importance of education and leadership. *Journal of Nursing Management, 18*(1), 70–77. doi:10.1111/j.1365-2834.2009.01060.x
Joyce, M.C.W.K. (1995). *Education, culture, and empire: Sir Gordon Guggisberg and pedagogical imperatives in the Gold Coast, 1919-1927* [Unpublished master's thesis]. Queen's University at Kingston, Canada.
Kirk-Greene, A. (1989). Badge of office? Sport and his excellency in the British empire. *The International Journal of the History of Sport, 6*(2), 218–241. doi:10.1080/09523368908713689
Komabu-Pomeyie, S.G.M.A. (2020). Disability, culture, and technology: Issues, challenges, and applications in the Ghanaian classroom. In M. Grassati & J. Zoino-Jeannetti (Eds.), *Next generation digital tools and applications for teaching and learning enhancement* (pp. 159–178). IGI Global.
Lugard, F.D. (1965). *The dual mandate in British tropical Africa*. Oxon.
McElligot, T.E. (1950). *Education in the Gold Coast colony 1920–1949* [Unpublished doctoral dissertation]. Stanford University.

McWilliam, H.O.A., & Kwamena-Poh, M.A. (1975). *The development of education in Ghana: An outline*. London: Longman.

Mensah, C (2016). *The use of sports as a tool for diplomacy: The case of Ghana since independence* [Unpublished doctoral dissertation]. University of Ghana.

Mereku, D.K. (2019). Sixty years of teacher education in Ghana: Successes, challenges and the way forward. *African Journal of Educational Studies in Mathematics and Sciences*, *15*(2), 69–74.

Mumford, B.N. (1929). Education and social adjustment of the primitive peoples of Africa to European culture. *Africa: Journal of the International African Institute*, *2*(2), 138–161. doi:10.2307/1155823

Nabie, M.J. (2008). *Cultural games in Ghana: Exploring mathematics pedagogy with primary school teachers* [Unpublished doctoral dissertation]. University of Alberta.

Newell, S. (2002). *Literary culture in colonial Ghana: 'How to play the game of life'*. Manchester University Press.

Ocansey, R. (2013). Setting a new agenda for sports development and teaching physical activity optimize-health for sports excellence. *Ghana Physical Education and Sport Thinktank-Exercise Medicine Ghana* [brochure].

Ocansey, R., Sofo, S., & Baba, J. (2013). Perspectives of physical education and after-school sports in Ghana. In J.R. Chepayator-Thomson & S. Hsu (Eds.), *Global perspectives on physical education and after-school sport programs*, 13–20. Lanham, MD: University Press of America.

Opoku-Fianko, K. (1985). *The growth and development of physical education and sports in Ghana* [Unpublished doctoral dissertation]. The Ohio State University.

Pic, M., Lavega-Burgués, P., & March-Llanes, J. (2019). Motor behaviour through traditional games. *Educational Studies*, *45*(6), 742–755. doi:10.1080/03055698.2018.1516630

Rodger, P.J. (1909). The Gold Coast of today. *Journal of African Society*, *9*(33), 1–19.

Sofo, S., Kpebu, D., & Belcher, D. (2007, February). A postcolonial perspective of secondary physical education teachers' value orientations in Sub-Sahara Africa: The case of Ghana. *Research Quarterly for Exercise and Sport*, *78*(1), A74–A74.

Stoffle, R.W., & Baro, M.A. (2016). The name of the game: Oware as men's social space from Caribbean slavery to post-colonial times. *International Journal of Intangible Heritage*, *11*, 142–156.

Thomas, R.G. (1974). Education in northern Ghana, 1906–1940: A study in colonial paradox. *The Journal of African Historical Studies*, *7*(3), 427–467. doi:10.2307/217253

Van Dalen, D.B., & Bennett, B.L. (Eds.). (1971). Physical education in Australia. In *A world history of physical education: Cultural, philosophical, comparative* (pp. 631–639). Prentice Hall.

Whitehead, N., & Hendry, L.B. (1976). *Teaching physical education in England: Descriptions and analysis*. Lepus Books.

Wilson, J.P. (2014). International human resource development: Learning, education and training for individuals and organisations (3rd ed.). *Development and Learning in Organizations*, *28*(2). doi:10.1108/DLO-02-2014-0010

9
THE RE-ASSIMILATION OF INDIGENEITY IN EDUCATION

A Long-Term Journey

Takako Mino and Elaine Alowo-Matovu

We have all heard the phrase 'Africa doesn't work' one too many times. It has been discussed extensively that part of the reason why Africa fails is that, as we pursue all forms of development goals, we find ourselves stuck with systems that were not developed within the context of our peculiar circumstances (Mamdani, 2018; Rodney, 2018). What is worse is the increasing number of inhabitants on the continent who are being educated at home and abroad to solve these problems, yet by education systems built on the same worldviews that are alienated from African realities (Shizha, 2014; wa Thiong'o, 1992). Colonial education has deliberately separated educated Africans from Indigenous knowledges. Thus, the decolonising of higher education requires transforming all aspects of the university, including teaching, research, and community engagement. As previous chapters have clarified ways forward, we offer an application of their recommendations: How can one African university be structured to enact this decolonial challenge? As collaborators in creating Musizi University, a new university in Uganda, we believe that encouraging the exploration and integration of Indigenous ways of knowing and being will help students construct a foundational worldview to better understand themselves, reflect on their place within a global context, strengthen their voices, and develop the confidence and creativity to approach local and world problems with homegrown solutions.

We have heard the drumbeats that call for sustainable models of development if Africa, and indeed, the world, is to survive beyond our immediate future. What can be done to centre the intentional, sustainable survival of Africa's future generations, and what is the role of higher institutions of learning in collective survival? In the case of Africa, whose natural development path and core philosophies were interrupted and destabilised by colonialism, we aim to re-introduce value systems that centre our hearts and minds, offering a model of Obuntu

Bulamu, or 'healthy humanness,' to the rest of the world (Murphy, 1972 as cited in Karlström, 1996). Within the Ugandan context, the ethos of Obuntu Bulamu is demonstrated through compassion, consideration, and good manners towards others. Lubogo (2020) describes Obuntu Bulamu:

> Altruism (a regard for and devotion to the interest of others)…not to measure one's life by what you have attained in terms of your desires, but these small moments of integrity, compassion, rationality, and even self sacrifice because in the end the only way we can measure the significance of own lives is by valuing the lives of others.
>
> *(p. 12)*

Across a Southern African context, Obuntu Bulamu is closely related to Ubuntu, a philosophy of communality and interdependence, which has been heavily theorised and applied to education (Tutu, 1999; Venter, 2004). While Obuntu Bulamu is a Luganda term that refers to the philosophy of humaneness towards others in the community, numerous ethnic groups in Uganda also value this concept. At Musizi, we hope to recentre Obuntu Bulamu as a sustainable development model for all participants to engage and carry forward.

In his 2005 inaugural address, University of Kwazulu-Natal Vice-Chancellor Makgoba declared, 'The African university draws its inspiration from its environment, as an Indigenous tree growing from a seed that is planted and nurtured in African soil' (p. 15). Similarly, while we embark on the first steps of building Musizi University, we seek deep roots with local communities, serving as catalysts to celebrate and elevate our collective strengths. Obuntu Bulamu—a foundational concept to our university culture and ethos—intentionally re-assimilates Indigeneity. We use the term re-assimilation because what we seek to do was once a way of life and is not a complete reinvention of the wheel. The Baganda have a tongue twister proverb: 'Amazzi gakulukutira gyegaali gatakulukutilanga? Nedda! Mbadde, amazzi gakulukutira gyegaali gakulukutidde!' This saying roughly translates to, 'Does water flow, where it never flowed before?' and answers, 'No! Water always flows where there were once riverbeds.' Similarly, the lack of a value-based ethos in higher education may be seen as a dry riverbed, and the re-assimilation, therefore, is an attempt to restore the river to where it once flowed.

As we write this chapter, we are in the beginning stages of creating Musizi: We are conducting a feasibility study, developing a business plan, searching for land, and looking for funding. This chapter focuses on what we intend to accomplish through Musizi University as we look forward to welcoming our first class of students. In what comes next, we introduce our collective story as a foundation for Musizi. Next, we discuss the complexities of Indigeneity in Uganda. Then we frame the recentring of Indigeneity in higher education and Musizi's approach of constantly referencing the past to inform the present and the future. This is followed by our argument for the importance of reviving

Obuntu Bulamu in higher education. We then share our thoughts on fostering the culture of Obuntu Bulamu through converging all aspects of the university on community engagement, which then shapes our teaching and research.

Ti koro nko agyina

Elaine was born and educated in Uganda in a family descending from educators. From a young age, Elaine learned the value of a pursuit of reading beyond what school had taught her. Beginning at the age of eight, Elaine spent the long school holidays with her paternal grandparents in Tororo. For hours on end, she scoured through old books on a wide range of subjects that she then barely understood, from the teachings of Karl Marx's *The Communist Manifesto* to literature like Chinua Achebe's *Things Fall Apart* and her favourite Black James Bond equivalent, Lance Spearman, in a bi-weekly comic, *The Spear*. Reading a lot of things she didn't quite understand would lead to her long conversations with the adults around her to explain some of what she was reading. Arguably the greatest value that came from these reading experiences was the curiosity and freedom they created to ask questions. When she was studying history in school, Elaine often asked her teachers what Uganda was like before the arrival of the missionaries. She came to the conclusion quite early that she would not get the answers to why Uganda's history began with the coming of white people, and she sought opportunities to learn other versions of Uganda's history and Indigenous knowledges. Elaine also experienced firsthand the limitations of Uganda's higher education system, where corruption and apathy were rampant. Although she studied law at university and became a successful corporate lawyer, she felt disillusioned by the entrenched injustices that she encountered in the courts. Seeking to put her efforts into something to help transform Uganda's trajectory, Elaine eventually co-founded an affordable international school in Kampala. The school quickly grew from 30 students to over 600 within 4 years. Elaine was sure that a university would be the next logical step to continue paving the path to education that allowed space for critical thinking, questioning, and independent learning.

Meanwhile, on the other side of the world, Takako was born in Japan and grew up in the U.S. She, too, remembers the important role of history in understanding her identity and purpose. When she learned about World War II in the fourth grade, her grandmother, an atomic bomb survivor, told her story for the first time in 50 years and expressed her wish that no human being suffers in the way she had. This was contrary to what was often taught in schools—that the bomb was a justified move in securing America's victory. Takako often felt conflicted between what she learned from school and what she learned from her family, and she sometimes looked down upon her Japanese culture; but she eventually realised that she did not have to be confined to one culture. She could learn from the strengths and weaknesses of diverse cultures and embrace herself for the unique person that she was.

Inspired by her grandmother's story, Takako decided that she wanted to become someone who could contribute to world peace. While she studied international relations at college, moreover, she studied abroad in Uganda, where she was touched by people's warmth and humanity. She saw how much Ugandans valued education as the way to change their destiny, and she returned several times to implement education programs in rural areas. To repay her debt of gratitude to Uganda and as her contribution to a more peaceful world, Takako wished to support the development of education in Uganda. This dream eventually became a goal to start a new university in Uganda. Over the course of 10 years, she went back to the U.S. to gain experience as a high school teacher, obtained her doctorate, and later moved to Ghana to work as a lecturer at a Ashesi University to build her understanding of education from multiple angles.

When the pandemic hit in early 2020 and most of the world went on lockdown, Elaine and Takako were virtually introduced to each other through a mutual friend. From the first time we spoke on the phone, there was a synergy, as we both wished to create an education that cultivated students' humanity and built on the strengths of Uganda's Indigenous cultures. And we both recognised the tremendous youth potential in Uganda, where around three-quarters of the population is under 30 years old (Daumerie & Madsen, 2010). After speaking regularly for months, we made the leap to work together. Takako moved to Uganda in October 2020, and from there, we began to craft our shared vision into what has now become the foundation of Musizi. An Akan proverb cautions, 'Ti koro nko agyina,' which means, 'One head cannot hold council.' Together, we are wiser and stronger.

These are our stories, but we know that we are part of a much bigger story of Uganda. We are tributaries joining a majestic river. Uganda is the seat of innovations that have changed the world; Indigenous healers in Uganda performed the first known caesarean sections (US National Library of Medicine 2013), and Uganda sits at the source of the Nile River, which has been called 'the great, great grandfather of human civilisation' (Hamdan, 1967, as cited in Hassan & Rasheedy, 2007). Uganda historically served as an East African hub for higher education and continues to send professionals to neighbouring countries, such as Somalia, South Sudan, Rwanda, Burundi, and the Democratic Republic of Congo. Uganda's oldest university, Makerere University, educated post-independence African leaders including Julius Nyerere, Joseph Kabila, and Mwai Kibaki as well as leading writers such as Ali Mazrui, Ngugi wa Thiong'o, and Nurudin Farah. The inspiration for many big ideas was produced in this space, and we are standing on the shoulders of these giants as we strive to build upon this proud legacy.

Indigenous Complexity in Uganda

Indigeneity is closely intertwined with the dynamics of language, culture, and power in Uganda. There exists in Uganda a struggle for dominance along these fault lines. According to the 1995 Uganda Constitution, Uganda officially recognises 65 ethnic groups. From before colonisation, some ethnic groups were organised in kingdoms such as Buganda, Bunyoro, Toro, Ankole, and Busoga, while others were organised in paramount chieftaincies such as Acholi, Iteso, and Lango. The largest ethnic group are the Baganda, or those in the Buganda kingdom.

Additionally, Uganda welcomes a substantial number of refugees across Africa, about 1.4 million (UNHCR, 2021), making the population even more diverse as refugee populations settle and contribute their cultures to the country. Ethnic identity continues to play an important role in people's lives but has also been mobilised to divide the nation, as reflected in the history of military coups, ethnic conflicts, and colonially enforced divisions (Kibanja, Kajumba, & Johnson, 2012; Lindemann, 2011; Rohner, Thoenig, & Zilibotti, 2013). Indigeneity is thus a difficult topic in Uganda, and an attempt at re-assimilating it into higher education begs the question of whose Indigeneity to centre.

The history of language colonisation in Uganda further complicates these divisions. From pre-colonial times, there was no unifying language among the diverse sociolinguistic groups in the region. Colonial Britain gave Buganda a preferential status, allowing for Luganda to become the unofficial lingua franca of the protectorate. English was the official language but was almost exclusively spoken among the school-educated elite; the rest of the protectorate outside Buganda and the 'less-educated' tended to use Kiswahili (Nyaigotti-Chacha, 1987). That the British then gave most of the civil servants' jobs to the English-speaking Baganda—and the jobs in the military and the police to Kiswahili-speaking others—further exacerbated ethnic power dynamics (Nyaigotti-Chacha, 1987). As Mamdani (2018) explains, 'Every institution touched by the hand of the colonial state was given a pronounced regional or nationality character. It became a truism that a soldier must be a northerner, a civil servant a southerner and a merchant an Asian' (as cited in Amone, 2014). Built into the structure of Ugandan society, this painful colonial context has always hindered a clear, inclusive language policy.

This colonial dynamic continued after independence. While Luganda was and continues to be the most widely spoken Indigenous language in Uganda, there was pushback against Luganda becoming a national language because other groups felt this would entrench the Baganda's dominance and marginalise the others who did not speak the language; on the other hand, many highly placed Baganda were in strong opposition to Kiswahili, which they feared would empower the Luo-dominated, Kiswahili-speaking military and police (Nyaigotti-Chacha, 1987). In the end, the government haphazardly decided on English, even though most ordinary people did not speak it (Nyaigotti-Chacha, 1987). The Ugandan experience is in stark contrast to our neighbours in Tanzania, where a comprehensive language policy set Kiswahili as a national language and where first Tanzanian President Nyerere enforced the teaching of Kiswahili in schools and the resettlement of Tanzanians from their original ancestral homes through Ujamaa and villagisation policies. While Nyerere at the time was greatly criticised for what seemed like a great failure, today we can see that he succeeded in the creation of a Tanzania defined and identified first by their nationhood before their ethnic group, and therefore the existence of a Swahili culture and nation (Mazrui & Mazrui, 1995). This is not the case in Uganda, where most Ugandans identify first with their ethnic groups rather than with the nation as a whole, as reinforced by current language policy and practice.

There are different levels of preserving Indigenous knowledge and culture within various ethnic groups. In some ways, the culture and language of the Baganda are more well-known than others because of their historical advantage and tradition of assimilating those from other groups. Buganda is located centrally and envelops Kampala, Uganda's capital city, which has attracted people from around the country. Today, Asians and other non-Baganda are welcomed, many of whom have been given Luganda names. Luganda has evolved to be the base language of popular culture, music, and trade, particularly in Kampala. The wide use of Luganda beyond Buganda can also be attributed to religion. Buganda was a strong ally in the spread of Christianity and colonial subjugation of other ethnic groups within Uganda in a story often summarised as the flag following the cross (Wrigley, 1959). Until recently, in the Anglican Church, all non-English services were held in Luganda. If colonisation is the subjugation of one culture by another, the Baganda may be seen to have subjugated other ethnic groups within this context.

Due to this complicated context, we at Musizi must be very careful about how we recentre Indigeneity; our founding purpose is to embrace all ethnic groups, while keeping these tensions at the forefront. We hope to empower students with the confidence to draw values from all of the 65 ethnic groups that exist within Uganda or any African or world culture. This localised globalism is especially needed considering that Uganda not only represents a very diverse group of Indigenous people but also is home to continual resettlements of immigrants and refugees. Every student that comes to Musizi should have the confidence to dip into their Indigeneity and those of others, regardless of where they are from, through an introspective, research orientation.

Musizi University: Recentring Indigeneity

Musizi University was named after the Musizi tree, an Indigenous tree in Uganda. Musizi, translated from Luganda to English, means 'the sower.' It is a tree that protects and supports life. Traditionally, coffee plantations in Uganda are strewn with Musizi trees, which provide the right amount of shade and light for the coffee plant to flourish. We aspire for students to become like Musizi trees, firmly planted in the realities of their societies and contributing to the improvement of others' lives with a strong undergirding of authentic confidence, a confidence that allows them to constantly interrogate essential life questions: Who am I? Where do I come from? And where am I going? These questions are not just limited to exploring ethnic and linguistic identity but also constructing an understanding of one's personhood based on all facets of life. Our school motto—'Better Me. Better World'—illustrates how an individual's transformation based on this fundamental identity work connects to changes in the wider community.

As each student engages in this process of self-discovery and self-realisation—a process of awakening, meaning-making, and becoming—they can pursue a 'Better Me' and by doing so create a 'Better World.' This echoes Buddhist philosopher Daisaku Ikeda's (1987) framework of human revolution, or the inner transformation of an individual. Ikeda explains that

> just as our shadow is cast on the ground in a form matching that of our body, all of human society is a reflection of humanity's inner life. Without a transformation of humanity, there can be no transformation of our social environment.
>
> *(pp. 247–248)*

Each person's thriving in their own uniqueness will enable all of us to thrive. This bettering also speaks to a sustainable model where the progress of one need not come at the cost to another and that consideration for others need not mean less for one. Just like the Musizi trees that grow so tall as to be noticeable from a distance in a flourishing coffee plantation, there are ways to pursue better versions of ourselves while contributing to the betterment of others. We believe that Musizi students should develop the necessary skills and contribute to the body of world knowledge on how to actualise this collective thriving in addressing global challenges such as climate change.

Recentring Indigeneity calls for a balanced interrogation into why our Indigenous systems worked, what about us worked, and how we worked, with a specific emphasis on processes we did right. This is especially so as it is often misleading to look into the past without balancing views. Nigerian writer Chimamanda Ngozi Adichie (2009) emphasises that the common habit of telling a single story can form one-dimensional perspectives and drown out other equally valid positions and realities. This is not to say that history must be viewed through only rose-tinted glasses, but rather to underscore what we miss out on if we are not intentional about highlighting the history that reflects the highest version of ourselves. That highest version becomes the basis for us to forge forward into an unknown future, holding onto our strongest virtues and using our past strengths to write new stories that we and those who come after us can be proud of. This exploratory and reflective process creates a cycle, where each generation endeavours to do better than the one before by refining the worthwhile practices of our ancestors and ensuring that we yield fairer and more widely beneficial outcomes for as many members of society as possible.

We are also mindful that some of our Indigenous practices, which worked excellently in traditional African contexts, if applied today without critical scrutiny and mindfulness, might not always create value. For instance, there is a restorative justice practice among the Acoli of northern Uganda called Mato Oput (drinking of the bitter root). This ceremony was traditionally brought about to create reconciliation between the perpetrator of a crime and the victim. It began with the acknowledgement of wrongdoing by the perpetrator followed by a determination by traditional leaders about the appropriate compensation and actions the perpetrator should provide to the victim. Both parties drink the bitter root, which signifies that they will let go of their bitterness and move forward. This works when both parties are fully cognisant and spiritually invested in the ritual, allowing the victims' families an opportunity to heal and move on from the loss, while enabling the perpetrator to receive true forgiveness and relieve themselves of the burden of guilt. This system was used successfully to reconcile child soldiers with their communities after they had been saved from the rebel camps of Joseph Kony in the war in northern Uganda. However, with the existence of a parallel legal system where certain offences like defilement would attract a death sentence, a system like Mato Oput may be abused and manipulated to allow perpetrators to make cash settlements with influential family members, leaving the victims feeling cheated and in greater pain.

What held systems like Mato Oput above reproach? Indigenous systems in traditional African societies worked because community members had high levels of self-consciousness in which they saw themselves as part of a greater whole. Individuals had a strong sense of pride and a great fear of the shame that would befall their household, clan, and village in the event of any social impropriety that debased human life on their part. This philosophical foundation served to bring order and harmonious coexistence within society. In traditional Buganda society, this moral foundation was articulated as Obuntu Bulamu.

Obuntu Bulamu

Because principles like Obuntu Bulamu had enabled the functioning of Indigenous societies, we believe that it is important to return to these principles in developing the foundation of Musizi.

(In Takako's voice) During my time in Uganda, I have often met people being described as *humble*, which is how Obuntu Bulamu is usually translated into colloquial English. I was surprised at how closely the concept of humility (Obuntu Bulamu) mirrors the Japanese culture of putting others before oneself. This is manifested in the way Japanese people refrain from being noisy, ranging from the volume of one's voice to the loudness of one's outfit, and go out of one's way to make sure that others are comfortable and not burdened by one's presence. I imagined if this aspect of our way of being could be summarised in one Japanese word, and if that Japanese word was then translated into a single English word, how deeply stripping of meaning this would be. Would one be able to understand the full meaning of a way of being by simply reading the dictionary definition of 'humility'?

(In Elaine's voice) Often, when one asks for a reference on a service provider, it is not uncommon to get the response 'Oyo omusajja Muntu Mulamu bambi, aja kukolera bulungi,' which translates to, 'That man is a Muntu Mulamu, he will work well for you.' Or if a girl were getting married to a boy, and her family inquired about his family, it is not uncommon to hear the response, 'Abo abantu Bantu Balamu bambi, omwana aja kufumba,' meaning, 'Those people are Bantu Balamu, the child will cook (sustain the marriage).' In this context it becomes clear that Obuntu Bulamu is not *humble*.

Obuntu Bulamu describes a person who is modest, kind, warm, considerate, welcoming, truthful, reliable, and trustworthy. Obuntu Bulamu—Buntu meaning humanness and Bulamu meaning life—roughly translates to 'what keeps a human being alive.' In other words, what makes us alive is being a true human being with a sense of responsibility to others' well-being. Obuntu Bulamu can also be translated as 'humanness is a part of life.' In other words, regardless of anything, anyone who is alive is human and therefore must be accorded respect. Even if someone commits a crime, there is a sense of 'we see you for who you are outside of what you have done.'

(In our collective voice) This is why we believe that Obuntu Bulamu, as a way of being, is a classic example of lost Indigenous knowledge. Obuntu Bulamu is a rather profound concept that is often flattened into the single conceptualisation, *humility*, which results in a one-dimensional understanding of the concept. This in turn has a long-term effect of a loss of a way of being. If, because of this limited understanding, humility then becomes the only aspect to which a community aspires in attaining Obuntu Bulamu, what happens to the other aspects of the ideal such as a concern for others and respect for humanity? This watering down could make Obuntu Bulamu essentially meaningless as a means of defining a society. We thus recognise that foundational efforts at Musizi can help re-establish this shared meaning.

We argue that there must be a return to full understanding, a re-definition that extends beyond the single word *humility*. While there are some publications about Obuntu Bulamu, including its application to law (Lubogo, 2020) and disability inclusion (Bannink Mbazzi et al., 2020), it is often described as the same as Ubuntu. Our application of Obuntu Bulamu to higher education is in alignment with what Chapter 2 in the book calls Ubuntu-based education. Nevertheless, there remains more work to explore what Obuntu Bulamu means as lived reality, as well as how it differs from similar regional conceptions. For instance, while Confucian values have influenced cultures across East Asia, they are viewed and practised in subtly different ways in China, Korea, Japan, and Taiwan (Zhang, Lin, Nonaka, & Beom, 2005). This is also the case with different African cultures. Rather than conflating Obuntu Bulamu as Ubuntu, we believe that this is an important opportunity to invest in researching Obuntu Bulamu's manifestation, transformation, and applications in Uganda in order to ground the principle within the academic space as a subject to be analysed and within social spaces for practice in campus life and beyond.

We cannot return to the times of yore, and simply inserting Indigenous knowledge will not solve the fundamental problems of African higher education. At Musizi, we think that while the Indigenous context may no longer hold in some instances, the raison d'etre of Indigenous norms remains the same. Since we know how important the underlying values are in the development of student confidence and identity, we can infuse the underpinnings of Indigenous knowledge into education through Obuntu Bulamu in a way that is compelling for students. Thus, in our university manifesto poem, we end by saying, 'Take your place. You are Musizi.' We want to instill in students that they are part of something bigger, have their own place of honour within our community, and play an essential role in creating our collective culture. Obuntu Bulamu as part of higher education allows us to pursue the ideals of excellence while reminding us that we cannot all be in the same place or pace at the same time. Obuntu Bulamu says I have the patience to hear and understand where you are in your journey and the time to explain where I am and that I sit with you as an equal as we both pursue our shared ideals. Obuntu Bulamu says everyone is enough, and every person's voice matters. This philosophical grounding can serve as a powerful organising principle of our university in all our functions.

Community Engagement

Post-colonial African literature and film are strewn with storylines that speak of the alienation of Africans who have pursued a Western education that diminishes their ability to relate to their communities (Ansah, Bucknor, Collier, & Misa, 2007; p'Bitek, 1984; Sembene, 1968). The locus classicus of this case is portrayed by Lakunle in Wole Soyinka's (1962) *Lion and the Jewel*. The supposedly 'modernised' man, Lakunle, is mocked by the rest of the village as he clumsily attempts to woo a beautiful girl without engaging in what he believes to be the 'savage' tradition of bride-price. This separation of school-educated Africans and traditionally educated Africans plays out in today's African societies, where the more school-educated we are, the more far removed we become from the realities of most people and the greater the tendency to other those who did not get the opportunity to get a formal education. At Musizi, we seek to combat this discrimination and division by centring ourselves on community engagement as a lifestyle, not as a separate task of the university. This means that benefiting the wider communities will become the central focus of everything we do at the university, both for the staff and the students. Indeed we must exist for the benefit of those who never had the chance to attend university.

At Musizi, we aim to foster a community where everyone, including students and staff, has a personal responsibility to ensure that our actions move the collective forward through asking the following questions in curricula and all university functions: Who am I impacting? How are other people affected? How is the environment impacted? Am I benefiting at the expense of another?

Does this benefit everyone? By asking these kinds of questions about the kind of impact we want to make, we can become a part of our communities in a more meaningful manner.

In order to model a community engagement culture across academics and research, Musizi wishes to include community leaders into planning processes. Showing respect to community members should be modelled from the top to the bottom. The culture of Obuntu Bulamu must extend to all those who work at the university, whether they are the gardeners, security guards, cleaners, or other workers. We hope to create a kind, warm-hearted community, where everyone feels that they belong and are accepted for who they are by integrating this ethic of care to guide how we think about human resources, governance, and other aspects of the university.

As articulated in Chapter 1 by Knaus, Mino, and Seroto, we see community engagement as the starting point and teaching and research as existing in support of community engagement. In the following sections, we elaborate on what this might look like.

Teaching

We have decided to take a liberal arts approach to provide a broad-based, interdisciplinary, and holistic education, breaking down the barriers between different subjects and affording students the opportunity to understand who they are from multiple lenses including culture, literature, philosophy, and language. There is a tendency to think about a liberal arts education as a Western concept, for example, in the context of an American liberal arts degree. We would like to refute this misconception. For instance, India has a rich Indigenous tradition of liberal arts, espoused by its oldest universities and contemporary thinkers—these intellectual and spiritual traditions have contributed to the development of contextually relevant liberal arts education for India (Mino, 2021). Similarly, a liberal arts degree can be rooted in African philosophies. Allowing for differing conceptions of liberal arts is part of the decolonising process—we are reclaiming the liberal arts for ourselves in the pursuit of building an African liberal arts tradition drawing from the wisdom of our people. As we build our own liberal arts tradition, our curriculum will include core components such as storytelling, language study, project-based learning, and business orientation based on a philosophy of care and collaboration, inspired by Obuntu Bulamu.

Care

As expressed in Isabirye in Chapter 4, the relationship between teachers and students in Indigenous pedagogy is characterised as one that inspires joy, passion, and agency. At Musizi, we will strive to emulate this, knowing that we are fostering each seedling Musizi into a great tree. This means getting to know and deeply caring for each student, sharing meals, playing games, exchanging stories, making jokes, and creating a warm atmosphere of care and inclusion in our classrooms so that students experience self-fulfilment and develop into excellent human beings.

Collaboration

Ugandan cultures are collectivistic. Whether for birth, schooling, marriage, or funerals, families and communities work together to support most aspects of a person's life. Collaboration is a difficult skill that needs intentional development, and we envision that students will practise this essential skill by frequently working in teams on projects. Teaching can be structured in a way that reflects the collaboration we expect from students. Faculty from different disciplines can collaborate to co-teach and contribute their different expertises to facilitate learning. We believe that this co-teaching approach will help faculty members broaden their minds beyond disciplines and model collaborative interdisciplinarity for the students.

Storytelling

Storytelling is a core aspect of traditional Ugandan societies. This is how older generations share with younger generations about the history, art, and values of their people. Typically, in the evening, all the generations of a family sit under the moonlight and listen to stories told by the elders. This storytelling skill continues to carry importance today in order to articulate who we are to ourselves and to contribute our distinct rhythms to the symphony of the world. For this reason, we want students at Musizi to engage in identity narrative writing and oral literature in a storytelling course. This process necessitates engaging in personal reflection, identifying points of inflection and change, and expressing deeper meaning to others as well as conducting research into one's not-yet-explored backgrounds. Such storytelling is a creative, inward-looking process that helps one better understand oneself and proudly share that self with others. In addition, students can learn how to tell the story of someone else by stepping into the viewpoint of another person and developing the imaginative empathy required to tell that person's story with the dignity and accuracy they deserve. Since we recognise that we are all on journeys of self-discovery together, we hope to challenge faculty to participate in storytelling processes and share about their lives as one way to humanise teacher-learner relationships.

Language Study

Treasure troves of Indigenous knowledge are hidden in our languages, and studying language enables us to tap into cultural wisdom that may not be obvious at the surface level. At Musizi, we want to encourage all students to study at least one Indigenous language and delve into its different forms such as proverbs, folktales, songs, and riddles. Through Indigenous language, students can explore Obuntu Bulamu's expression, role, and nuances in various Ugandan cultures and embark on research to conceptualise and revive this vital ethos beyond our current understanding. This endeavor involves studying African philosophy, sociology, anthropology, among other fields, to build on one's understanding of Indigenous contexts, linking students with communities, rather than being isolated from them. We want students to appreciate that the classroom is not limited to the campus; rather, Musizi is part of the world. Similarly, we can invite stewards of Indigenous knowledge to Musizi as integrated elders to learn from their talents and experiences.

Project-based Learning

If Musizi exists for the sake of communities, we need to address the challenges facing Uganda. For many courses, we will take a project-based approach, where students work on a collaborative activity to learn in a contextually relevant and interdisciplinary fashion, similar to how African Indigenous pedagogy took place within everyday life interactions. As students work on a project, they will acquire the necessary theories and skills for completing their inquiry rather than learning the theories out of context. For instance, a course could centre on the challenge of electrifying villages in rural Uganda, where students take the lead in conducting research across a variety of disciplines such as electrical engineering, economics, politics, and policy studies in order to develop a holistic understanding of the issue at hand and to generate a preliminary solution. In a course on law, for instance, another project could be an exploration of the right to sovereignty over natural resources in Africa. The faculty will act as facilitators of learning, help students ask thoughtful questions, avoid over-simplified thinking, and share content expertise while learning alongside students. Modelling curiosity and lifelong learning helps show students how we can all learn, every day. We desire that students strengthen their instincts to find out what they don't know for themselves. Rather than only relying on what is taught in the course, students should find information in its different forms and understand that learning is not limited to schooling. These experiences will engrain lifelong learning habits among students, in preparation for their roles as changemakers within their community.

Business Orientation

Uganda has been ranked as having the highest youth entrepreneurial propensity in the world with an estimated 55.4 per cent of youth involved in new or established businesses. Unfortunately, however, most of these businesses add little to job creation and are financially unsustainable (Singer, Amoros, & Moska, 2015). The entrepreneurial drive is there but needs to be backed up with the capacity to transform ambition into a viable and Obuntu Bulamu-centred enterprise. Regardless of what degree students pursue, we would like each to develop a fundamental business orientation. Utilising Obuntu Bulamu as an ethical framework for analysing businesses, students can learn how to ask the right questions to determine whether a business practises empathy in its interactions with its workers, customers, and general public or whether it creates harmful effects in the pursuit of maximising profit. We believe that if students have the opportunity to carry out research on societal problems—such as the inequities and shortfalls of the education system, the impact of global warming on agriculture, and the rise of asthma with urbanisation—and experience starting and running a small business to address these issues in teams, even failing at them, it will provide a more realistic understanding of team dynamics, conflict management, ethics, and financial decision-making in order to prepare them for the world of work and to bring their humanising abilities to make the business world more beneficial to communities.

Research

A Kiswahili proverb foretells, 'Until the Lion tells his side of the story, the tale of the hunt will always glorify the Hunter.' A quick review of our documented history as taught across the various levels of education will show a bias towards the victors, namely the colonialists, and a greater emphasis on our failures. We are taught that we have no history of our own until the advent of colonialism. This is of little surprise as politics has been described as 'an intellectual and moral creation characterised by the contents of its ideals, theories, slogans and propaganda' (Gedlu, 2000, p. 91). This results in a school curriculum that distorts African history, thereby reinforcing Black inferiority.

At Musizi, we seek to be intentional about inquiring into our history and our culture to study the aspects that reflect the best versions of ourselves as a people. We want to change the dominant narrative in Uganda, as a place without a history. This research by, for, and with our communities can then be fed back into the curriculum. Because such curricular content is not yet created and most of what we have available at our disposal is Western knowledge, we must engage in a continual cycle of contextually relevant knowledge production and curriculum development. Uncovering our forgotten histories so that the lion's story of the hunt is told is a gargantuan task that requires the mobilisation of funds and resources so that students, community members, and staff alike can engage in this pursuit of lost knowledge. Musizi, first of all, must amass the required funding in order to create opportunities for the university community to engage in meaningful research with relevance to the wider community. This self-discovery allows us to meet events that reflect higher versions of our ancestry, encouraging us to greater heights and changing the rhetoric that nothing good can come from Uganda. This knowledge production contributes to culture production. In the same way that the concept of もったいない (Mottainai, or 'what a waste' in Japanese) has become part of the global rallying cry for sustainability and was adopted in Kenya for a campaign against single-use plastic bags, we believe that the concept of Obuntu Bulamu can be an important cultural contribution from Uganda to help the entire world revive our humanity. If, as a Ugandan, we had the luxury of looking at a piece of art like the Luzira Head, which is presently sitting somewhere in a British museum, what would that do for our artistic inspiration? This would be so in the same way that in the 1800s, young Vincent van Gogh, now considered to be the second-greatest Dutch painter after Rembrandt, had the luxury to be inspired by his predecessor Rembrandt's *The Night Watch* masterpiece painted in 1642. It is said that Van Gogh spent hours sitting at the foot of Rembrandt's painting looking in amazement at the artistry from over two centuries before. This example highlights the importance of having access to the documented triumphs of our predecessors in our history.

We can learn from African universities challenging the application of community-centredness to research. At Wangari Maathai Institute in Kenya, students are taught to actively engage the community in the research process from the beginning to the end; while they are formulating their research questions and plans, they engage the community to seek their input, and once they have completed their data collection and analysis, they go back to the community to present their findings and seek their feedback again. Students are continually challenged to ask themselves 'Who will benefit from the research you conduct?' (Mino, 2020, p. 77). We can turn to such existing frameworks for inspiration, while continually interrogating our research methods using Obuntu Bulamu as a guide.

We hope that research at Musizi will expand our ways of knowing through exploring aspects of life that are traditionally excluded from academia. One way Musizi may achieve this is through conducting research on popular culture. For instance, in Ghana, at Ashesi University, Oduro-Frimpong (2021) analyses African popular culture, ranging from funeral posters, vehicle inscriptions, hip-life music, to satirical cartoons, as a way of validating the legitimacy of these modes of expression in academia. He also challenges students to go out into the community to find their own examples of popular culture, analyse them, and present them in exhibitions. These are aspects of culture that we see in everyday life but are not given the same respect as the Western literary canon. However, thinking about these ordinary artefacts enables us to uncover the different layers of depth in a culture. Studying popular culture as one aspect of Indigeneity creates an academic space to talk about and validate the importance of things we routinely exclude from the academic setting.

We envision Musizi as a public hub, where people come and learn, share their stories, be inspired, and aspire to apply what they have learned to transform our challenges and invent new ideas to build upon our highest versions. This means creating historical archives, data banks, and Indigenous knowledge repositories where we document, analyse, and disseminate research. We can also create opportunities for funding for community members, students, and staff to conduct research together on new ways of applying Indigenous knowledge. Only through finding ways to apply Indigenous knowledge can this important wisdom survive to represent the best of Ugandan and other cultures and identities.

Conclusion

We share Musizi University's ideas for an Obuntu Bulamu-centred higher education as a way to recentre Indigenous knowledge, inquire into our forgotten past, and draw inspiration from the best version of our people. We identify Obuntu Bulamu as an organising ethos common across ethnic groups in Uganda and acknowledge that we are building upon the legacies of hundreds and thousands of years of civilisations. Musizi seeks to revitalise our cultures, which may be quickly drying up, so that the river will flow where it once flowed again. Towards this end, Musizi focuses on nurturing our hearts through habitual introspection into oneself and understanding one's interdependence with and contribution to others. We ground Musizi in community engagement as a culture that influences the way that we teach and produce knowledge, so that we ensure that our existence is for the sake of supporting the thriving of all life.

While we are in the startup stages of the university and have much more work to do before welcoming our first group of students, we hope to continue to analyse these ideas and engage with Ugandan and international community members about the kind of university that best supports the renaissance and flourishing of Uganda and the world, all while supporting the young people, whom we are fortunate to mould so that they live by the motto, 'Better Me. Better World.'

The chapters in this book argue for decolonising approaches, including but not limited to the language of instruction, curriculum framing, pedagogy, research, and service. As we aim to transform colonial infrastructures and approaches, we advocate to close the chapter on only-Western based education and offer this in-process foundation of not only a decolonial, but also an intentionally Indigenous university, grounded in Obuntu Bulamu. We seek to rebuild teaching and research through Obuntu Bulamu in the hopes of recreating a society based on the pursuit of fairness, respect for humanity, and sustainable progress for all, starting on our campus and spreading across the world.

References

Adichie, C.N. (2009). *The danger of a single story* [video]. https://www.ted.com/talks/chimamanda_ngosi_adichie_the_danger_of_a_single_story?language=en

Amone, C. (2014). The creation of Acholi military ethnocracy in Uganda, 1862 to 1962. *International Journal of Liberal Arts and Social Science*, 2(3), 141–150.

Ansah, K., Bucknor, K., Collier, I., & Misa, A. (2007, October 27). *Heritage Africa* [Drama]. Film Africa Production.

Bannink Mbazzi, F., Nalugya, R., Kawesa, E., Nambejja, H., Nizeyimana, P., Ojok, P., Van Hove, G., & Seeley, J. (2020). 'Obuntu Bulamu'–Development and testing of an Indigenous intervention for disability inclusion in Uganda. *Scandinavian Journal of Disability Research, 22*(1), 403–416. doi:10.16993/sjdr.697

Gedlu, M. (2000). Two contributions to the interpretation of Subsaharan Africa's colonial history: A review essay. *Perspectives, 15*, 91–111. https://www.jstor.org/stable/23615890

Hamdan, G. (1967). *Skakhsiyyat Masr* [The character of Egypt]. Irbid, Jordan: Dar al-Hilal.

Hassan, H.A., & Rasheedy, A.A. (2007). The Nile River and Egyptian foreign policy interest. *African Sociological Review/Revue Africaine de Sociologie, 11*(1), 25–37. https://www.jstor.org/stable/24487584

Ikeda, D. (1987). The Human Revolution: A prerequisite for lasting peace. *McGill Journal of Education/Revue Des Sciences de l'éducation de McGill, 22*(003). https://mje.mcgill.ca/article/view/7763

Karlström, M. (1996). Imagining democracy: Political culture and democratisation in Buganda. *Africa, 66*(4), 485–505. doi:10.2307/1160933

Kibanja, G.M., Kajumba, M.M., & Johnson, L.R. (2012). Ethnocultural conflict in Uganda: Politics based on ethnic divisions inflame tensions across the country. In D. Landis & R.D. Albert (Eds.), *Handbook of ethnic conflict* (pp. 403–435). Springer.

Lindemann, S. (2011). The ethnic politics of coup avoidance: Evidence from Zambia and Uganda. *Africa Spectrum, 46*(2), 3–41. https://www.jstor.org/stable/41336253

Lubogo, I.C. (2020). *Obuntu-bulamu and the Law: An extra textual aid statutory interpretation tool*. Marianum Press Ltd.

Makgoba, M.W. (2005). The African university: Meaning, penalties and responsibilities. In D. Chetty (Ed.), *Towards African scholarship* (pp. 11–19). University of Kwazulu-Natal.

Mamdani, M. (2018). *Citizen and subject: Contemporary Africa and the legacy of late colonialism*. Princeton University Press.

Mazrui, A.A., & Mazrui, A.M. (1995). *Swahili state and society: The political economy of an African language*. East African Publishers.

Mino, T. (2020). Humanizing higher education: Three case studies in Sub-Saharan Africa. *International Journal of African Higher Education, 7*(1). https://ejournals.bc.edu/index.php/ijahe/article/view/11249

Mino, T. (2021). Building a liberal arts tradition in India. *Revista Española de Educación Comparada, 39*, 123–137. doi:10.5944/reec.39.202i.30042

Murphy, J. (1972). *Luganda-English dictionary*. Catholic University of America Press.

Nyaigotti-Chacha, C. (1987). The Uganda problem: A linguistic perspective. *Ufahamu: A Journal of African Studies, 15*(3), 176–183. doi:10.5070/F7153016981

Oduro-Frimpong, J. (2021). "We dey beg": Visual satirical media discourses on contemporary Ghana-Sino relations. *Journal of African Cultural Studies, 33*(2), 218–229. doi:10.1080/13696815.2020.1824777

p'Bitek, O. (1984). *Song of Lawino & song of Ocol*. Heinemann.

Daumerie & Madsen. (2010). *The effects of a very young age structure in Uganda*.

Rodney, W. (2018). *How Europe underdeveloped Africa*. Verso Trade.

Rohner, D., Thoenig, M., & Zilibotti, F. (2013). Seeds of distrust: Conflict in Uganda. *Journal of Economic Growth, 18*(3), 217–252. https://www.jstor.org/stable/42635325

Sembene, O. (1968). *Mandabi* [Drama]. Filmi Domirev, Comptoir Français du Film Production (CFFP), StudioCanal.

Shizha, E. (2014). Rethinking contemporary Sub-Saharan African school knowledge: Restoring the Indigenous African cultures. *International Journal for Cross-Disciplinary Subjects in Education* 4(1), 1870–1878. doi:10.20533/ijcdse.2042.6364.2014.0260

Singer, S., Amoros, J. E., & Moska, D. (2015). *Global entrepreneurship monitor 2014 global report*. London: Global Entrepreneurship Research Association.

Soyinka, W. (1962). *The lion and the jewel*. Oxford University Press.

Tutu, D. (1999). *No future without forgiveness*. Image.

UNHCR. (2021). *UNHCR – Refugee statistics*. UNHCR. Retrieved October 2, 2021, from https://www.unhcr.org/refugee-statistics/

US National Library of Medicine. (2013). *Cesarean section – A brief history: Part 2* [Exhibitions]. U.S. National Library of Medicine. https://www.nlm.nih.gov/exhibition/cesarean/part2.html

Venter, E. (2004). The notion of ubuntu and communalism in African educational discourse. *Studies in Philosophy and Education*, 23(2–3), 149–160.

wa Thiong'o, N. (1992). *Decolonising the mind: The politics of language in African literature*. James Currey.

Wrigley, C.C. (1959). The Christian Revolution in Buganda. *Comparative Studies in Society and History*, 2(1), 33–48. doi:10.1017/S0010417500000530

Zhang, Y.B., Lin, M.-C., Nonaka, A., & Beom, K. (2005). Harmony, hierarchy and conservatism: A cross-cultural comparison of Confucian values in China, Korea, Japan, and Taiwan. *Communication Research Reports*, 22(2), 107–115. doi:10.1080/00036810500130539

INDEX

Adedeji, J. 131
Adum-Kyeremeh, K. 133
Africanising higher education 31–32, 46–47
Ainsley, G. 133
Ajisafe, M. 131
Akadinda 96, 99, 102, 104; see also Entenga music
Ampe 123, *123*
Anakwue, N. 23
Arnot, Frederick 74–75
Asare, E. 129–133

Badat, S. 45–46
Banks, J. 28
Bell, D. 27–28
Black consciousness 77; Black Consciousness Movement 56, 59
Booth, M. 131
Boughey, C., and McKenna, S. 41
Braun, V., and Clarke, V. 64
Britain: colonial history 76–77, 143; anti-colonial movements 77–78; physical education 129–133; see also colonial history of education; Ghana; Zambia
Brock-Utne, B. 29
Burton, R., and Westerfield, G. 110

Césaire, A. 10
Chaskele 125, *127*
Chivaura, V. 22

Christianity: colonial schooling 11, 15, 26, 76; religious teaching 127–129, 144
colonial history of education 26–29; British South African Company 76–77; pedagogy 49; see also missionary; modernisation; Zambia
colonialism 3–4, 9–11, 43, 49, 58, 127–129, 139, 152
coloniality 11–14, 42–46, 55–58, 61, 108–121
community engagement 33, 49–54, 78, 87, 148; see also Musizi University; University of Zambia (UNZA)
Cossa, J. 30
Coward, V., and Lane, T. 131
The Council on Higher Education (CHE) 44
COVID-19 1, 3, 40, 63, 102, 118
curriculum transformation 14, 37–52, 61; 4Rs 61–62; challenging Eurocentrism 71; discourse of 37; policy frameworks 42, 65

decolonisation: approaches to research 50–51; Black consciousness 77; and capitalism 117–118; collective African memory 12; coloniality of the mind 43; curricular 37–38, 43–46, 55–71; definitions of 11; of education 13–15, 44–45; establishment of universities 43, 65; #FeesMustFall movement 43, 55, 67–70; gods and religion 74;

Index

language recognition 113–115; localised knowledge 74–87; pedagogy 49; sports 131, 135–136; theory connected to practice 48; Western influences 12, 44, 76, 86, 135; *see also* curriculum transformation; language mixing; physical education; unity; white supremacy
Derrida, J. 74, 86–87
Djibouti: demographics 109; French colonisation of 108–109; languages spoken 108–111; politics and language education 111–113; *see also* language education; Somali

elders 11, 13, 25, 31, 71, 96, 150; *see also* Ubuntu
Endongo 106n1
Entenga music 91, 97; cultural identity 98, 106; instruments and players 97; performances of *102, 103*, 105; revival of 91, 98, 105; *see also* Indigenous music; Musisi; Uganda
epistemic violence 10, 12, 44, 61, 74, 76
epistemological diversity 23–25, 38, 83–88; access across disciplines 44, 48
epistemological Indigeneity 30, 32, 75, 78; significance of ancestors 25; *see also* Indigenous African; Indigenous knowledge; Ubuntu
Etta, E. and Asukwo, O. 23–25

Fafunwa, A. 127
Fanon, F. 10–11, 44
Fataar, A. 32
Fomunyam, K. 49
Freire, P. 8, 28–29, 95

Ghana 120–136; strategies to decolonise physical education 135–136; history and traditional games 122, 132–133; missionary education 126–128; national politics and sports 132–134; Real Republicans Sporting Club 133; *see also* Ampe; Chaskele; decolonisation, sports; Oware; Pilolo; Tumatu

globalisation 26, 29, 38–39; transnational corporations 38
Goma, L. and Tembo, L. 78
Gruenewald, D. 94

Hamminga, B. 25
humility 104, 146–147; *see also* Musisi; Obuntu Bulamu

Indigenous African: epistemologies 23; languages 12–13; patriarchy 14; philosophies 12–15, 23–24, 70; populations 12; religions 12–15, 26; spirituality 24; students 70
Indigenous knowledge 12, 75–87, 144–151; African philosophies 12–15, 23–24; *see also* epistemological Indigeneity; localised knowledge; Musizi University; Obuntu Bulamu; physical education; University of Zambia (UNZA); Ubuntu
Indigenous music: revival of 102, 105–106; pedagogy 94; teaching through participation and meaning making 91–92, 95–96, 100; Wenger 104; *see also* Akidanda; Entenga music; Musisi
Iroegbu, P. 23

Joseph, T. 62

Kelly, M. 76–77
Kenyatta, J. 94
knowledge economy 39, 41
Kyambogo University 91, 100, 102; Singing Wells 91–92, 98; students saving *Entenga* music traditions 91, 99, 103–105; *see also* Indigenous music; Uganda

language mixing 111–112; hegemony of English language 113–115; Ministry of Education 113; *see also* Djibouti; South Africa
Le Grange, L. 43–44, 61
localised knowledge: and epistemology 83–85; faculty discourse 79–86; and Indigenous knowledge 51–52, 78–83; Zambia 74–77
Lotz-Sisitka, H. 47
Lugard, Lord 127
Lumadi, M. 44, 48

Maldonado-Torres, N. 10, 13
Maringe, E., and Ojo, E. 47
Marsh, K. 94
Marumo, P., and Chakale, M. 23

massification of higher education 39
Mbembe, A. 30, 44
McElligot, T. 128
MacGregor, K. 40
McWilliam, H., and Kwamena-Poh, M. 129
missionary 26, 74–75; influence on education 76, 126–131; *see also* colonial history of education
modernisation 26–28, 115, 148
Morreira, S. 8, 11
Mukalazi Livingstone, Musisi: as student 91, 103; Indigenous pedagogy 100; interviews with 98, *99*; teaching music *100*, 104–105; *see also* Akadinda; Entenga music
Mukasa, D. 98
Muldoon, J. 58
Mullet, D. 45
Mumford, B. 128
Musizi University 139; centering Indigeneity 144–145, 148, 151; community engagement 148–149; foundation of 140, 142, 146; research 152–153; storytelling 150; *see also* Obuntu Bulamu
Mutekwe, E. 21, 26–27

Nattrass, N. 4–6
Ndlovu-Gatsheni, S. 10, 30, 62
Ndofirepi, A. 30–31
Nketia, J. 94
Nkoane, M. 47
Nkrumah, K. 11, 131–134
Nyerere, J. 11, 142–143

Obuntu Bulamu: business 152; higher education 141, 149; Indigenous knowledge 148, 151; organising ethos 140, 146, 153–154; translation as 147
Ocansey, R. 134
Okere, T., Njoku, C., and Devisch, R. 79
Ole 125, *128*
oral tradition 13, 24
Osman, R. and Petersen, N. 33
Osuagwu, M. 23
Oware 124, *126*
Ozumba, G. 23

pedagogy 49–50, 154; humanising 32; Indigenous 14, 92, 94, 100, 149, 151; music 91

physical education: Ghana 120–136; *see also* decolonisation, sports
Pilolo 124, *125*
Pond, S. 105

Ramose, M. 23–24
research 153; data analysis 80; focus group 81; and individualistic approach to knowledge 29; interviews 57, 63–64, 75, 83, 99; snowball sampling techniques 79–80; *see also* Musizi University
Rodger, J., Governor 129–130

Shay, S. 47
Somali 108–112, 115–118; *see also* Djibouti; language mixing
South Africa 1–5, 12, 43–45, 55–71; apartheid 27, 33; decolonisation of curriculum 71; Freedom Charter 60, 68–70; hegemony of English 113–115; South African Students Movement (SASM) 56; *see also* colonial history of education; curriculum transformation; language mixing; student protest movements
Spivak, G. 44, 76
Ssekamwa, J. 94
storytelling 91, 94, 110, 115, 122, 149–150; *see also* Musizi University
student protest movements 1–3, 43, 55–59, 62–71

Tia Mu Na Tow 122
Tumatu 123, *124*

Ubuntu 14, 25–27, 31, 52, 147; curriculum 44, 50; Obuntu Bulamu 140
Uganda: Buganda clans and society 96–97; Buganda cultural leaders 103–104; Entenga youth performing 103; Kabaka 93, 96, 102–104; Kirindi 104–105; Luganda 140, 143–144; political history 98; Western influence on higher education 94; *see also* Entenga music; Kyambogo University; Musisi Mukalazi Livingstone
unity 30, 116–117, 119, 122, 132–133; *see also* language mixing

Vorster, J. 49–50

wa Thiong'o, N. 12, 22, 44, 61, 70, 142
white supremacy 2, 6, 10–11, 22–23, 26–30
Whitehead, N., and Hendry, L. 131
World Intellectual Property Organisation (WIPO) 51

Zambia: centering Indigeneity 74, 76, 86–87; colonial history of education 76–77; community engagement 87; independence from Britain 77–78; Western influence on higher education 74–76, 81, 88; *see also* University of Zambia (UNZA)
Zambia, University of (UNZA) 75–78; faculty interviews 79–86; faculty recommendations 86–88; localised knowledge 74–79; Lockwood Commission 77–78; School of Education 83; *see also* Indigenous knowledge; localised knowledge
Zembylas, M. 30, 32

Printed in the United States
by Baker & Taylor Publisher Services